Deep Learning Methods for Image Object Detection and Recognition

Deep Learning Methods for Image Object Detection and Recognition

Pengfei Shi • Xinnan Fan • Yuanxue Xin

Hohai University, China

Gang Wan

China Yangtze Electric Power Co., Ltd., China

Qingying Wang

Beijing Institute of Space Electromechanical Technology, China

中国工信出版集团 電子工業出版社 PUBLISHING HOUSE OF ELECTRONICS INDUSTRY

World Scientific

NEW JERSEY • LONDON • SINGAPORE • BEIJING • SHANGHAI • HONG KONG • TAIPEI • CHENNAI • TOKYO

Published by

World Scientific Publishing Co. Pte. Ltd.
5 Toh Tuck Link, Singapore 596224
USA office: 27 Warren Street, Suite 401-402, Hackensack, NJ 07601
UK office: 57 Shelton Street, Covent Garden, London WC2H 9HE

Library of Congress Control Number: 2026020301

British Library Cataloguing-in-Publication Data
A catalogue record for this book is available from the British Library.

DEEP LEARNING METHODS FOR IMAGE OBJECT DETECTION AND RECOGNITION

ISBN 978-981-98-3334-4 (hardcover)
ISBN 978-981-98-3335-1 (ebook for institutions)
ISBN 978-981-98-3336-8 (ebook for individuals)

For any available supplementary material, please visit
https://www.worldscientific.com/worldscibooks/10.1142/14883#t=suppl

Desk Editors: Nambirajan Karuppiah/Veronica Lee

Typeset by Stallion Press
Email: enquiries@stallionpress.com

Preface

The report of the 20th National Congress of the Communist Party of China pointed out that "We should develop the marine economy, protect the marine ecological environment, and accelerate the building of a strong maritime country."

The ocean is the lifeblood of the Earth's habitability and a strategic location for maintaining human survival and high-quality development. Understanding and managing the ocean, as well as building a strong maritime country, particularly requires relying on scientific and technological innovation to drive development. The 2024 government work report proposed to carry out the "Artificial Intelligence +" initiative. All industries are accelerating their transformation and upgrading under the guidance of artificial intelligence, providing new impetus for the cultivation and development of new quality productivity.

Object detection technology is of extremely significant importance in fields such as marine resource exploration, marine environmental protection, underwater safety assurance, underwater archaeological research, military applications, and scientific research. It is a crucial technical means for promoting marine scientific research and protection, facilitating the development and utilization of marine resources, and ensuring underwater safety. The deficiencies of object detection technology in underwater applications mainly include issues such as lighting problems, camera shake, complex background interference, diverse object types, fast object movement speed, changes in background light sources, variations in the color and distribution of objects, changes in background areas caused by camera shake, object occlusion, and the large computational load for detecting and identifying moving objects.

To address the shortcomings of object detection technology, researchers have introduced deep learning into image object detection technology, but there are still problems, such as small and inaccurate datasets, poor quality of underwater images, and a decline in model recognition accuracy due to lighting effects.

This book focuses on underwater object detection scenarios, refining commonly employed deep learning-based detection techniques to enhance their suitability for submerged object identification. It systematically synthesizes over a decade of the author's research practice, covering the following principal aspects:

The "Introduction" chapter serves as an introduction, primarily outlining the research background and significance of deep learning in the field of underwater image object detection, alongside the current state of research both domestically and internationally.

Chapter 1 presents an image defogging algorithm based on U-Net. This chapter introduces a multi-scale feature fusion image defogging algorithm incorporating an attention mechanism. The algorithm adopts an encoder-decoder architecture similar to U-Net, directly learning an adaptive defogging model from the input data to achieve favorable defogging results.

Chapter 2 presents an image enhancement algorithm based on feature fusion Generative Adversarial Networks (GANs). This chapter primarily leverages the strengths of GANs to devise an underwater image enhancement algorithm employing feature fusion GANs. Through adversarial training between the generator and discriminator, a robust underwater image enhancement model has been developed.

Chapter 3 presents an image super-resolution reconstruction algorithm based on ESRGAN. This chapter primarily elaborates on the single-image super-resolution (SISR) algorithm ESRGAN, designing an underwater image super-resolution algorithm with exceptional reconstruction quality by optimizing its generator architecture.

Chapter 4 presents an image segmentation algorithm based on a nested U-Net. This chapter proposes Att_Nested_U-Net, a crack image segmentation model based on a nested U-Net incorporating self-attention mechanisms. Building upon the design philosophy of the U-Net architecture, it employs the U-Net++ model, which embeds multiple U-Net layers within one another. Attention mechanisms are integrated into each U-Net layer, significantly enhancing segmentation accuracy for crack images while suppressing noise and preserving fine details.

Chapter 5 presents an underwater dam crack image segmentation algorithm based on adversarial transfer learning. This chapter primarily achieves unsupervised domain adaptation for underwater dam crack features through multi-stage adversarial transfer learning, which effectively transfers the features extracted from terrestrial crack images to the segmentation of underwater dam crack images while ensuring detection accuracy.

Chapter 6 presents a marine organism detection algorithm based on an improved Faster-RCNN. This chapter replaces the VGG feature extraction network in Faster-RCNN with ResNet and adds Bidirectional Feature Pyramid Network (BiFPN) after ResNet, forming a ResNet-BiFPN structure to enhance the model's feature extraction and multi-scale feature fusion capabilities. It employs Enhanced Intersection over Union (EIoU) to replace the original Intersection over Union (IoU), incorporating a centerness weighting to reduce the proportion of redundant bounding boxes in the training data and improve bounding box quality. The K-means++ algorithm is used to generate more suitable anchor boxes. These improvements to Faster-RCNN have yielded positive results.

Chapter 7 presents an object detection algorithm based on YOLOv4. This chapter proposes an algorithm that incorporates PredMix, the Convolutional Block Attention Module (CBAM), and DetPANet into YOLOv4. Integrating CBAM into the CSPDarknet53 backbone enhances the algorithm's feature extraction capability. DetPANet augments the Path Aggregation Network (PANet) by adding intra-layer and cross-layer skip connections, thereby strengthening the multi-scale feature fusion ability. PredMix (Prediction-Mix) is introduced to improve the algorithm's robustness.

Chapter 8 presents a dense object detection algorithm based on RetinaNet. This chapter comprehensively considers the balance between detection accuracy and speed. Building upon the single-stage RetinaNet detector, it proposes specific improvements tailored for dense object scenarios in remote sensing imagery, ultimately achieving higher detection accuracy for densely distributed objects.

Chapter 9 presents a real-time video object detection algorithm based on LSTM networks. Addressing the limitations of traditional image-based detectors in processing video sequences, this chapter proposes a video object detection algorithm utilizing LSTM networks. By improving the memory-guided network and introducing a cross-detection framework, it fully leverages the temporal information from consecutive video frames, enhancing both the accuracy and speed of video object detection.

Chapter 10 is an embedded substation instrument detection algorithm based on improved YOLOv4. This chapter mainly aims at devices with limited performance, such as embedded platforms and mobile edge computing. It implements a lightweight network at the model design stage and reasoning stage, improves YOLOv4, reconstructs and optimizes the improved YOLOv4 using TensorRT, deploys the improved YOLOv4 to the embedded platform, and meets the real-time detection requirements of substation instruments.

The content of this book involves the research achievements of many projects, especially the National Key Research and Development Program (2022YFB4703400), Jiangsu Natural Science Foundation (BK20231186), Changzhou Science and Technology Support Program (Social Development) (CE20235053), Hubei Smart Hydropower Technology Innovation Center Open Research Fund Project (1523020038), Jiangsu Power Transmission and Distribution Equipment Technology Key Laboratory Project (2023JSSPD01), etc.

Pengfei Shi is responsible for compiling the content related to image target detection and recognition, Xinnan Fan is responsible for compiling the content related to image enhancement, Yuanxue Xin is responsible for compiling the content related to image target positioning, Gang Wan is responsible for compiling the content related to underwater dam crack detection, and Qingying Wang is responsible for compiling the content related to remote sensing image detection. Zhongkai Zhou, Xiaotian Wang, Jin Wan, Xudong Yang, doctoral students from Hohai University, and Jie Wang, Ruiyang Xue, Song Han, Liang Lu, Wei Yan, Xin Yang, Pengfei Cao, Xiaolong Fang, Fengting Zhu, Runkang Zhou, Weisheng Huang, master students from Hohai University participated in the proofreading of some chapters of this book, and I would like to express my heartfelt thanks to them!

Due to the limited theoretical level of the author and the limitations of the research work, especially the rapid development of in-depth learning, there are inevitably some shortcomings in this book, and readers are kindly requested to criticize and correct them.

About the Authors

Pengfei Shi, Ph.D., is an Associate Professor and Master Supervisor at Hohai University. He is selected into the "Dayu Scholar" program of Hohai University, a member of the CAA Networked Intelligence Special Committee, a member of CCF, and a member of IEEE. He has been long engaged in research in the fields of artificial intelligence and robotics, smart power systems, smart water conservancy, edge computing, machine vision, software and hardware development, etc. He has presided over 1 National Natural Science Foundation project, 1 sub-project of the National Key Research and Development Program, 1 Industry-University-Research Collaborative Education Project of the Ministry of Education, 2 Natural Science Foundation projects of Jiangsu Province, 2 Basic Research Programs of Changzhou City, and multiple entrusted scientific and technological projects from enterprises and institutions. He has published more than 100 papers, among which more than 50 are retrieved by SCI/EI, including many top journal papers and top conference papers in the fields of artificial intelligence and machine vision, such as IEEE Trans. on Instrumentation and Measurement and ICCV. He has applied for more than 30 invention patents, and 10 of them have been authorized. He has been invited to serve as the chair of sub-conferences of international academic conferences for many times. He has obtained more than 10 software copyrights. He has published a textbook named *Artificial Intelligence and Robotics.* He has won one third prize of the Jiangsu Science and Technology Award. He has guided students to participate in competitions and won one first prize and one second prize in provincial competitions, and one third prize in national competitions, etc.

Xinnan Fan, Ph.D., is a Professor and Doctoral Supervisor at Hohai University. His main research areas include information acquisition and processing, intelligent sensing technology, Internet of Things (IoT) technology and applications, and water conservancy informatization. He has led or participated in the completion of more than 30 projects, including those funded by the National Natural Science Foundation of China, the National "863" Program, and sub-projects of the National Key R&D Program. He has published over 100 academic papers (more than 30 of which are SCI-indexed), obtained 18 authorized invention patents, registered 10 software copyrights, authored one monograph, and received two provincial and ministerial-level science and technology awards, as well as four Jiangsu Provincial Outstanding Teaching Achievement Awards. He was also awarded the Baosteel Education Award for Outstanding Teachers. Currently, he serves as the Director of the Jiangsu Provincial Key Laboratory of Transmission and Distribution Equipment Technology, Deputy Secretary-General of the Jiangsu Transmission and Distribution Industry Technology Innovation Alliance, Outstanding Mid-Career Leader of the Jiangsu "Qinglan Project," and Head of the Water IoT and Sensing Center Team at the Jiangsu "World Water Valley" and Water Ecological Civilization Collaborative Innovation Center. He teaches undergraduate courses such as "Principles and Applications of Single-Chip Microcomputers."

Yuanxue Xin, Ph.D., is an Associate Professor and Master's Supervisor at Hohai University, as well as a member of the China Computer Federation (CCF) and has been recognized as a "Dayu Scholar" by Hohai University and a "Longcheng Talented Professional" in Changzhou. Her primary research focuses on spectral efficiency, energy efficiency and novel duplexing technologies in massive MIMO systems. She has presided over one National Natural Science Foundation of China (Youth Program) project and one Open Fund from the State Key Laboratory of Mobile Communications. As the first author, she has published 14 papers, including 7 SCI-indexed articles, four EI-indexed articles, and one top-tier conference paper in the field of communications. She has also obtained one authorized invention patent as the first inventor, with two additional patent applications under review. Additionally, she has participated in three international academic conferences and delivered one keynote presentation.

Gang Wan is a Senior Engineer at China Yangtze Power Co., Ltd. His main research areas include intelligent operation and maintenance of large hydropower stations, as well as intelligent management and digitalization of hydropower maintenance processes. He has participated in two national key research and development projects, serving as the lead of one specialized topic. He has received multiple awards, including first and third prizes for outstanding employee technological innovation achievements from organizations such as the China Electricity Council and the National Energy, Chemical, and Geological Systems. He has been granted over 50 patents, including 16 invention patents, and has published 12 papers, three of which are SCI-indexed. In the past three years, he has delivered two presentations at academic conferences.

Qingying Wang is a Senior Engineer at the Beijing Institute of Space Mechanics & Electricity. She has long been engaged in theoretical research, system design, and engineering development in the field of space remote sensing, achieving a series of innovative results in the structural design, simulation, testing, and experimentation of space cameras. She has participated in over ten National Major Science and Technology Projects, serving as the lead of two specialized topics. Her awards include the Third Prize of the National Defense Technology Invention Award, the Third Prize of the Corporate-level Science and Technology Invention Award, as well as multiple institute-level honors in research management, quality work, and "Five Small" outstanding innovation achievements. She has been granted more than ten patents and has published several papers in core journals and academic conferences. In the past three years, she has delivered one presentation at an academic conference.

Contents

Preface v

About the Authors ix

Introduction **1**

1 Research Background and Significance 1
2 Research Status at Home and Abroad 3
2.1 Methods for underwater image quality enhancement 4
2.2 Research on deep learning-based object detection algorithms 8
2.3 Research on crack image segmentation algorithms 11
3 The Main Content and Chapter Arrangement of This Book 14
References 19

1. Image Dehazing Algorithm Based on U-Net **25**

1.1 Introduction 25
1.2 The Algorithm 27
1.2.1 Feature extraction layer 27
1.2.2 Network structure 27
1.2.3 Loss function 32
1.3 Experimental Results and Analysis 32
1.3.1 Experimental environment 32
1.3.2 Experimental dataset 32

1.3.3 Evaluation metrics 33
1.3.4 Parameter settings 33
1.3.5 Experimental results 34
1.3.6 Comparison of running time 38
1.4 Conclusion 40
References 40

2. GAN-Based Image Enhancement Algorithms 43

2.1 Introduction 43
2.2 Generative Adversarial Network Model 44
2.2.1 Basic concept 44
2.2.2 Representation of mathematical models 44
2.3 Underwater Image Enhancement with Feature Fusion Generative Adversarial Networks 46
2.3.1 Color correction 47
2.3.2 Generative network architecture 51
2.3.3 Discriminating network structure 53
2.3.4 Loss function selection 54
2.4 Experimental Comparison and Result Analysis . . . 56
2.4.1 Experimental data and training 57
2.4.2 Experimental results 59
2.4.3 Ablation experiments 62
2.5 Conclusion 66
References 66

3. ESRGAN-Based Image Super-Resolution Reconstruction Algorithm 69

3.1 Introduction 69
3.2 ESRGAN Methodology 69
3.3 Improved ESRGAN for Super-Resolution Reconstruction of Underwater Images 73
3.3.1 Generating network structures 73
3.3.2 Discriminant network structure 78
3.3.3 Loss function selection 78
3.4 Comparison of Experiments and Analysis of Results 80
3.4.1 Experimental data and training 80
3.4.2 Results 81

3.5 Conclusion 85
References 85

4. The Image Target Segmentation Algorithm Based on a Nested U-Net 89

4.1 Introduction 89
4.2 Convolutional Neural Network-Related Technologies 90
4.3 Fully Convolutional Neural Network (FCN) 92
4.4 U-net Model 95
4.5 Crack Image Segmentation Model Att_Nested_Unet 97
4.5.1 Related research 97
4.5.2 Att_Nested_Unet algorithm 98
4.5.3 Experiments and results 102
4.6 Conclusion 106
References 106

5. Underwater Dam Crack Image Segmentation Algorithm Based on Adversarial Transfer Learning 109

5.1 Introduction 109
5.2 Related Work 111
5.2.1 Crack image segmentation 111
5.2.2 Underwater crack image segmentation . . . 112
5.2.3 Transfer learning 113
5.3 Proposed Method 114
5.3.1 Network model 114
5.3.2 Adversarial transfer learning 117
5.3.3 Loss function 118
5.4 Experiment and Results 120
5.4.1 Datasets 120
5.4.2 Training strategy 120
5.4.3 Experimental results 121
5.4.4 Evaluation indicators 123
5.5 Conclusion 124
References 125

6. Marine Organism Detection Algorithm Based on an Improved Faster-RCNN 129

6.1 Introduction 129
6.2 Related Work 130
6.3 Marine Organism Detection Algorithm Based on an Improved Faster-RCNN 132
6.3.1 ResNet-BiFPN 132
6.3.2 Effective intersection over union (EIoU) 135
6.3.3 K-means++ clustering algorithm 138
6.4 Experiment 141
6.4.1 Experiment configuration and dataset . . . 141
6.4.2 Evaluation metrics 142
6.4.3 Experimental results 142
6.5 Conclusion 146
References 147

7. Real-Time Object Localization and Recognition Algorithm for Video Images Based on YOLOv4 149

7.1 Introduction 149
7.1.1 Basic concept of overlay analysis 149
7.2 The Underwater Target Detection Algorithm That Combines Data Augmentation with Improved YOLOv4 153
7.2.1 CBAM-CSPDarknet53 153
7.2.2 DetPANet 156
7.2.3 PredMix 157
7.3 Experiment 160
7.3.1 Experimental configuration and dataset 160
7.3.2 Experimental results 161
7.4 Conclusion 166
References 167

8. RetinaNet-Based Algorithm for Image Dense Target Detection 169

8.1 Introduction 169
8.2 Remote Sensing Image Target Detection Algorithm Based on Multidimensional Attention Module . . . 171

8.2.1 Algorithm body framework 171
8.2.2 Multidimensional attention module 173
8.2.3 Weak non-maximal value suppression algorithm 175
8.2.4 Loss function 179
8.3 Experimentation and Analysis Faster-RCNN 180
8.3.1 Experimental environment and data sets 180
8.3.2 Experimental parameters and evaluation indicators 183
8.3.3 Experimental procedures and analysis of results 184
8.4 Conclusion 191
References 192

9. Real-Time Detection Algorithm of Video Image Object Based on LSTM 195

9.1 Long Short-Term Memory Network and Memory Guide Network 197
9.1.1 Long short-term memory network 197
9.1.2 Memory guide network improvement 200
9.2 Construction of Cross Detection Model 203
9.2.1 Cross detection model idea 203
9.2.2 Cross detection model selection 204
9.3 Model Training and Experimental Analysis 206
9.3.1 Model training strategy 206
9.3.2 Experimental analysis 208
9.4 Conclusion 214
References 215

10. Embedded Substation Instrument Detection Algorithm Based on Improved YOLOv4 217

10.1 Introduction 217
10.2 Methodology 220
10.2.1 YOLOv4 network 220
10.2.2 Improved YOLOv4 substation instrument detection algorithm 221
10.3 Experimental Results and Analysis 226
10.3.1 Dataset and experimental platform 226

10.3.2 Experimental parameter settings 228
10.3.3 Comparison of computational complexity and model parameters 228
10.3.4 Comparison of detection accuracy and detection speed 229
10.4 Conclusion 233
References 234

Index 237

Introduction

1 Research Background and Significance

With the vigorous development of the global economy and technology, human demand for material resources continues to increase. The limited terrestrial resources will gradually fail to meet human needs, prompting humans to turn their attention to the vast ocean. The ocean covers approximately 71% of the Earth's surface and harbors an abundance of biological, mineral, chemical, and dynamic resources. China is a major maritime nation, with a total area of internal seas and territorial waters of approximately 370,000 square kilometers and a jurisdictional maritime area of around 3 million square kilometers. It possesses rich marine resources, yet it has not yet reached the standard of a maritime power. China's development and utilization of resources mainly remain land-based, with the exploitation of marine resources being merely a drop in the ocean. Therefore, promoting the efficient and rational development and utilization of marine resources and enabling them to serve humanity is of great significance for the development of China's technology, economy, and military. To fully understand the ocean and enhance the extent of marine resource development and utilization, acquiring ocean information is an indispensable step.

First, optical images, as one of the important carriers of marine information, play a crucial role in obtaining such information. However, due to the attenuation of light in water and the varying degrees of attenuation experienced by light of different wavelengths, the resulting underwater images often suffer from severe color distortion. Among them, red light is the most severely attenuated, capable of propagating only about 2–3 meters at most, while blue and green light attenuate more slowly and can travel longer distances in water, causing underwater images to often exhibit an overall bluish or greenish tint. Additionally, the scattering of light by suspended particles in water results in the superimposition of scattered light from both within and outside the camera's field of view onto the acquired images, leading to reduced image clarity and contrast. Apart from being affected by the external environment, images may also suffer from low resolution and unclear details due to compression caused by limitations in network transmission systems and imaging equipment. Such issues similarly lead to a degradation in image quality. Low-quality underwater images significantly reduce the amount of information that can be extracted from them, severely impeding tasks such as underwater exploration, underwater archaeology, and underwater biological research. Meanwhile, they pose great challenges to some underwater computer vision tasks, such as object detection and recognition. Therefore, how to effectively enhance the quality of underwater images has become a current hot topic. Effectively improving the quality of underwater images can provide substantial assistance for subsequent underwater operations and accelerate the process of marine development.

Second, marine organisms are an important component of the marine ecological environment. Marine ecological protection organizations perform tasks such as tracking and population counting of marine organisms through methods like manual diving or underwater robot photography. By studying the distribution and living habits of marine organisms, targeted measures are taken to maintain the healthy and sustainable development of the marine ecological environment. However, the complex underwater environment severely degrades the quality of captured videos or images, making it difficult for researchers to accurately identify targets with the naked eye and easily leading to deviations in population counts. Hence, there is an urgent need for a method to detect and identify marine organisms that can replace the naked eye. Traditional object detection methods suffer from poor recognition performance, low accuracy, and slow recognition speed, making effective marine organism detection challenging. In recent years, deep learning has made significant breakthroughs in the field of object detection. In many scenarios, deep learning-based object detection can achieve considerable success. However, general object detection network models do not perform well in marine environments; the complexity of the marine environment and marine organisms can severely interfere with the effectiveness of marine organism detection. Therefore, how to effectively improve the detection accuracy of underwater targets has become a current hot topic, thereby deepening the understanding of marine scenes.

Finally, with continuous technological advancements, water conservancy and hydropower construction have made significant progress. As extremely important infrastructure in water conservancy and hydropower projects, dikes have profound significance for agricultural irrigation, hydroelectric power generation, and disaster prevention and flood control. However, dam cracks are a major hidden danger that threatens the normal operation of dikes. The presence of dam cracks can affect the strength and lifespan of the dam body and even lead to problems such as leakage and breach. Cracks not only exist on the surface of the dam but can also extend inward. The disasters they cause are unpredictable and are one of the main triggers of dangers, worsening disasters, and inducing tragedies. Timely and accurate detection and identification of dam cracks are of profound significance for danger diagnosis, dam reinforcement and repair, and ensuring the normal operation of the dike system. Traditional manual detection methods, due to their slow speed, low accuracy, and susceptibility to the subjective emotions of inspectors, have gradually been replaced by vision-based detection methods using underwater robots. Currently, the latter has become one of the most important non-destructive testing methods in the field of structural crack detection. Its typical workflow involves using underwater robots to collect images, then processing and analyzing the crack images to obtain the type, location, and size of the cracks, thereby providing guidance for dam health diagnosis and reinforcement repair.

2 Research Status at Home and Abroad

Improving the quality of images taken by underwater robots, followed by detection and recognition, is essential for understanding underwater scenes. This section reviews methods for underwater image quality enhancement and subsequent techniques for target recognition and crack segmentation.

2.1 *Methods for underwater image quality enhancement*

Underwater image quality enhancement methods mainly include restoration algorithms and enhancement algorithms.

Underwater image restoration algorithms: These algorithms construct degradation models of underwater images based on the propagation characteristics of light in water. By estimating the parameters in the model and inverting the degradation process, they ultimately obtain a clear image before degradation [1]. Since the degradation principles of underwater images are similar to those of hazy images, after He *et al.* [2] proposed the Dark Channel Prior (DCP) algorithm to address the degradation problem of hazy images with remarkable results, many researchers combined DCP with the attenuation characteristics of underwater images and subsequently proposed numerous underwater image restoration methods. In 2013, Drews *et al.* [3] proposed an improved DCP-based underwater image restoration algorithm, which applies DCP only to the blue and green channels to reduce the influence of the red component. This approach effectively improves the visual quality of underwater images, though its applicability is limited. In 2015, Galdran *et al.* [4], considering the poor performance of directly applying DCP due to the selective attenuation of different wavelengths of light in water, proposed a red channel restoration algorithm. This method reverses the background light and pixel intensity of the red channel, then estimates transmission using DCP. The improved algorithm restores realistic scene colors and enhances image clarity. In 2016, Li *et al.* [5] estimated the red channel transmission based on the principle of minimal information loss, then calculated the blue and green channel transmission according to their relationship with the red channel, finally reconstructing natural-colored and clear restored images using the underwater imaging model. In 2019, Ueki *et al.* [6] introduced an iterative restoration algorithm based on the Generalization of Dark Channel Prior (GDCP). They first enhanced the image through GDCP iteration, and to address color distortion and noise in background areas, fused the iteratively enhanced images with the initially enhanced image. This algorithm effectively improves image contrast and clarity, but the iterative process significantly increases computational cost. In 2020, Lin *et al.* [7] proposed a restoration method based on a modified scattering model. The technique incorporates background light into the underwater imaging model, introduces an inverse red channel model, and employs DCP to estimate transmission, thereby restoring underwater images prior to degradation. This algorithm effectively improves contrast and reveals more details. Traditional underwater image enhancement methods can improve contrast and clarity, enhancing visual quality. However, as they fail to account for the inherent characteristics of underwater imaging, the enhanced results may suffer from color distortion, artifacts, or noise amplification in certain scenarios. With the rise of deep learning, researchers have integrated it with image restoration techniques by employing convolutional networks to learn parameters of the underwater imaging model. The main procedure involves estimating the transmission map of underwater images using convolutional networks and then restoring the original image through the imaging model. In 2017, Wang *et al.* [8] synthesized underwater image datasets using an underwater imaging model, then trained a convolutional neural network to estimate the transmission map and the attenuation rates of red, green, and blue light. The restored images achieved both high clarity and pleasing visual effects. In 2018, Cao *et al.* [9] designed two neural network architectures to separately estimate background light and scene depth. Transmission was then computed by combining light attenuation coefficients in water with scene depth, and the degraded image was restored using the imaging model. The algorithm yielded vibrant colors and high contrast. In 2019, Wang *et al.* [10] proposed a parallel convolutional neural network-based underwater image restoration algorithm. This structure estimated the blue channel transmission and background light, then inferred the red and green channel transmission based on inter-channel relationships. Trained on a constructed dataset, the method produced restored images with natural colors and high clarity. In 2020, Yang *et al.* [11] introduced a novel background light estimation scheme to mitigate the effect of artificial light sources on the physical model. In this method, depth information estimated by a convolutional neural network was combined with DCP to obtain background light, which was then used with DCP to restore degraded images. This algorithm alleviated color distortion and improved contrast, although its performance is constrained by the accuracy of depth estimation.

Underwater Image Enhancement Algorithms: These algorithms primarily address issues such as poor underwater image quality by directly modifying the pixel values within the image. To address degradation in underwater imagery, experts and scholars have proposed numerous enhancement algorithms. In 2017, Perez *et al.* [12] employed degraded underwater images and their corresponding clear counterparts as a training set. They then utilized a convolutional neural network to learn the mapping from degraded to clear ones, thereby accomplishing the task of underwater image enhancement. In the same year, Ding *et al.* [13] proposed a deep learning-based enhancement strategy. They first applied an adaptive color correction algorithm to address color distortion in underwater images, followed by a super-resolution convolutional neural network model to remove blurring. Since the introduction of Generative Adversarial Networks (GANs) [14] in 2014, their robust learning capabilities and adaptability have led to widespread application across various fields [15, 16]. In recent years, numerous scholars have employed GANs to address distortion issues in underwater imagery. In 2017, Li *et al.* [17] proposed WaterGAN, an unsupervised GAN algorithm for underwater image enhancement. WaterGAN first obtains corresponding underwater images from clear images and their depth information. It then employs a depth estimation network to estimate the depth information of the underwater images, feeding both the depth estimates and the underwater images into a color correction network. This ultimately yields enhanced images. The algorithm effectively resolves color bias issues in underwater images, restoring the scene's true colors. In 2018, Fabbri *et al.* [18] proposed the Underwater Generative Adversarial Network (UGAN) tailored for underwater scenes. To address the scarcity of underwater image datasets, they employed the Cyclic Generative Adversarial Network (CycleGAN) to generate datasets. Training the generative adversarial network under conditions of sufficient data effectively enhanced the visual quality of underwater images. In 2020, Li *et al.* [19] proposed an underwater image enhancement algorithm based on an improved CycleGAN. This approach suppresses alterations in edge structures between input and output images by designing an edge structure similarity function. Concurrently, it employs a combined network architecture of weak and strong supervision alongside a two-stage learning model to ensure color consistency between generated and target images. The algorithm effectively enhances image contrast while restoring the scene's true colors. In the same year, Islam *et al.* [20] introduced FUnlE-GAN, a real-time underwater image enhancement model based on fully convolutional conditional generative adversarial networks. By integrating a multimodal objective function, the enhanced images demonstrated significantly improved contrast and clarity while boosting perceived image quality. Also in 2021, Dudhane *et al.* [21] proposed a generative adversarial network model for underwater image restoration. Addressing the distortion characteristics of underwater images, they designed a color-channel-based feature extraction module and a dense residual network to tackle blurring in degraded underwater images. Combined with their proposed loss function, this algorithm effectively restores colors, preserves scene detail structures, and generates more realistic edge information when processing underwater images. In 2021, Yong *et al.* [22] proposed a weakly supervised underwater image enhancement algorithm incorporating an attention mechanism to address challenges such as the difficulty of obtaining paired samples. Within this algorithm, the attenuation map of the red channel serves as the attention map, with both the original underwater image and the attention image fed simultaneously into the generative network. Finally, adversarial training enables the generative network to output images with enhanced contrast and clarity. This algorithm demonstrated favorable results for underwater images exhibiting color distortion and low contrast, yet performed poorly on turbid underwater imagery. In the same year, addressing issues of blurriness, low contrast, and color distortion in underwater imagery, Li *et al.* [23] proposed DeWaterNet, a fusion generative adversarial network. In this algorithm, the generative network is constituted by two convolutional networks. Each of these networks extracts features from the fusion-enhanced image and the original underwater image, respectively. The sum of these outputs serves as the generative network's final output, thereby effectively enhancing the visual quality of underwater imagery.

2.2 Research on deep learning-based object detection algorithms

Object detection refers to the task of locating specific objects within an image or video, typically by delineating them with bounding boxes. If multiple object categories are present, the task also involves classifying the detected objects. For humans, vision enables the recognition of object categories and their locations. Similarly, object detection aims to address two fundamental problems in computer vision applications: what the object is and where it is located.

Due to its broad application prospects, object detection has attracted significant attention and plays a crucial role in various tasks such as face recognition [24], gait recognition [25], crow counting [26], security surveillance [27], autonomous driving [28], and drone scene analysis [29]. Research areas within object detection include edge detection [30], multi-object detection [31–33], and salientobject detection [34, 35].

With advancements in deep learning, the field of object detection has also developed rapidly. Most object detection methods rely on deep learning networks as their backbone, where models extract features, perform classification, and localization from input images. Deep learning-based object detection algorithms can generally be divided into two categories: two-stage object detection algorithms and one-stage object detection algorithms. Two-stage algorithms, proposed earlier, are characterized by high detection accuracy but slower detection speed. One-stage algorithms, on the other hand, offer faster detection speed but slightly lower accuracy. Currently, both one-stage and two-stage algorithms are advancing toward the goal of being both fast and accurate. The following section discusses the research status of these two types of object detection algorithms.

(1) Two-stage object detection algorithms: Two-stage object detection algorithms involve first generating candidate regions through a certain method, then classifying the contents of these regions to determine whether they contain the target object, and finally refining these regions. Since the process consists of two steps—candidate region generation and candidate region detection—it is referred to as a two-stage object detection algorithm.

In 2014, Ross B. Girshick proposed RCNN [36], which uses selective search to partition images and generate candidate regions.

These regions are then input into a CNN model pre-trained on ImageNet to extract features, replacing the traditional sliding window method. Finally, a linear SVM classifier is used to predict the object category within each candidate region. This approach enables RCNN to achieve very high detection accuracy. However, RCNN also has significant drawbacks: due to the large number of overlapping regions among candidates, the computations performed on these overlapping regions are highly redundant, which severely slows down the detection speed. Additionally, all candidate regions in RCNN must be resized to fixed dimensions, leading to unwanted geometric distortions.

In 2014, He *et al.* proposed the Spatial Pyramid Pooling Network (SPPnet) [37] to address the redundant computation issue in RCNN. Unlike RCNN, which directly partitions candidate regions on the image, SPPnet selects candidate regions on the extracted feature maps of the image, thereby reducing redundant computations. To handle candidate regions of varying sizes, the algorithm maps convolutional features of any size to a fixed-dimensional fully connected input, avoiding the geometric distortion problems caused by resizing candidate regions as in RCNN. SPPnet achieves a detection speed that is twenty times faster than RCNN without any loss in detection accuracy. However, SPPnet also has its limitations: backpropagation through the SPP layer is highly inefficient for training samples of different images, preventing the update of weights below the SPP layer and limiting improvements in detection accuracy. In 2015, Ross B. Girshick proposed Fast RCNN [38]. This algorithm uses bounding box regression and non-maximum suppression to obtain non-redundant bounding boxes with the highest prediction scores. Compared to RCNN, Fast RCNN significantly improves both detection accuracy and speed. However, due to the constraints of candidate region detection, the detection speed of Fast RCNN still cannot be greatly enhanced. In 2015, Ren *et al.* proposed Faster RCNN [39]. The Region Proposal Network (RPN) in Faster RCNN separates the localization and classification operations in object detection. The workflow of Faster RCNN is as follows: features are extracted using a VGG network model; candidate regions are generated from the extracted features via the RPN; these regions are then assessed to determine whether they contain objects or background, and are refined accordingly; finally, ROI Pooling is applied to classify the candidate regions screened and refined by the RPN. Compared to Fast RCNN, Faster RCNN achieves a significant breakthrough in detection speed.

(2) Single-stage object detection algorithms: Single-stage object detection algorithms accomplish both object localization and classification tasks in a single stage. The entire process of single-stage object detection algorithms is more streamlined, requiring less detection time and better meeting real-time requirements in terms of detection speed.

In 2015, Joseph *et al.* proposed YOLOv1 [40]. YOLOv1 also uses a convolutional neural network to extract features, then divides the entire image into a grid. For each grid cell, it predicts a certain number of bounding boxes and the probabilities of belonging to different categories. Each bounding box has five vectors: four coordinate values describing the position and the confidence score for each category. YOLOv1 combines the prediction of the target region with the prediction of the target category, significantly improving detection speed. However, YOLOv1 can only predict one object per grid cell, and its detection accuracy is quite limited. Since YOLOv1 does not utilize shallow features rich in detailed information for prediction, it performs poorly in detecting small objects.

In 2016, Liu *et al.* proposed SSD [41] (Single Shot MultiBox Detector) to address issues such as the low accuracy of small object detection in YOLOv1. Compared to YOLOv1, SSD performs object detection directly after the CNN model, rather than after the fully connected layers as in YOLOv1. SSD extracts features at different scales for object detection: for small objects, SSD uses shallow features rich in positional and detailed information; for large objects, SSD uses deep features rich in semantic information. SSD also fixes the aspect ratios and sizes of anchor boxes, checking whether each feature contains a target within a fixed number of anchor boxes. With these modifications, SSD achieves both higher detection accuracy and faster detection speed than YOLOv1, and it also performs well in detecting small-scale objects.

In 2017, Redmon *et al.* incorporated the advantages of SSD into YOLOv1 and made improvements, proposing YOLOv2 [42]. In YOLOv2, Redmon J designed a new convolutional neural network to extract image features, used a clustering algorithm to cluster the sizes of labeled boxes in the dataset to determine anchor box dimensions, and added batch normalization to convolutional layers to reduce overfitting and effectively improve model convergence. Compared to YOLOv1, YOLOv2 was trained on higher-resolution ImageNet and then fine-tuned using detection datasets. The authors also added a multi-scale training method to YOLOv2, enabling it to detect objects at multiple scales. In 2018, Redmon *et al.* made further improvements based on YOLOv2 and proposed YOLOv3 [43]. YOLOv3 designed a more powerful feature extraction convolutional neural network—Darknet53—and improved the clustering algorithm to obtain more accurate anchor box sizes. YOLOv3 adopted the multi-scale prediction idea of feature pyramids, making predictions at three scales, with each scale corresponding to three candidate boxes. YOLOv3 also used multi-label classification, allowing each candidate box to predict multiple categories. By replacing pooling layers with increased convolutional kernel strides, YOLOv3 reduced the number of model parameters. Although YOLOv3 is slightly slower than YOLOv2, overall, YOLOv3 was the state-of-the-art single-stage object detection algorithm at the time. In 2020, Alexey improved upon YOLOv3 and proposed YOLOv4 [44]. YOLOv4 screened and applied various techniques (tricks) that had been used in various object detection models since the release of YOLOv3 to improve detection accuracy. Additionally, YOLOv4 replaced YOLOv3's backbone network, Darknet53, with CSPDarkNet53, which has stronger feature extraction capabilities, added SPPnet to expand the receptive field size, and used the Path Aggregation Network (PANet) for multi-channel feature fusion.

2.3 *Research on crack image segmentation algorithms*

Crack image segmentation algorithms can be divided into two categories: morphological methods and deep learning methods [45]. The former is an algorithm for image segmentation that researchers used to implement using knowledge of digital image processing, topology, mathematics, etc. before the popularity of deep learning methods [46]. This type of method is easily affected by factors such as image quality and noise, and has high requirements for the usage environment. Compared with deep learning methods, its applicability is poor, and there are also certain gaps in segmentation performance.

With the continuous development of deep learning, more and more researchers have chosen to apply it to crack image segmentation tasks [47]. Due to the relatively complex texture features of cracks, high requirements are placed on the segmentation performance of the model. Currently, the fully convolutional network (FCN) and its variants are more commonly used in the field of crack image segmentation [48]. FCN was proposed by Jonathan Long *et al.* in 2015 [49]. This network consists of an encoder sub-network and a decoder sub-network. Among them, the encoder sub-network is used to extract image features, while the decoder sub-network is responsible for classifying the pixels of the image. Limited by the overly simple decoder sub-network of FCN, its segmentation effect is not ideal, and misjudgment often occurs.

Olaf Ronneberger *et al.* proposed the Unet network based on FCN [50], which realizes the semantic fusion of features at different layers of medical images through skip connections. Similarly, there is also the SegNet network [51], which uses the indices generated by the pooling operations of the encoder network to achieve the fusion of image semantic features. Compared with FCN, these improved algorithms change the network to a symmetric structure, enrich the semantic features output by the decoder, and effectively improve the segmentation accuracy of the image.

Although the proposed U-net and SegNet were not designed to solve the crack image segmentation problem, their effectiveness has been proven. Huyan Ju *et al.* [52] proposed an improved road crack image segmentation network CrackU-net based on U-net. With the help of the padding operation, this scheme can keep the size of the feature map unchanged. Jierong Cheng *et al.* [53] proposed a pixel-level road crack image segmentation scheme based on the classic U-net. By introducing a new loss function based on distance transform, this method achieved outstanding pixel-level accuracy. Shengyuan Li *et al.* [54] incorporated Dense Block into SegNet and proposed a new concrete structure crack detection algorithm. Qin Zou *et al.* [55] applied multi-scale cross-layer fusion to the SegNet network and proposed a crack detection algorithm called DeepCrack.

Although these methods can effectively improve the segmentation accuracy of ground crack images, there are still some problems when directly applying them to the underwater crack image segmentation task. Since these methods are all supervised learning methods, their model training requires a large amount of labeled data. Given the difficulty in obtaining underwater crack images and the time-consuming and laborious annotation of the dataset, it is difficult to implement supervised learning for underwater crack image segmentation.

Underwater crack images are different from ground crack images. Due to the limitations of the image acquisition system, the quality of most underwater images is poor [56]. Underwater crack images have low contrast, contain less information, and have a lot of random noise and black dots, which brings great difficulties to crack feature extraction and image segmentation [57]. The conventional method for processing underwater crack images is to first enhance the original image and then segment the enhanced image. Jinxiang Ma *et al.* [58] proposed an adaptive enhancement algorithm for dam underwater crack images based on the improved dark channel prior, which can effectively suppress the noise of underwater images and increase the clarity of the images. Wenjing Chen *et al.* [59] proposed a Retinex algorithm based on guided filtering, which effectively retains the edge information of the image while filtering the underwater image. Congping Chen *et al.* [60] proposed a new algorithm for crack detection in dam images, which converts the 2D crack image into a 3D space surface according to pixel intensity and detects cracks by analyzing curvature features. Although these algorithms have improved the detection effect of underwater crack images to a certain extent, the accuracy still needs to be improved.

The combination of image enhancement and morphological methods is the most common method for dealing with the underwater crack image segmentation problem, but the segmentation performance of this method is greatly affected by the image enhancement effect and has poor adaptability. Therefore, this paper hopes to achieve underwater crack image segmentation through deep learning methods to improve the adaptability and segmentation accuracy of the algorithm. At present, there are few open-source underwater crack image datasets. Deep learning has high requirements for datasets, and insufficient datasets are likely to lead to insufficient model training and ultimately poor underwater crack image segmentation results. Therefore, when using deep learning methods to process the underwater crack image segmentation task, the problem of insufficient underwater samples needs to be considered.

Since directly using supervised learning methods to handle various learning tasks often faces the problem of insufficient data samples, researchers have proposed some solutions, such as semi-supervised learning, few-shot learning, and transfer learning, etc. Semi-supervised learning [61]. By extracting and learning the features of labeled data and unlabeled data with the same distribution, while reducing the demand for the number of sample labels, the performance of the model is guaranteed. Few-shot learning [62] belongs to a type of transfer learning. By further training the pre-trained model on a small amount of labeled target domain data, the learning of specific tasks on the target domain is achieved. Transfer learning [63] is a learning method with a relatively wide range of applications. This method can apply the prior knowledge learned when the model is pre-trained on the source domain to the learning tasks of the target domain, which can effectively shorten the training duration and ensure the accuracy of the model. Compared with semi-supervised learning, its advantage is that the data distributions of the labeled source domain data and the unlabeled target domain data can be inconsistent. After years of development, transfer learning has spawned multiple branches. Deep transfer learning has achieved satisfactory results in many fields such as image classification [64] and semantic segmentation [65].

3 The Main Content and Chapter Arrangement of This Book

(1) To address issues in traditional image dehazing algorithms, such as being easily constrained by prior knowledge and color distortion, a multi-scale feature fusion image dehazing algorithm incorporating an attention mechanism is proposed. This network uses downsampling layers to extract feature maps at multiple scales from the image and fuses feature maps of different scales through skip connections. Meanwhile, during the skip connection process, a feature attention module composed of a channel attention submodule and a pixel attention submodule

is incorporated to focus more on important channels and pixel regions in the hazy image. Experiments show that this algorithm can overcome the shortcomings of traditional single image dehazing algorithms, which are prone to being constrained by prior knowledge and color distortion, producing relatively clear haze-free images with minimal color distortion and outperforming several comparative dehazing algorithms.

(2) To address problems in underwater optical images, such as color distortion, low contrast, and low clarity caused by the unique underwater environment, an underwater image enhancement algorithm based on a feature fusion generative adversarial network is proposed. Given the proposal and development of generative adversarial networks (GANs), to further improve the performance of underwater image enhancement algorithms, this paper leverages the advantages of GANs to design an underwater image enhancement algorithm based on a feature fusion generative adversarial network. Through adversarial training between the generator and discriminator, a highly robust underwater image enhancement model is obtained. The main components include an improved color correction algorithm, the structure of the feature fusion generative network, the structure of the discriminative network, and the loss function of the model during training. Finally, through ablation experiments on the loss function and model, as well as comparative analysis with other algorithms, it is concluded that the proposed algorithm effectively enhances underwater image quality.

(3) To address the problems of low resolution and small information content in underwater images caused by compression during acquisition and transmission due to limitations of imaging equipment or network transmission speed and bandwidth, which make feature extraction difficult, this paper designs a higher reconstruction quality underwater image super-resolution algorithm based on the Single Image Super-Resolution (SISR) algorithm ESRGAN by improving its generator network structure. Firstly, the super-resolution algorithms SRGAN and ESRGAN based on generative adversarial networks are described, along with the main improvements of ESRGAN over SRGAN. Secondly, the improved ESRGAN-based

underwater image super-resolution algorithm proposed in this paper is introduced, detailing the structures and roles of the generator and discriminator networks, as well as the loss function of the model during training. Finally, by comparing the proposed algorithm with other typical super-resolution algorithms, the effectiveness of the improvements is demonstrated.

(4) To address the inability of traditional methods to perform large-scale detection of cracks in real-time crack detection systems with high timeliness requirements, and to segment crack images more quickly and accurately, this paper adopts a nested Unet method combined with an attention mechanism for pavement crack image segmentation. The network model follows the Unet design philosophy, utilizing a Unet++ model that nests multiple layers of Unet, and incorporates an attention mechanism into each Unet layer. Through training on a dataset of 8700 crack images and validation on a test set of 1290 crack images, the proposed method is shown to be superior to the Unet++, Att_Unet, and Unet algorithms in terms of both subjective visual effects and objective performance metrics, achieving accurate detection of crack images with different morphologies and under various background conditions.

(5) To address the challenges in underwater crack image segmentation tasks, such as the scarcity of available datasets, the time-consuming and labor-intensive nature of manual annotation, and the difficulty of achieving supervised learning, this paper proposes an unsupervised domain adaptation scheme based on deep adversarial transfer. By constructing a multi-level feature adversarial network, features extracted from the source domain (annotated ground crack images) are applied to the underwater crack image segmentation task, effectively reducing the reliance on annotated underwater datasets while maintaining segmentation accuracy to a certain extent.

(6) To address the issue of poor underwater imaging quality, complex seabed environments, and the varying sizes, shapes, overlaps, and occlusions of marine organisms that limit the performance of traditional deep learning–based detection algorithms, this paper proposes an improved Faster R-CNN–based method for marine organism detection. It replaces the original VGG backbone feature extraction network with ResNet and

incorporates BiFPN to enhance the model's feature extraction and multi-scale feature fusion capabilities. The Effective IoU (EIoU) is used to replace IoU to reduce redundant bounding boxes, and the k-means++ clustering algorithm is employed to generate suitable anchor boxes. Experiments show that the proposed detection algorithm effectively improves the detection accuracy of marine organisms.

(7) To address the issues of low-quality underwater imaging, varying sizes and shapes of underwater objects, and overlapping or occlusion of underwater objects leading to low detection accuracy, this paper proposes an underwater object detection algorithm combining data augmentation and an improved YOLOv4. The convolutional block attention module (CBAM) is added to the CSPDarknet53 backbone feature extraction network in YOLOv4 to enhance the model's feature extraction capability. Skip connections within the same layer and cross-layer skip connections are incorporated into the Path Aggregation Network (PANet) to improve multi-scale feature fusion. The data augmentation method PredMix (Prediction-Mix) is used to simulate scenarios where underwater organisms are partially visible due to overlapping or occlusion, thereby enhancing the model's robustness. Experimental results demonstrate that the proposed algorithm, which combines data augmentation and improved YOLOv4, effectively improves underwater object detection accuracy.

(8) To address the challenge of detecting densely arranged objects in remote sensing images, this paper proposes an object detection algorithm based on RetinaNet with a multi-dimensional attention module, built upon the RetinaNet object detection algorithm. First, to mitigate the interference of noise information between densely packed objects, a multi-dimensional attention module composed of spatial and channel attention submodules is incorporated to suppress noise. Then, a weakened non-maximum suppression algorithm is used to replace the standard non-maximum suppression algorithm to prevent the removal of detection boxes for certain densely packed objects. Ablation experiments show that the improved algorithm outperforms the baseline algorithm in detection accuracy, while comparative experiments indicate that the

proposed algorithm achieves better detection performance than six other classic object detection algorithms. Therefore, the proposed algorithm offers high detection accuracy for densely arranged objects in remote sensing images. To some extent, addresses the challenging issue of densely packed objects in such images.

(9) To address the issue of missed detections in sonar video caused by motion blur and noise when using traditional image object detection algorithms, this paper proposes a sonar video object detection algorithm based on a memory-guided network. First, the original memory-guided network is improved to achieve inter-frame feature propagation and aggregation. Meanwhile, to enhance the model's inference speed, a strategy of cross-detection using models of different sizes is proposed: a large model is responsible for improving accuracy, while a small model is responsible for improving speed. End-to-end training is ultimately achieved on a sonar dataset. Experimental results show that, compared to single-frame object detection algorithms, the proposed algorithm solves the issue of missed detections caused by abnormal motion object postures, complex background interference, and partial object occlusion. Moreover, it achieves comparable or superior performance compared to other video object detection algorithms.

(10) To address the issues of large parameter sizes, high resource consumption, and difficulty in deploying object detection models to embedded devices, this paper proposes an embedded substation instrument detection algorithm based on an improved YOLOv4. Lightweight improvements are made to the YOLOv4 algorithm: MobileNet V3 is adopted as the backbone feature extraction network, depthwise separable convolution is introduced, and a transfer learning strategy is used for network training. TensorRT is utilized to optimize the model, making it more suitable for deployment on embedded devices with limited performance. Experimental results show that the proposed method exhibits good robustness and real-time performance for instrument detection in substation environments, meeting the requirements of substation instrument detection tasks and facilitating migration and deployment across different substations, demonstrating strong practical application value.

References

[1] Guo JC, Li Y, Guo CL, Chen S. Research progress on underwater image enhancement and restoration methods. *Journal of Image and Graphics*, 2017, 22(03): 273–287.

[2] He K, Sun J, Tang X. Single image haze removal using dark channel prior. *IEEE Transactions on Pattern Analysis and Machine Intelligence*, 2010, 33(12): 2341–2353

[3] Drews P, Nascimento E, Moraes F, *et al.* Transmission estimation in underwater single images. *Proceedings of the IEEE International Conference on Computer Vision Workshops.* 2013: 825–830.

[4] Galdran A, Pardo D, Picón A, *et al.* Automatic red-channel underwater image restoration. *Journal of Visual Communication and Image Representation.* 2015, 26: 132–145.

[5] Li CY, Guo JC, Cong RM, *et al.* Underwater image enhancement by dehazing with minimum information loss and histogram distribution prior. *IEEE Transactions on Image Processing*, 2016, 25(12): 5664–5677.

[6] Ueki Y, Ikehara M. Underwater image enhancement based on the iteration of a generalization of dark channel prior. *2019 IEEE Visual Communications and Image Processing (VCIP).* IEEE, New York, 2019: 1–4.

[7] Lin S, Bai Y, Li WT, Tang YD. Underwater image restoration based on modified model and dark channel prior. *Robot*, 2020, 42(04): 427–435.

[8] Wang Y, Zhang J, Cao Y, *et al.* A deep CNN method for underwater image enhancement. *2017 IEEE International Conference on Image Processing (ICIP).* IEEE, New York, 2017: 1382–1386.

[9] Cao K, Peng YT, Cosman PC. Underwater image restoration using deep networks to estimate background light and scene depth. *2018 IEEE Southwest Symposium on Image Analysis and Interpretation (SSIAI).* IEEE, New York, 2018: 1–4.

[10] Wang K, Hu Y, Chen J, *et al.* Underwater image restoration based on a parallel convolutional neural network. *Remote Sensing*, 2019, 11(13): 1591.

[11] Yang S, Chen Z, Feng Z, *et al.* Underwater image enhancement using scene depth-based adaptive background light estimation and dark channel prior algorithms. *IEEE Access*, 2019, 7: 165318–165327.

[12] Perez J, Attanasio AC, Nechyporenko N, *et al.* A deep learning approach for underwater image enhancement. *International Work-Conference on the Interplay between Natural and Artificial Computation.* Springer, Cham, 2017: 183–192.

[13] Ding X, Wang Y, Liang Z, *et al.* Towards underwater image enhancement using super- resolution convolutional neural networks. *International Conference on Internet Multimedia Computing and Service.* Springer, Singapore, 2017: 479–486.

[14] Goodfellow IJ, Pouget-Abadie J, Mirza M, *et al.* Generative adversarial networks. arXiv preprint arXiv: 1406.2661, 2014

[15] Knyaz VA, Kniaz V, Remondino F. Image-to-Voxel model translation with conditional adversarial networks. *Proceedings of the European Conference on Computer Vision (ECCV) Workshops.* 2018.

[16] Li M, Huang H, Ma L, *et al.* Unsupervised image-to-image translation with stacked cycle- consistent adversarial networks. *Proceedings of the European Conference on Computer Vision (ECCV).* 2018: 184–199.

[17] Li J, Skinner KA, Eustice RM, *et al.* WaterGAN: Unsupervised generative network to enable real-time color correction of monocular underwater images. *IEEE Robotics and Automation Letters*, 2017, 3(1): 387–394.

[18] Fabbri C, Jahidul Islam M, Sattar J. Enhancing underwater imagery using generative adversarial networks. *2018 IEEE International Conference on Robotics and Automation (ICRA).* IEEE, New York, 2018: 7159–7165.

[19] Li QZ, Bai WX, Niu J. Underwater image color correction and enhancement based on improved cycle-consistent generative adversarial networks. *Acta Automatica Sinica*, 2023, 49(4): 820–829.

[20] Islam MJ, Xia Y, Sattar J. Fast underwater image enhancement for improved visual perception. *IEEE Robotics and Automation Letters*, 2020, 5(2): 3227–3234.

[21] Dudhane A, Hambarde P, Patil PW, *et al.* Deep underwater image restoration and beyond. *IEEE Signal Processing Letters*, 2020, 27: 675–679.

[22] Yong ZY, Guo JC, Li CY. Weakly-supervised underwater image enhancement algorithm incorporating attention mechanism. *Journal of Zhejiang University (Engineering Science)*, 2021, 55(03): 555–562.

[23] Li H, Zhuang P. DewaterNet: A fusion adversarial real underwater image enhancement network. *Signal Processing: Image Communication*, 2021, 95:116220.

[24] Chen YD, Wang LM. Face recognition method based on convolutional neural network. *Journal of Northeast Normal University (Natural Science Edition)*, 2016, 48(02):70–76.

[25] He YW, Zhang JP. Deep learning for gait recognition: A survey. *Pattern Recognition and Artificial Intelligence*, 2018, 31(5): 442–452.

[26] Lan HL. A survey of crowd counting algorithms. *Computer Products and Circulation*, 2019(7): 91 + 93.

[27] Gu WT, Yu XW, Li Y, Qiu Z, Zhuo Y, Dong Y. Research on safety helmet detection and monitoring based on deep learning. *Power Equipment Management*, 2020(05):42–43 + 49.

[28] Zhang XY, Gao HB, Zhao JH, Zhou M. A review of deep learning-based autonomous driving technology. *Journal of Tsinghua University (Science and Technology)*, 2018, 58(04):438–444.

[29] Du J. Water Body Identification from UAV remote sensing images based on deep learning. *Jiangxi Science*, 2017, 35(1): 158–161 + 170.

[30] Wang T, Chen Y, Qiao M, *et al.* A fast and robust convolutional neural network-based defect detection model in product quality control. *The International Journal of Advanced Manufacturing Technology*, 2018, 94(9): 3465–3471.

[31] Xu X, Tanvir A. Research on multi-object detection based on faster R-CNN. *Computer and Digital Engineering*, 2020, 48(10): 2393–2399.

[32] Xu YJ. Video multi-target pedestrian detection and tracking based on deep learning. *Modern Information Technology*, 2020, 4(12): 6–9.

[33] Brys T, Harutyunyan A, Vrancx P, *et al.* Multi-objectivization and ensembles of shapings in reinforcement learning. *Neurocomputing*, 2017, 263: 48–59.

[34] Gao SH, Tan YQ, Cheng MM, *et al.* Highly efficient salient object detection with 100k parameters. *European Conference on Computer Vision*. Springer, Cham, 2020: 702–721.

[35] Fan DP, Zhai Y, Borji A, *et al.* BBS-Net: RGB-D salient object detection with a bifurcated backbone strategy network. *European Conference on Computer Vision*. Springer, Cham, 2020: 275–292.

[36] Girshick R, Donahue J, Darrell T, *et al.* Rich feature hierarchies for accurate object detection and semantic segmentation. *Proceedings of the IEEE Conference on Computer Vision and Pattern Recognition*. 2014: 580–587.

[37] He K, Zhang X, Ren S, *et al.* Spatial pyramid pooling in deep convolutional networks for visual recognition. *IEEE Transactions on Pattern Analysis and Machine Intelligence*, 2015, 37(9): 1904–1916.

[38] Girshick R. Fast r-cnn. *Proceedings of the IEEE International Conference on Computer Vision*. 2015: 1440–1448.

[39] Ren S, He K, Girshick R, *et al.* Faster r-cnn: Towards real-time object detection with region proposal networks. arXiv preprint arXiv:1506.01497, 2015.

[40] Redmon J, Divvala S, Girshick R, *et al.* You only look once: Unified, real-time object detection. *Proceedings of the IEEE Conference on Computer Vision and Pattern Recognition*. 2016: 779–788.

[41] Liu W, Anguelov D, Erhan D, *et al.* SSD: Single shot multibox detector. *European Conference on Computer Vision.* Springer, Cham, 2016: 21–37.

[42] Redmon J, Farhadi A. YOLO9000: Better, faster, stronger. *Proceedings of the IEEE Conference on Computer Vision and Pattern Recognition.* 2017: 7263–7271.

[43] Redmon J, Farhadi A. YOLOv3: An incremental improvement. arXiv preprint arXiv:1804.02767, 2018.

[44] Bochkovskiy A, Wang CY, Liao HYM. YOLOv4: Optimal speed and accuracy of object detection. arXiv preprint arXiv:2004.10934, 2020.

[45] Wang W, Wang M, Li H, *et al.* Pavement crack image acquisition methods and crack extraction algorithms: A review. *Journal of Traffic and Transportation Engineering (English Edition)*, 2019, 6(6): 535–556.

[46] Cao W, Liu Q, He Z. Review of pavement defect detection methods. *IEEE Access*, 2020, 8: 14531–14544.

[47] Kang D, Benipal SS, Gopal DL, *et al.* Hybrid pixel-level concrete crack segmentation and quantification across complex backgrounds using deep learning. *Automation in Construction*, 2020, 118: 103291.

[48] Dung CV. Autonomous concrete crack detection using deep fully convolutional neural network. *Automation in Construction*, 2019, 99: 52–58.

[49] Long J, Shelhamer E, Darrell T. Fully convolutional networks for semantic segmentation. *Proceedings of the IEEE Conference on Computer Vision and Pattern Recognition.* 2015: 3431–3440.

[50] Ronneberger O, Fischer P, Brox T. U-net: Convolutional networks for biomedical image segmentation. *International Conference on Medical Image Computing and Computer-Assisted Intervention.* Springer, Cham, 2015: 234–241.

[51] Badrinarayanan V, Kendall A, Cipolla R. Segnet: A deep convolutional encoder-decoder architecture for image segmentation. *IEEE Transactions on Pattern Analysis and Machine Intelligence*, 2017, 39(12): 2481–2495.

[52] Huyan J, Li W, Tighe S, *et al.* CrackU-net: A novel deep convolutional neural network for pixelwise pavement crack detection. *Structural Control and Health Monitoring*, 2020, 27(8): e2551.

[53] Cheng J, Xiong W, Chen W, Gu Y, Li Y, "Pixel-level Crack Detection using U-Net," TENCON 2018 - 2018 IEEE Region 10 Conference, Jeju, Korea (South), 2018, pp. 0462–0466, doi: 10.1109/TENCON.2018.8650059.

[54] Li S, Zhao X. Automatic crack detection and measurement of concrete structure using convolutional encoder-decoder network. *IEEE Access*, 2020, 8: 134602–134618.

[55] Zou Q, Zhang Z, Li Q, *et al.* Deepcrack: Learning hierarchical convolutional features for crack detection. *IEEE Transactions on Image Processing*, 2018, 28(3): 1498–1512.

[56] O'Byrne M, Pakrashi V, Schoefs F, *et al.* Semantic segmentation of underwater imagery using deep networks trained on synthetic imagery. *Journal of Marine Science and Engineering*, 2018, 6(3): 93.

[57] Fan X, Wu J, Shi P, *et al.* A novel automatic dam crack detection algorithm based on local-global clustering. *Multimedia Tools and Applications*, 2018, 77(20): 26581–26599.

[58] Ma JX, Fan XN, Wu ZX, Zhang XW, Shi PF, Wang GR. Dam underwater crack image enhancement algorithm based on dark channel prior. *Journal of Image and Graphics*, 2016, 21(12): 1574–1584.

[59] [59] Chen WJ. *Research on Detection Methods for Underwater Dam Crack Images.* North China University of Water Resources and Electric Power, 2019.

[60] Chen C, Wang J, Zou L, *et al.* A novel crack detection algorithm of underwater dam image. *2012 International Conference on Systems and Informatics (ICSAI2012).* IEEE, New York, 2012: 1825–1828.

[61] Van Engelen JE, Hoos HH. A survey on semi-supervised learning. *Machine Learning*, 2020, 109(2): 373–440.

[62] Sung F, Yang Y, Zhang L, *et al.* Learning to compare: Relation network for few-shot learning. *Proceedings of the IEEE Conference on Computer Vision and Pattern Recognition.* 2018: 1199–1208.

[63] Tan C, Sun F, Kong T, *et al.* A survey on deep transfer learning. *International Conference on Artificial Neural Networks.* Springer, Cham, 2018: 270–279.

[64] Pires de Lima R, Marfurt K. Convolutional neural network for remote-sensing scene classification: Transfer learning analysis. *Remote Sensing*, 2020, 12(1): 86.

[65] Wurm M, Stark T, Zhu XX, *et al.* Semantic segmentation of slums in satellite images using transfer learning on fully convolutional neural networks. *ISPRS Journal of Photogrammetry and Remote Sensing*, 2019, 150: 59–69.

Chapter 1

Image Dehazing Algorithm Based on U-Net

1.1 Introduction

The atmosphere contains particles such as fog, smoke, and dust, which refract and scatter light, often resulting in color distortion, low contrast, and blurriness in images captured in such conditions. These low-quality images can negatively impact advanced visual tasks like object detection and classification, making dehazing essential for restoring foggy images to clear ones. In recent decades, dehazing has garnered increasing attention as a preprocessing step in advanced visual tasks.

Traditional dehazing methods primarily rely on prior knowledge, such as the Dark Channel Prior (DCP) proposed by He *et al.* [1], which assumes that foggy images contain at least one channel with very low intensity. While effective, these methods can introduce color distortion in certain scenes. Other methods, like those by Meng *et al.* [2] and Zhu *et al.* [3], use boundary constraints and linear models to improve the dehazing process. Despite their contributions, many traditional methods have limitations, often leading to incomplete dehazing and color distortion due to reliance on prior information and manual feature extraction.

With the rapid development of deep learning, many dehazing methods based on this technology have emerged, primarily utilizing Convolutional Neural Networks (CNNs) to create trainable dehazing networks. For instance, Cai *et al.* [4] proposed DehazeNet, which estimates the mapping between foggy images and transmission maps by learning features from the foggy images, introducing an end-to-end dehazing network. Ren *et al.* [5] introduced the Multi-Scale Convolutional Neural Networks (MSCNN), which uses a large-scale network for overall transmission estimation and a small-scale network for refinement, resulting in more accurate transmission maps. Li *et al.* [6] rederived the atmospheric scattering model to estimate transmission and atmospheric light parameters. While these deep learning methods improved dehazing performance, they often separate the task into two steps rather than achieving true end-to-end processing. To address this, some methods now directly or iteratively estimate clear images using deep CNNs. For example, Ren *et al.*'s Gated Fusion Network (GFN) estimates a weight map to guide the fusion of the input image [7], while Chen *et al.*'s Gated Context Aggregation Network (GCAN) focuses on direct recovery of clear images [8], employing advanced techniques to mitigate grid artifacts. Despite these advancements, the algorithms may inadequately focus on dense fog regions and crucial channel information, impacting overall dehazing effectiveness.

This paper addresses the shortcomings of existing methods by proposing a multi-scale feature fusion image dehazing algorithm that incorporates an attention mechanism. The algorithm utilizes an encoder-decoder structure similar to U-Net to directly learn an adaptive dehazing model. Specifically, the encoder employs a convolutional neural network to obtain feature maps at different scales, while the decoder sequentially recovers image details from the encoded feature maps. To fully leverage input information and accurately estimate structural details, skip connections link the encoder and decoder feature maps for fusion across scales. Additionally, a novel feature attention module, composed of channel and pixel attention sub-modules, is cleverly integrated into the encoder–decoder structure. This module enhances the network's focus on important channels and pixels, concentrating attention on dense fog regions and critical channel information. The feature attention module improves the network's flexibility in handling diverse types of information, allowing the proposed algorithm to effectively process foggy images with high density and rich details.

1.2 The Algorithm

1.2.1 *Feature extraction layer*

According to the imaging principles of foggy images, researchers typically use the atmospheric scattering model to simulate the imaging process of foggy images. Therefore, this model is also an important basis for image dehazing. The expression of the atmospheric scattering model is given in Eq. (1.1):

$$I(x) = J(x)t(x) + A(1 - t(x)) \tag{1.1}$$

In this context, $J(x)$ represents the foggy image obtained by the imaging device; $I(x)$ represents the dehazed image; denotes the atmospheric light value; A and $t(x)$ represents the transmission map. To clarify the dehazing process, Eq. (1.1) can be further expressed as Eq. (1.2):

$$J(x) = \frac{I(x) - A}{t(x)} + A \tag{1.2}$$

From Eq. (1.2), it is clear that image dehazing can be performed based on the estimation of the atmospheric light value A and the transmission map $t(x)$. Therefore, the core task of dehazing algorithms is to estimate these two prior pieces of information. In some deep learning-based dehazing algorithms, transmission maps are estimated first using convolutional neural networks, followed by traditional methods for estimating the atmospheric light value. While these algorithms perform well, they do not constitute true end-to-end image dehazing methods. This paper, however, utilizes the U-Net architecture to directly estimate the transmission map, atmospheric light value, and clear image, aiming to develop a model that learns an adaptive dehazing process directly from the input.

1.2.2 *Network structure*

This paper proposes a multi-scale feature fusion image dehazing algorithm that incorporates an attention mechanism. The network structure of this algorithm is illustrated in Fig. 1.1.

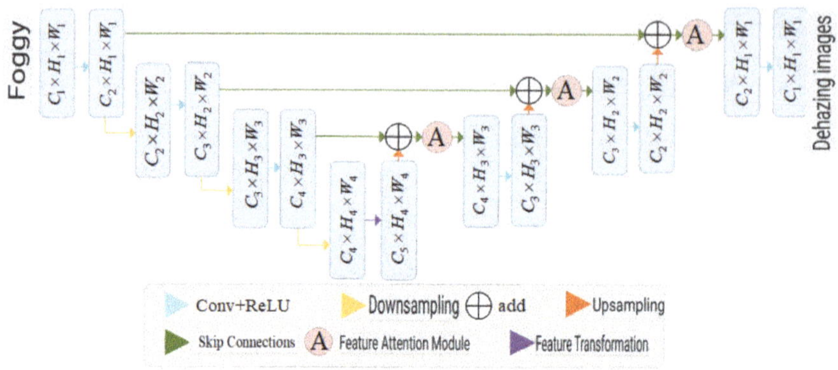

Figure 1.1. Network structure diagram of this method.

From Fig. 1.1, it can be seen that the main structure of this algorithm employs an encoder-decoder network similar to U-Net, consisting of four modules: the encoder module, feature transformation module, feature attention module, and decoder module. In this algorithm, convolutional neural networks are first used to extract feature maps at multiple scales from the images. Then, skip connections are employed to fuse feature maps of different scales, ensuring that the final feature map contains both deep and shallow features, which enhances the algorithm's ability to express features. Additionally, a feature attention module, composed of channel attention and pixel attention sub-modules, is integrated into the network, allowing it to focus more on dense fog pixel regions and important channel information. The following sections will provide a detailed description of each module in the proposed multi-scale feature fusion image dehazing algorithm that incorporates the attention mechanism.

1.2.2.1 *Encoder module*

The encoder module consists of convolutional layers and downsampling layers. The convolutional layers perform two operations: first, a convolution operation using a kernel with a stride of 2 and a size of 3×3. The choice of a 3×3 kernel is due to its effectiveness in extracting features while also reducing the number of parameters in the network, thereby improving computational efficiency. After the convolution operation, a ReLU activation function is applied.

Following this, downsampling is performed to obtain feature maps at multiple scales, encoding the image information in this manner.

1.2.2.2 *Feature transformation module*

As is well known, the main advantage of deep networks lies in their ability to represent very complex functions and learn deeper, more abstract features, thereby enhancing the network's feature expression capability. Early researchers aimed to improve network performance by increasing its depth, but eventually found that performance declined after reaching a certain depth. This phenomenon is attributed to the vanishing gradient problem during backpropagation, which prevents the adjustment of weights in earlier layers. The introduction of residual networks addressed this issue by using identity mappings, allowing for deeper feature extraction without degradation in performance as the network deepens. To balance network performance and computational efficiency, this paper employs a feature transformation module consisting of 18 residual blocks for feature learning. Each residual block contains two convolution operations with 3×3 kernels and a ReLU activation function. The structure of the feature transformation module is illustrated in Fig. 1.2.

1.2.2.3 *Feature attention module*

Most existing dehazing networks do not differentiate between different channel and pixel features, yet numerous studies have shown that different channel features carry distinct weighting information. Additionally, the distribution of fog concentration in foggy images

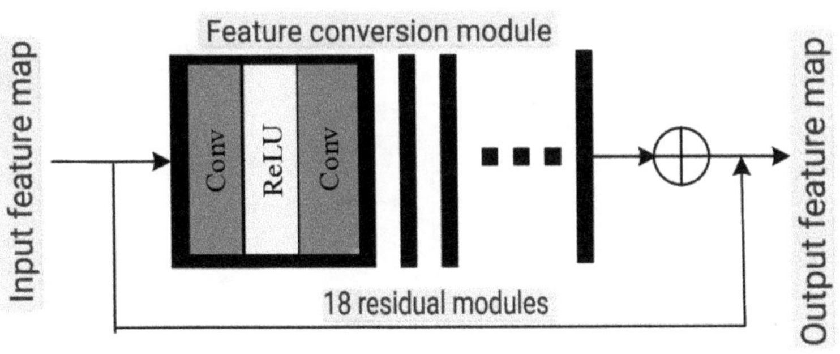

Figure 1.2. Point feature conversion module.

is uneven, resulting in different pixel weights for areas of light and heavy fog. Treating channel and pixel features equally may lead to the waste of computational resources on unnecessary information while neglecting critical details, ultimately limiting the network's representational capacity. Since the introduction of attention mechanisms has proven effective in various studies, many researchers have started incorporating them into their models. This paper integrates a feature attention module, composed of channel and pixel attention sub-modules, into the encoder-decoder network. This module enables the network to focus more on important channels and pixels, concentrating attention on dense fog pixels and crucial channel information. This flexibility significantly enhances the dehazing performance for foggy images with high concentration and rich details. The structure of the feature attention module is illustrated in Fig. 1.3.

1. **Channel attention sub-module:** In this paper, global spatial information within channels is described using average pooling, as shown in Eq. (1.3):

$$g_c = H_p(F_c) = \frac{1}{H \times W} \sum_{i=1}^{H} \sum_{j=1}^{W} X_c(i, j) \tag{1.3}$$

   In this context, F_c represents the feature map of the c-th channel, $H_p(\cdot)$ denotes the pooling function, g_c represents the output feature map of the c-th channel, H and W represent the height and width of the feature map, respectively. The value at the pixel location (i, j) in the c-th channel's feature map is denoted as $X_c(i, j)$. After this transformation, the dimensions of the feature map change from $C \times H \times W$ to $C \times 1 \times 1$ (C is the number of channels). The feature map is then processed through two convolution

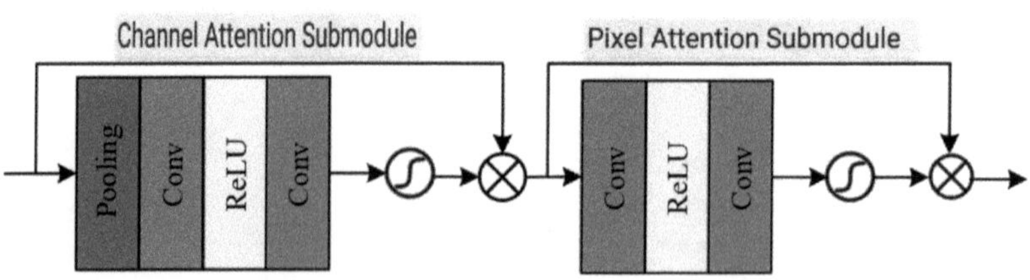

Figure 1.3. Feature attention module.

layers, followed by a ReLU activation function and a sigmoid activation function, as shown in Eq. (1.4):

$$CA_c = \sigma\{Conv\{\delta[Conv(g_c)]\}\} \tag{1.4}$$

In this context, $\delta(\cdot)$ denotes the ReLU activation function, $\sigma(\cdot)$ represents the sigmoid activation function, and CA_c denotes the weight for the c-th channel. Finally, the output feature map from the channel attention sub-module is obtained by multiplying CA_c with the input feature map F_c, as shown in Eq. (1.5):

$$F_c^* = CA_c \times F_c. \tag{1.5}$$

2. **Pixel attention submodule:** After passing the feature map output from the channel attention sub-module through two convolution layers, followed by a ReLU activation function and a sigmoid activation function, the dimensions change from $C \times H \times W$ to $1 \times H \times W$, as shown in Eq. (1.6):

$$PA = \sigma\{Conv\{\delta[Conv(F_c^*)]\}\} \tag{1.6}$$

In this context, $\delta(\cdot)$ denotes the ReLU activation function, $\sigma(\cdot)$ represents the sigmoid activation function, and PA_c denotes the weight for the c-th channel. Finally, the output feature map from the pixel attention sub-module is obtained by multiplying PA_c with the input feature map F_c^*, as shown in Eq. (1.7):

$$\bar{F} = F_c^* \times PA_c. \tag{1.7}$$

1.2.2.4 *Decoder module*

The decoder module consists of three upsampling layers and three convolution layers. In contrast to the encoder, the upsampling layers in the decoder sequentially restore image details, ultimately producing the dehazed image. To maximize the information flow between different levels, skip connections are used to link the feature maps between the encoder and decoder. Simultaneously, the feature attention module is integrated into these skip connections, allowing the network to focus more on important channel and pixel information within the image.

1.2.3 *Loss function*

The loss function used in the proposed network is the smooth loss, which quantitatively describes the difference between the foggy image and the ground truth image. This loss function is less sensitive to outliers, effectively preventing the issue of gradient explosion. The smooth loss function is shown in Eq. (1.8):

$$L = \frac{1}{N}\sum_{p=1}^{N}\sum_{c=1}^{3} F(\bar{y}_c(p) - y_c(p)) \tag{1.8}$$

In this context, N represents the total number of pixels in an image, p denotes the pth pixel, and c indicates the cth channel. Thus, $\bar{y}_c(p)$ represents the pixel value of the pth pixel in the cth channel of the predicted image, while $y_c(p)$ denotes the pixel value of the pth pixel in the cth channel of the ground truth image. The function $F(\cdot)$ can be expressed as shown in Eq. (1.9):

$$F(x) = \begin{cases} 0.5x^2, & \text{if } |x| < 1 \\ |x| - 0.5, & \text{otherwise} \end{cases} \tag{1.9}$$

1.3 Experimental Results and Analysis

1.3.1 *Experimental environment*

The computer processor used in this experiment is an Intel Core i7-7700, with 128GB of RAM and 12 GB of GPU memory, utilizing an NVIDIA TITAN V GPU. The implementation is based on Python 3.6, with the deep learning framework being PyTorch 1.0.0.

1.3.2 *Experimental dataset*

In general, it is challenging to collect a large number of real-world foggy images along with their corresponding clear images. Therefore, synthetic foggy images are often used to evaluate the dehazing performance of algorithms. These foggy images are generated by adding appropriate scattering coefficients and atmospheric light values to real clear images. This paper first uses the commonly employed RESIDE synthetic dataset to validate the performance of the proposed algorithm. The dataset includes the NYU Depth V2 dataset and the Middlebury Stereo dataset. The RESIDE indoor training set (ITS) is composed of 1,399 clear images, generating foggy images with atmospheric light values ranging from [0.7, 1.0] and scattering coefficients ranging from [0.6, 1.8], with each clear image producing 10 foggy images. Thus, the indoor dataset contains a total of 13,990 synthetic foggy images, with 13,000 for training and the remaining 990 for validation. The RESIDE outdoor training set (OTS) consists of 8,477 clear images, with atmospheric light values ranging from [0.8, 1.0] and scattering coefficients from [0.04, 0.2]. The outdoor dataset contains a total of 296,695 synthetic foggy images. The test set used in this paper is the Synthetic Objective Testing Set (SOTS) from the RESIDE dataset, which includes 500 indoor images and 500 outdoor images. Additionally, to further demonstrate the effectiveness and robustness of the proposed method, two vividly colored images from the Middlebury Stereo dataset (MSD) were synthesized into foggy images using the atmospheric scattering model, primarily to validate whether the algorithms cause color distortion in the images after dehazing. Finally, comparative experiments were conducted on real foggy images to verify the dehazing effectiveness of the proposed algorithm in real-world scenarios.

1.3.3 *Evaluation metrics*

Since subjective judgment cannot fully demonstrate the effectiveness of the proposed method, this paper uses Peak Signal to Noise Ratio (PSNR) and Structural Similarity Index (SSIM) to quantify the recovery quality of dehazed images in comparison with existing dehazing methods. PSNR represents the ratio of the maximum signal power to the noise power, with a higher PSNR value indicating that the dehazed image is closer to the clear image. SSIM measures the similarity between two images, with a higher SSIM value indicating a lower degree of distortion in the dehazed image.

1.3.4 *Parameter settings*

The important experimental parameters of this study are provided in Table 1.1.

The optimizer used is Adam, with the parameters β_1 and β_2 set to their default values of 0.9 and 0.999, respectively. The batch size

Table 1.1. Experimental parameters.

Parameters	Values
Optimizer	Adam
Batch size	1
Epoch	100
Learning rate	0.0001

is set to 1, meaning that only one image is trained at a time. The number of epochs for the training set is set to 100. The initial learning rate is set to 0.0001, and a cosine annealing function is employed to adjust the learning rate. The learning rate adjustment function is shown in Eq. (1.10):

$$\eta_t = \frac{1}{2}\left(1 + \cos\left(\frac{t\pi}{T}\right)\right)\eta \tag{1.10}$$

In this context, η represents the initial learning rate, η_t denotes the current learning rate, T represents the total number of batches, and t indicates a specific batch.

1.3.5 *Experimental results*

To verify the effectiveness of the proposed algorithm, this section conducts both qualitative and quantitative comparisons of its dehazing performance with several popular dehazing algorithms, including DCP, DehazeNet, MSCNN, AOD-Net, and GFN. To ensure a fair comparison, all methods follow the same training approach. The dehazing performance of each algorithm is then tested on the SOTS dataset, MSD dataset, and real foggy images.

1.3.5.1 *Experiments on the synthetic dataset*

First, the proposed algorithm is quantitatively compared with the other algorithms on the SOTS dataset, and the experimental results are presented in Table 1.2.

From Table 1.2, it can be seen that the PSNR and SSIM values of the dehazed images produced by the proposed method are higher than those of the other comparison algorithms, demonstrating that the proposed dehazing algorithm outperforms the others.

Table 1.2. Comparison of evaluation metrics for each algorithm.

	Indoor		Outdoor	
Method	PSNR/dB	SSIM	PSNR/dB	SSIM
DCP	16.62	0.8179	19.13	0.8148
DehazeNet	21.14	0.8472	22.46	0.8514
MSCNN	19.84	0.8327	22.06	0.9078
AOD-Net	19.06	0.8504	20.29	0.8765
GFN	24.91	0.9186	28.29	0.9621
Proposed algorithm	28.24	0.9440	29.42	0.9710

Note: The bold font indicates the optimal values in each column.

Next, a qualitative comparison of the proposed algorithm with the other algorithms on the SOTS dataset is conducted, and the results are shown in Fig. 1.4. As illustrated in Fig. 1.4, the DCP method fails to accurately estimate fog thickness, often resulting in dehazed images that are darker than the actual images (e.g., the desktop and wall areas in the first image of Fig. 1.4(b)), and it also leads to severe color distortion (e.g., the sky area in the third image of Fig. 1.4(b)), ultimately affecting visual quality.

The three deep learning-based methods, DehazeNet, MSCNN, and AOD-Net, generally perform better than traditional methods, as they are not constrained by prior knowledge. However, these methods overlook the structural information of foggy images during feature learning, leading to significant errors in the estimated transmittance and resulting in images that appear overly white after dehazing (e.g., Figs. 1.4(c), (d), and (e)). The GFN method achieves good dehazing results, effectively removing most of the fog, but still struggles in areas with high fog concentration (e.g., the region between chairs in the first image of Fig. 1.4(f)). In contrast, the proposed method demonstrates the best dehazing performance. The inclusion of the feature attention module allows it to effectively handle high fog concentration areas while preserving image details and minimizing color distortion.

Finally, a qualitative comparison of the proposed algorithm with the other algorithms on the MSD dataset is conducted, and the results are shown in Fig. 1.5. From Fig. 1.5, it can be observed that the DCP method results in significant color distortion and overall darkening of the dehazed images. The DehazeNet and AOD-Net

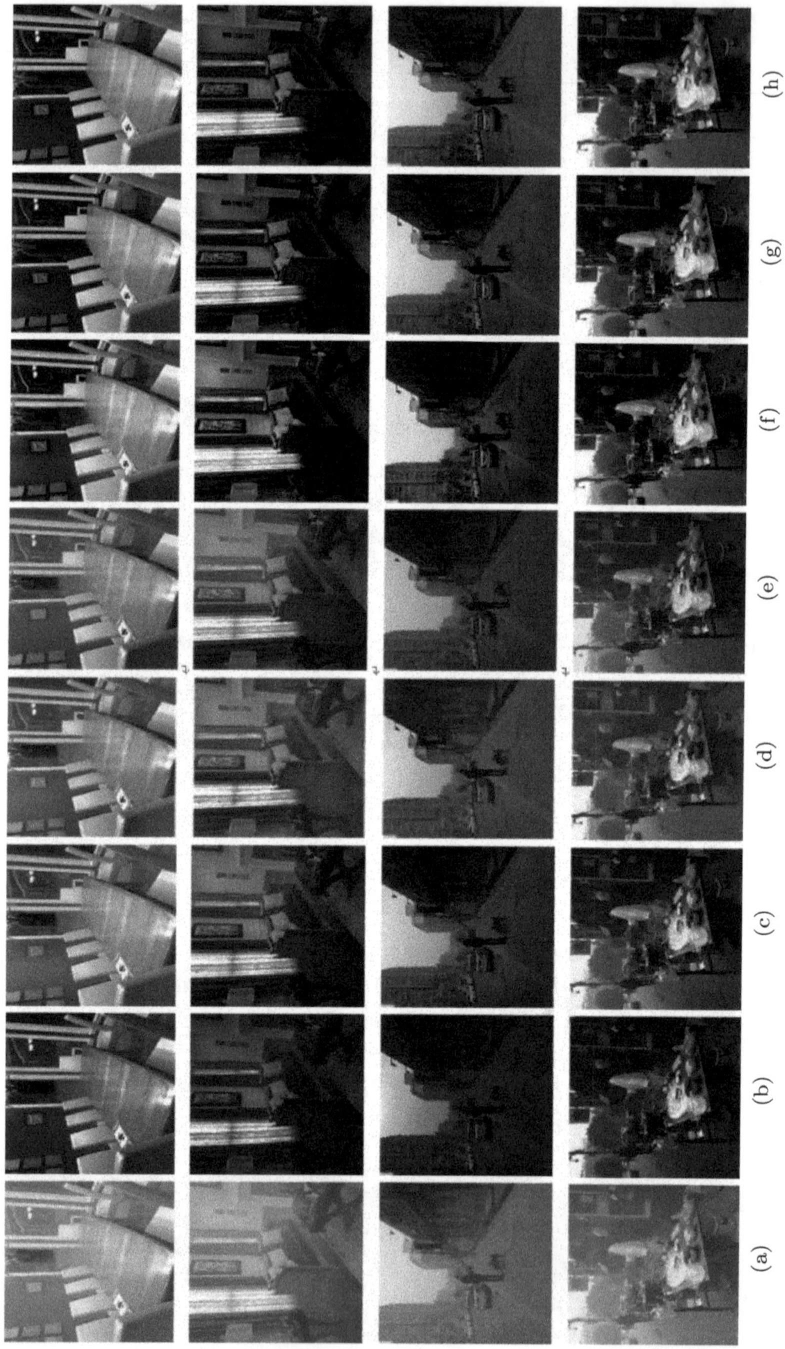

Figure 1.4. Dehazing results of various algorithms on the SOTS dataset. (a) Foggy, (b) DCP, (c) DehazeNet, (d) MSCNN, (e) AOD-Net, (f) GFN, (g) Methods, (h) Ground Truth.

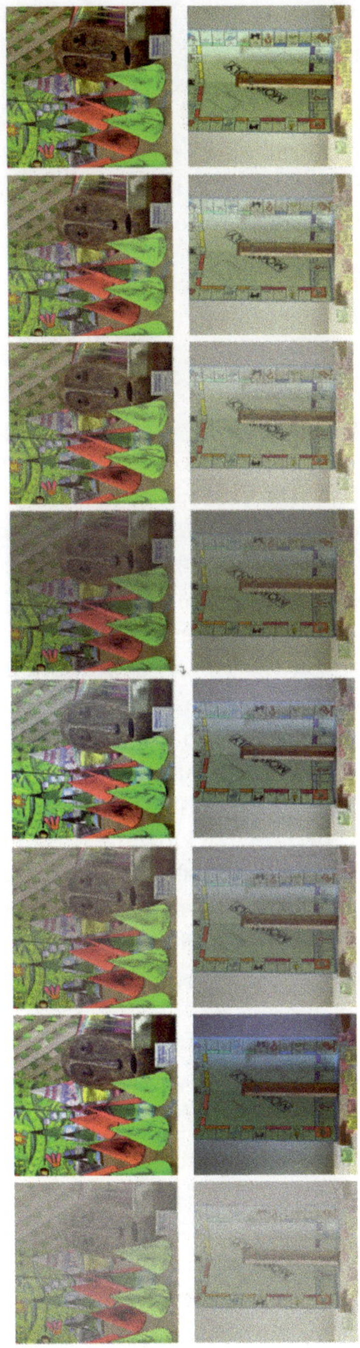

(a) (b) (c) (d) (e) (f) (g) (h)

Figure 1.5. Dehazing results of various algorithms on the MSD dataset. (a) Foggy, (b) DCP, (c) DehazeNet, (d) MSCNN, (e) AOD-Net, (f) GFN, (g) Methods, (h) Ground Truth.

methods produce images that are not thoroughly dehazed, resulting in an overall white tint that leads to color distortion. The MSCNN method also suffers from severe color distortion, with the overall tone significantly deviating from the ground truth images.

The GFN method maintains good color fidelity after dehazing; however, due to the high fog concentration in the original images, some fog remains. In contrast, the proposed method exhibits the best color fidelity among the compared algorithms, along with effective dehazing performance.

1.3.5.2 *Experiments on real fog images*

To validate the proposed algorithm's dehazing effectiveness in real scenarios, a qualitative comparison is conducted on three classic real fog images, with results shown in Fig. 1.6. From Fig. 1.6(b), it can be seen that the image processed by the DCP method still suffers from darkness issues, primarily due to its inability to accurately estimate fog concentration, leading to inaccurate transmission map estimates (e.g., the girl's skin tone appearing dark in the first image and the mountain region being dark in the third). Additionally, DCP causes significant color distortion in the dehazed images (e.g., overly blue sky in the third image), negatively impacting visual quality.

Figures 1.6(c), (d), and (e) show that DehazeNet, MSCNN, and AOD-Net still struggle with poor dehazing performance, particularly in removing fog from distant backgrounds. Although the GFN method (Fig. 1.6(f)) performs well in color retention and dehazing, it still leaves some fog in heavily affected areas. In contrast, Fig. 1.6(g) demonstrates that the proposed method effectively removes fog while preserving the image's color integrity, resulting in more natural and visually appealing dehazed images.

1.3.6 *Comparison of running time*

Table 1.3 shows the average processing time for each algorithm when handling a single fog image.

From Table 1.3, it can be observed that the DCP method has the longest average dehazing time due to its traditional approach, which requires more time for feature extraction. In contrast, the AOD-Net method has the shortest average dehazing time, as its lightweight

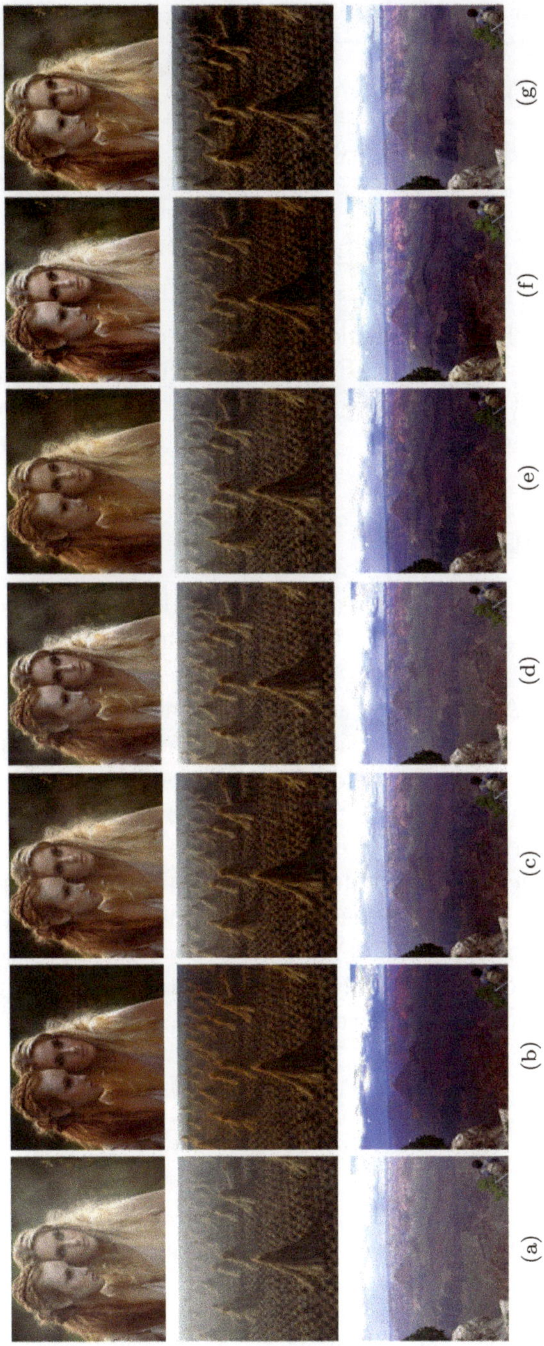

Figure 1.6. Dehazing results of various algorithms on real fog images. (a) Foggy, (b) DCP, (c) DehazeNet, (d) MSCNN, (e) AOD-Net, (f) GFN, (g) Method.

Table 1.3. Comparison of average running time for each algorithm.

Method	DCP	DehazeNet	MSCNN	AOD-Net	GFN	Proposed algorithm
Time(s)	1.53	0.30	0.26	0.08	0.37	0.20

architecture is often combined with advanced vision tasks like object detection. Among the compared algorithms, the proposed method ranks second in dehazing efficiency, with an average processing time of 0.20 seconds, just after AOD-Net. This efficiency is primarily due to the simpler network framework and fewer involved modules in the proposed method.

1.4 Conclusion

This chapter presents an effective end-to-end dehazing network similar to the U-Net architecture. The network utilizes downsampling layers to extract multi-scale feature maps and merges them through skip connections. Additionally, a feature attention module, consisting of channel and pixel attention submodules, is incorporated to focus on important channels and pixel regions in the hazy images. The model is trained using the publicly available RESIDE dataset, and the trained model is tested on the SOTS, MSD, and real image datasets. Experimental results demonstrate that the proposed algorithm overcomes the limitations of traditional single-image dehazing methods, which are often constrained by prior knowledge and prone to color distortion, yielding clearer dehazed images with minimal color distortion, outperforming several comparative dehazing algorithms.

References

[1] He KM, Sun J, Tang XO. Single image haze removal using dark channel prior. *IEEE Transactions on Pattern Analysis and Machine Intelligence*, 2011, 33(12): 2341–2353.

[2] Meng GF, Wang Y, Duan JY, *et al.* Efficient image dehazing with boundary constraint and contextual regularization. *Proceedings of the*

2013 IEEE International Conference on Computer Vision, Sydney, Australia, 8–12 April, 2013: 617–624.

[3] Zhu QS, Mai JM, Shao L. A fast single image haze removal algorithm using color attenuation prior. *IEEE Transactions on Image Processing*, 2015, 24(11): 3522–3533.

[4] Cai BL, Xu XM, Jia K, *et al.* Dehazenet: An end-to-end system for single image haze removal. *IEEE Transactions on Image Processing*, 2016, 25(11): 5187–5198.

[5] Ren WQ, Liu S, Zhang H, *et al.* Single image dehazing via multi-scale convolutional neural networks. *Proceedings of the 2016 European Conference on Computer Vision, Amsterdam, Netherlands*, 11–14 October, 2016: 154–169.

[6] Li BY, Peng XL, Wang ZY, *et al.* Aod-net: All-in-one dehazing network. *Proceedings of the 2017 IEEE International Conference on Computer Vision, Venice, Italy*, 22–29 October, 2017: 4780–4788.

[7] Ren WQ, Ma L, Zhang JW, *et al.* Gated fusion network for single image dehazing. *Proceedings of the 2018 IEEE/CVF Conference on Computer Vision and Pattern Recognition, Salt Lake City, USA*, 18–23 June, 2018: 3253–3261.

[8] Chen DD, He MM, Fan QN, *et al.* Gated context aggregation network for image dehazing and deraining. *Proceedings of the 2019 IEEE Winter Conference on Applications of Computer Vision, Waikoloa Village, USA*, 7–11 January, 2019: 1375–1383.

Chapter 2

GAN-Based Image Enhancement Algorithms

2.1 Introduction

Underwater optical images are typically degraded by the unique underwater environment, exhibiting issues such as color distortion, low contrast, and reduced sharpness. These problems severely diminish the visual quality of underwater images and create significant challenges for subsequent processing tasks. In recent years, generative models—particularly the development of Generative Adversarial Networks (GANs) [1], have achieved remarkable success in image restoration [2] and image-to-image translation [3]. This success is attributed to GANs' ability to learn semantically meaningful loss functions through discriminators, which surpass traditional pixel-level difference metrics [4]. To advance underwater image enhancement algorithms and obtain higher-quality results, this paper leverages the strengths of GANs to design a feature fusion-based generative adversarial network for underwater image enhancement. Through adversarial training between the generator and discriminator, we develop a robust underwater image enhancement model that effectively addresses the complex degradation patterns in underwater environments. Our framework strategically integrates multi-scale feature fusion mechanisms to enhance color fidelity, contrast restoration, and detail preservation in challenging underwater scenarios.

2.2 Generative Adversarial Network Model

2.2.1 *Basic concept*

The Generative Adversarial Network (GAN) is fundamentally a generative model that employs a novel framework for estimating generative models through an adversarial process. A GAN typically consists of at least two subnetworks: a generator and a discriminator. The generator is designed to learn the distribution of real data, aiming to make the generated data distribution as consistent as possible with the real data distribution. The discriminator, essentially a binary classifier, is tasked with determining whether the input sample is from the real data or the generated data. During the training phase, the generator's objective is to produce data that closely resembles the real distribution to "deceive" the discriminator, while the discriminator's goal is to maximize its accuracy in distinguishing between real and generated data. The GAN is trained through an alternating process where the two subnetworks compete against each other. The GAN reaches a stable state when the discriminator becomes unable to determine the source of the input data, at which point the generator is capable of recovering the real data distribution. The structure of the GAN is illustrated in Fig. 2.1.

2.2.2 *Representation of mathematical models*

The training process of a GAN corresponds to a minimax game, where the generator aims to produce outputs that are as realistic as possible, thereby minimizing the discriminator's accuracy in distinguishing between real and generated data. Conversely, the discriminator strives to maximize its accuracy in determining the origin

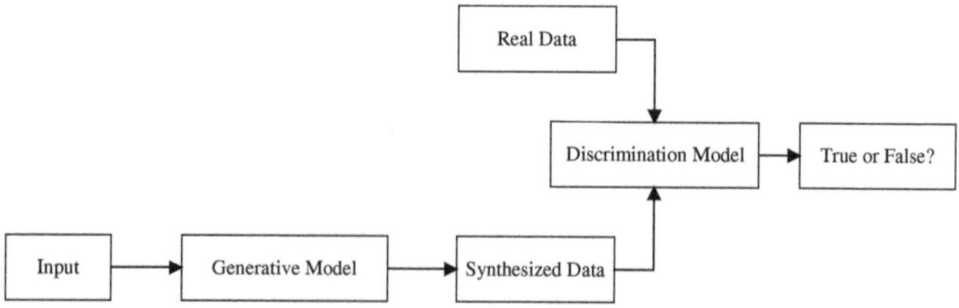

Figure 2.1. Block diagram for generating an adversarial network.

of the input samples. Through this adversarial training process, the generator progressively improves its ability to generate realistic outputs. In traditional GANs, the objective function is formulated using cross-entropy, which can be expressed as:

$$\min_G \max_D V(G, D) = E[\log D(y)] + E[\log(1 - D(G(z)))] \quad (2.1)$$

In this context, y represents the real data from the training set, and z denotes the random input signal to the generator network. G and D represent the generator network and the discriminator network, respectively. During the adversarial training process, the discriminator D aims to minimize the probability of misclassification by predicting the real data y as 1 and the output of the generator $G(z)$ as 0. On the other hand, the generator G strives to continually improve the similarity between the generated data and the real data, thereby reducing the accuracy of D and causing D to predict the input $G(z)$ as 1.

The whole GAN optimization process is carried out in an alternating manner with two sub-networks, and when optimizing the discriminating network, the parameters of the generative network are fixed and its parameters are optimized by a small batch gradient ascent algorithm, whose parameter updating process is shown below:

$$\theta_d \leftarrow \theta_d + \alpha \nabla_{\theta_d} \frac{1}{m} \sum_{i=1}^{m} [\log D(y^{(i)}) + \log(1 - D(G(z^{(i)})))] \quad (2.2)$$

Here, θ_d represents the parameters of the discriminator network, m represents the number of samples in a mini-batch, α represents the learning rate, $\{x(1), \ldots, x(m)\}$ are m real data points, and $\{z(1), \ldots, z(m)\}$ are m random input signals.

When optimizing the generator network, the parameters of the discriminator are fixed, and its parameters are optimized using the mini-batch gradient descent algorithm. The parameter update process is as follows:

$$\theta_g \leftarrow \theta_g - \alpha \nabla_{\theta_g} \frac{1}{m} \sum_{i=1}^{m} \log(1 - D(G(z^{(i)}))) \quad (2.3)$$

where θ_g represent generated network parameters.

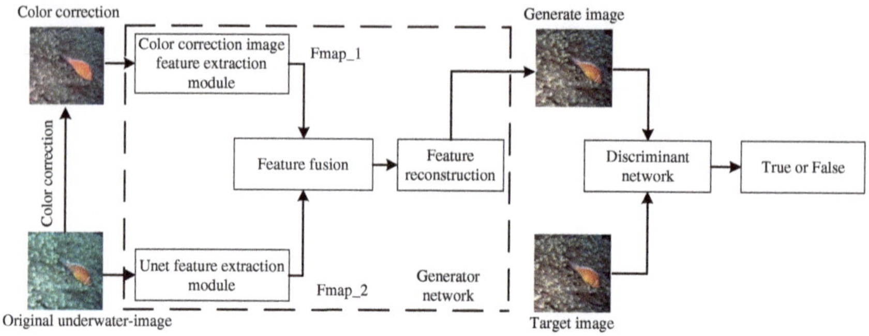

Figure 2.2. Block diagram of feature fusion to generate adversarial network structure.

2.3 Underwater Image Enhancement with Feature Fusion Generative Adversarial Networks

To address issues such as low contrast, reduced clarity, and color distortion in underwater images, this paper proposes an underwater image enhancement algorithm based on a Feature Fusion Generative Adversarial Network (FFGAN). The notable feature of this algorithm lies in its utilization of a feature fusion generator network, whose structure is illustrated in Fig. 2.2.

As shown in Fig. 2.2, the proposed algorithm first addresses the color cast issue in underwater images through an improved color correction method. The color-corrected image and the original underwater image are then used as inputs to the generator network. Among them, the feature Fmap_1 of the color-corrected image is obtained through a simple convolutional network, while the feature Fmap_2 of the original underwater image is extracted using a feature extraction network based on the U-Net structure [5]. At the final stage of the generator network, the features of the color-corrected image and the original underwater image are fused by performing element-wise multiplication, and the fused features are reconstructed into an enhanced image through a convolutional layer. Finally, the target image and the output image from the generator network are fed into the discriminator network. The discriminator evaluates the performance of the generator and guides its optimization process.

2.3.1 *Color correction*

Considering the issue of color distortion in underwater images, to enhance the robustness of the generative network model for underwater image enhancement in complex scenes, the features of color-corrected images are incorporated into the generative network. Both the original degraded underwater image and the color-corrected image are used as inputs to the generative network. Therefore, the proposed algorithm first addresses the color cast problem in underwater images.

To address the color cast problem in underwater images, this paper considers the following typical color correction algorithms: Gray World [6], Max RGB [7] and Gray Edge [8]. Among these white balance algorithms, the Gray World algorithm assumes that in a color-rich image, the average reflectance of the three color channels is equal, allowing the estimation of the light source color through the mean value of each color channel. The Max RGB algorithm assumes that the brightest point in the image perfectly reflects all incident light and estimates the light source color based on the maximum response of each color channel. The Gray Edge algorithm assumes that the average difference of edges in the scene is achromatic, and calculates the scene light source color by applying the Minkowski norm framework to the derivative structure of image color channels. Figure 2.3 shows the results of these three types of color correction algorithms applied to underwater images.

As shown in Fig. 2.3, when the color distortion in underwater images is relatively severe, the Max RGB and Gray Edge algorithms often fail to eliminate the color cast problem, and the overall color tone of the processed underwater images remains almost unchanged. The Gray World algorithm can effectively remove the blue or green tint in underwater images. However, as also observed in Fig. 2.3, images processed by the Gray World algorithm exhibit over-saturation in red in certain local areas. This phenomenon occurs because the average value of the red channel in underwater images is often very low. As a result, the Gray World algorithm tends to overcompensate the red channel in areas with significantly high red pixel values.

To address this issue, following previous research on improving underwater image quality [9], this paper adopts a strategy where the

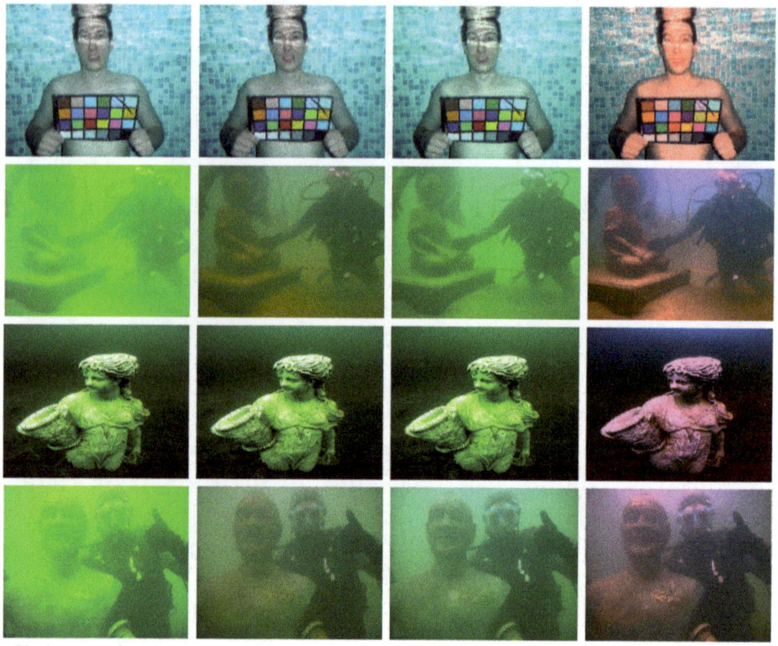

Figure 2.3. White balance algorithm processing results.

attenuation of the red channel is first compensated, followed by the application of the Gray World algorithm to obtain the color-corrected image. Ancuti *et al.* [10] proposed the following principles to mitigate the issue of local overcompensation in the red channel when applying the Gray World algorithm directly to underwater images with a strong blue tint: (1) Adding a portion of the green channel values to the red channel can effectively restore the full color spectrum while preserving the natural background; (2) According to the Gray World assumption that the average values of all color channels are equal in a natural scene, the red channel compensation should be proportional to the difference between the average values of the green and red channels; (3) To avoid localized over-saturation in red after applying the Gray World algorithm, compensation should be limited to areas where the red pixel values are relatively low, while areas with significantly high red pixel values should not be compensated. Based on these principles, the compensation value for each pixel (I, j) in the red channel can be expressed as:

$$I_r'(i,j) = I_r(i,j) + \alpha \cdot \left(\bar{I}_g - \bar{I}_r\right) \cdot I_g(i,j) \cdot (1 - I_r(i,j)) \quad (2.4)$$

Here, I_r and I_g denote the normalized red and green channels of the image I, respectively, $\bar{I}_r$ and $\bar{I}_g$ are the mean values of I_r and I_g, respectively, and α is a constant parameter for adjusting the compensation value.

For underwater images with a blue tint, the red channel compensation strategy in Eq. (2.4) can be applied, followed by the use of the Gray World algorithm, which effectively corrects the image color and suppresses the over-saturation phenomenon in areas with significantly high red channel values. However, when this strategy is directly applied to underwater images with a green tint, local over-compensation of the red channel may still occur, as shown in Fig. 2.5. This phenomenon arises because the pixel values in the green channel of green-tinted underwater images are relatively high. If the green channel values are partially transferred to the red channel, and the compensation amount for the red channel is proportional to the difference in mean values between the green and red channels, over-compensation will still occur in regions where the red pixel values are large, given the compensation rate that is related to the red channel pixel intensity $(1 - I_r(i,j))$. To extend Eq. (2.4) to address the color cast problem in green-tinted underwater images, this paper modifies the red channel pixel intensity-related compensation rate in Eq. (2.4). This modification further reduces the compensation rate in areas with high red channel pixel values, concentrating the compensation mainly in regions with lower red channel pixel values. The modified compensation rate is expressed as:

$$\text{Ratio} = 1/(1 + e^{\beta I_r(i,j) - \gamma}) \quad (2.5)$$

Here, β and γ are constants, and based on experimental results, we set $\beta = 13.15$ and $\gamma = 3.79$. Figure 2.4 shows the compensation rate curves for the red channel before and after the improvement. The horizontal axis represents the normalized pixel intensity values of the red channel, while the vertical axis represents the compensation rate related to the red channel pixel values. The blue curve represents the compensation rate of the method proposed by Ancuti *et al.* [10], and the red curve represents the improved compensation rate curve introduced in this paper. It can be observed that,

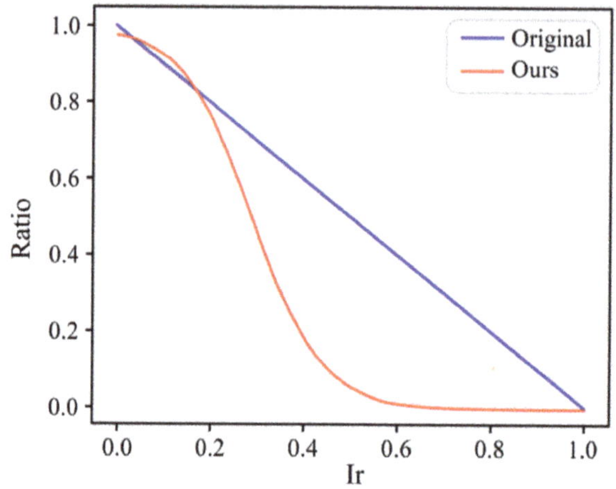

Figure 2.4. Original vs. improved red channel compensation rate curves.

compared to the original compensation rate, the compensation rate in regions with significantly high red channel pixel values is greatly reduced in the proposed method. On the other hand, the compensation rate in regions where the red channel pixel values are less prominent is slightly increased, with the compensation being mainly concentrated in areas with lower red channel pixel values.

Ultimately, the improved red channel compensation formula in this paper is as follows:

$$I_r'(i,j) = I_r(i,j) + \alpha \cdot \left(\bar{I}_g - \bar{I}_r\right) \cdot I_g(i,j) / \left(1 + e^{\beta I_r(i,j) - \gamma}\right) \quad (2.6)$$

After applying the red channel compensation, the Gray World algorithm is used to correct the color cast in underwater images. Figure 2.5 shows the results of color correction using the Gray World algorithm, the color correction algorithm proposed by Ancuti *et al.* [10], and the improved color correction algorithm introduced in this paper.

As shown in Fig. 2.5, the pre-improved color correction algorithm in this paper somewhat suppresses the overcompensation in the red channel caused by the Gray World algorithm. However, the issue still persists in green-tinted underwater images, as seen in the sculptures in images 3 to 5 in Fig. 2.5. In contrast, the improved algorithm proposed in this paper effectively suppresses the overcompensation of the red channel in green-tinted underwater images. Additionally, for

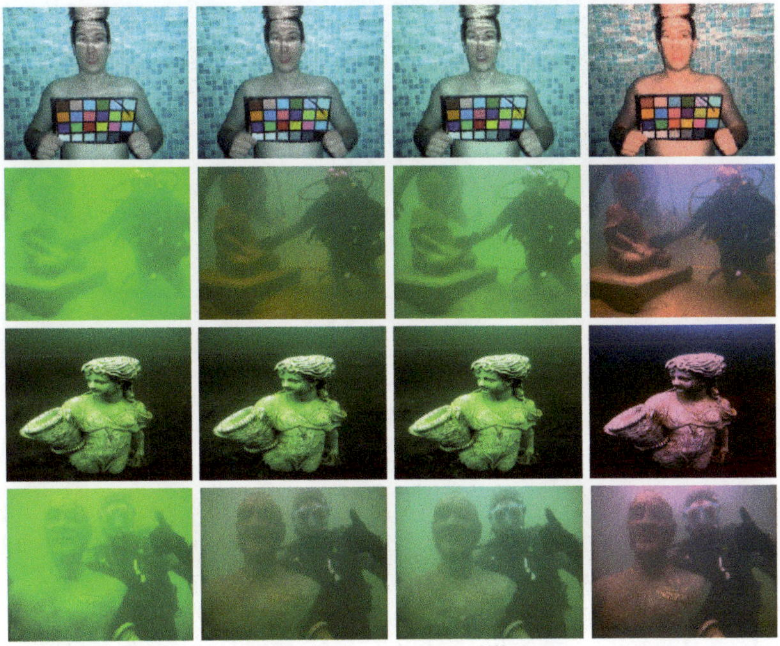

Figure 2.5. Comparison of color correction results for underwater-images.

blue-tinted images, it also reduces information loss to some extent, as shown in the bottom-right corner of the second image. The proposed improved color correction algorithm achieves good results for both blue-tinted and green-tinted underwater images.

2.3.2 *Generative network architecture*

This paper adopts a feature fusion-based generative network architecture, which mainly includes the color correction image feature extraction module, the original underwater image feature extraction module based on the U-Net structure, and the feature reconstruction module.

(1) Color-corrected image feature extraction module: To extract features from the color-corrected image, this paper employs a simple convolutional neural network structure. The architecture consists of two convolutional layers, each using a 3×3 kernel

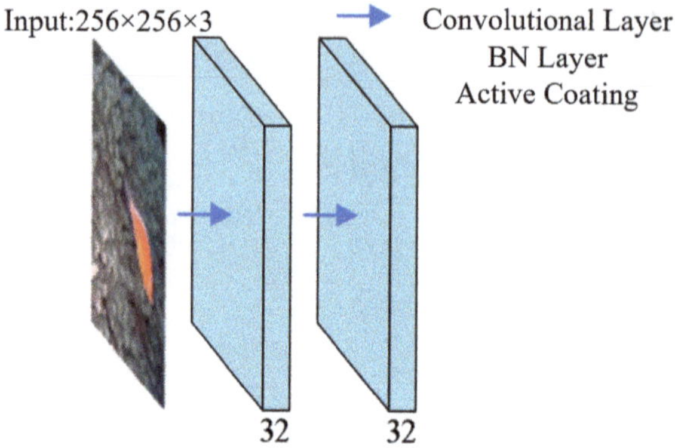

Figure 2.6. Color-corrected image feature extraction module.

with a stride of 1. After the convolutional layers, batch normalization [12] (BN) and Leaky ReLU activation layers are added. The BN layer accelerates network convergence while helping to prevent gradient explosion or vanishing to some extent. For an input color-corrected image of size $256 \times 256 \times 3$, the module outputs features of size $256 \times 256 \times 32$. The structure is shown in Fig. 2.6, with the numbers at the bottom of the figure representing the number of features.

(2) U-net feature extraction module: For feature extraction from the underwater degraded images, this paper uses a U-Net-based feature extraction network structure. The architecture adopts a symmetric encoder-decoder structure, with skip connections between feature channels of corresponding sizes in the encoder and decoder. Specifically, the output of each encoder is concatenated with the output of the corresponding decoder. Figure 2.7 illustrates the U-Net-based feature extraction network structure designed in this paper. In the U-Net feature extraction network designed in this paper, the encoder consists of down sampling units, while the decoder consists of up sampling units. The down sampling units are composed of two convolutional layers, with both convolutional layers using a kernel size of 3. The convolution stride is 1 for the first layer and 2 for the second. The up sampling units consist of one convolutional layer and one deconvolutional layer, both using a kernel size of 3. The convolution stride is 1 for the convolutional layer and 2 for the deconvolutional layer. After the convolutional and deconvolutional

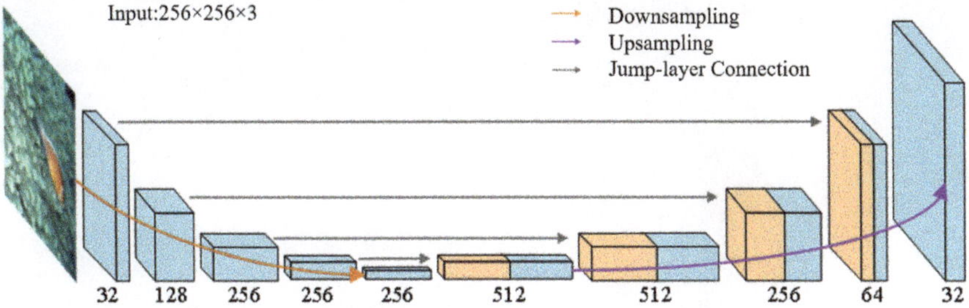

Figure 2.7. U-net feature extraction network structure.

layers, batch normalization (BN) layers and Leaky ReLU activation layers are added.

In the U-Net feature extraction network structure used in this paper, the encoder consists of 5 down sampling units. An underwater image of size $256 \times 256 \times 3$ is passed through the encoder of this feature extraction network and is mapped to 256 features of size 8×8. The decoder uses 5 up sampling units, where each up sampling unit, based on the output features from the previous layer and the skip connections from the encoder part, ultimately produces features of size $256 \times 256 \times 32$.

(3) Feature reconstruction module: After obtaining the color-corrected image features and the original underwater image features through the feature extraction modules, the two features are fused using element-wise multiplication. Finally, the fused features are mapped into the enhanced underwater image through the feature reconstruction module. In the generative network proposed in this paper, the feature reconstruction module consists of a convolutional layer with a kernel size of 1 and a stride of 1, followed by a Tanh activation layer.

2.3.3 *Discriminating network structure*

The discriminator network in this paper adopts a Markov discriminator (PatchGAN) [13], which outputs a 2D tensor, where each element corresponds to a local patch of the input image, and the value of each element represents the score for that local region. This design is beneficial for capturing local texture features of the image.

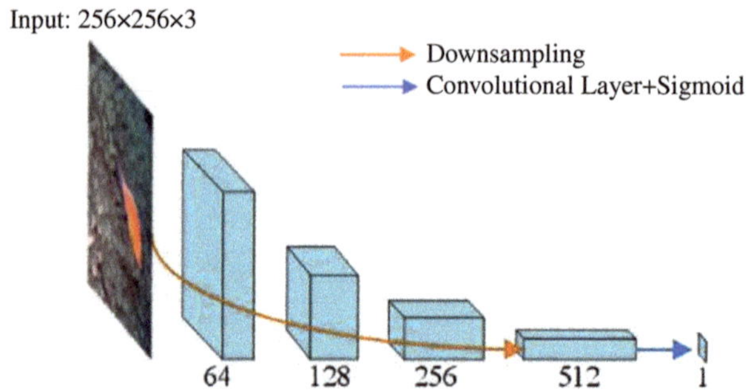

Figure 2.8. Discriminant network structure.

The discriminator network designed in this paper consists of five convolutional layers, and its structure is shown in Fig. 2.8.

Among them, the first four convolutional layers use convolutional kernels with a size of 3 and a stride of 2, with the number of kernels doubling at each layer. Batch normalization (BN) layers are added after each convolutional layer, followed by Leaky ReLU activation functions. The final layer uses a convolutional kernel of size 3 with a stride of 1 and applies a Sigmoid activation function. The discriminator network outputs a 16×16 matrix, where each element has a receptive field of 63×63. In other words, each element in the output matrix corresponds to the properties of a 63×63 region in the input image.

2.3.4 *Loss function selection*

Considering the stability of GAN training, the visual quality of the enhanced images, and the preservation of detailed features, the generative adversarial network model in this paper adopts a linear combination of multiple loss functions during training. The formulation is shown as follows:

$$L = \min_G \max_D L_{\mathrm{WGAN}}(G, D) + \lambda_1 L_{L1} + \lambda_2 L_{\mathrm{VGG}} + \lambda_3 L_{\mathrm{E}} \quad (2.7)$$

where L_{WGAN} represents the adversarial loss, L_{L1} denotes the global loss, L_{VGG} refers to the perceptual loss, and $\mathrm{L_E}$ represents the edge loss. The terms λ_1, λ_2 and λ_3 are the weighting coefficients for each loss function.

(1) Adversarial loss function: In traditional GANs, when the discriminator network uses cross-entropy as the loss function, the training balance between the discriminator network and the generator network is often suboptimal. In practical applications, as the discriminator network is optimized, the gradient of the generator network tends to vanish. Moreover, the better the performance of the discriminator network, the more severe this gradient vanishing problem becomes, making it difficult for training to continue. To address this issue, this paper adopts the Wasserstein-GAN (WGAN) [14] formula, which constructs a value function using Earth-Mover (EM) distance or Wasserstein(W) distance through the Kantorovich-Rubinstein dyad. In the WGAN framework, the W distance is approximated by a set of functions that satisfy the k-Lipschitz condition, and this set of functions is modeled as a neural network. Specifically, to ensure that the fitted functions satisfy the k-Lipschitz condition, this paper uses the Wasserstein-GAN with Gradient Penalty (WGAN-GP) [15]. Thus, the adversarial loss function is expressed as:

$$\hat{x} = \varepsilon y + (1 - \varepsilon)G(x) \tag{2.8}$$

$$\begin{aligned} L_{\text{WGAN}}(G, D) = {} & E[D(y)] - E[D(G(x))] \\ & + \lambda_{\text{GP}} E[(\|\nabla_{\hat{x}} D(\hat{x})\|_2 - 1)^2] \end{aligned} \tag{2.9}$$

where $\hat{x}$ denotes the sample obtained by interpolation between the distribution of the generated network output and the corresponding distribution of the clear reference images in the training set, ε is a random number between 0 and 1, G and D represent the generative network and the discriminator network, respectively, and x and y represent the underwater degraded images and the corresponding clear target images in the training set. λ_{GP} is the weight for the gradient penalty term, which is set to 10 as per the original paper.

(2) Content loss function: To ensure that the output of the generative network maintains consistency in image information with the reference images in the training set, this paper adds the $L1$ [13] distance between the generated image and the reference image from the training set as one of the loss functions to optimize the generative network. This can be expressed as:

$$L_{L1} = E[\|y - G(x)\|_1] \tag{2.10}$$

where x represents the original underwater degraded image, y denotes the corresponding clear reference image in the training set, and $G(\cdot)$ is the output of the generative network.

(3) Perceptual loss function: To ensure that the enhanced image has the same feature representation as the target reference image, thereby improving the visual quality of the enhanced image, inspired by previous work [16], this paper introduces the pre-trained VGG19 network. By extracting high-level features from the output of the third convolutional layer (Conv4_3) before the fourth max-pooling operation in the VGG19 network, a perceptual loss function is constructed. Its definition is as follows:

$$L_{\mathrm{VGG}} = E\left[\|\Phi(y) - \Phi(G(x))\|_2^2\right] \tag{2.11}$$

where $\Phi(\cdot)$ denotes the high-level features extracted from the input image by the Conv4_3 layer of the pre-trained VGG19 network model.

(4) Edge loss function: The generative network often outputs images with blurry detail features. To address this, this paper employs the Sobel operator to extract the horizontal and vertical edges of the generated image $G(x)$ and the reference image y from the training set. By penalizing the differences in edges along the horizontal and vertical directions, the network is encouraged to suppress the blurriness in the output image. The formulation is as follows:

$$L_E = E\left[\|y \otimes \boldsymbol{S}_h - G(x) \otimes \boldsymbol{S}_h\|_1 + \|y \otimes \boldsymbol{S}_v - G(x) \otimes \boldsymbol{S}_v\|_1\right] \tag{2.12}$$

where $\otimes$ represents the convolutional operation, S_h and S_v are size 3 transverse and longitudinal Sobel operators, respectively, denoted as:

$$\boldsymbol{S}_h = \begin{bmatrix} -1 & 0 & +1 \\ -2 & 0 & +2 \\ -1 & 0 & +1 \end{bmatrix}, \quad \boldsymbol{S}_v = \begin{bmatrix} +1 & +2 & +1 \\ 0 & 0 & 0 \\ -1 & -2 & -1 \end{bmatrix}$$

2.4 Experimental Comparison and Result Analysis

In this section, to validate the effectiveness of the proposed algorithm, we compare it with traditional and deep learning-based algorithms. The experimental results are analyzed both subjectively and objectively. Additionally, to evaluate the contributions of the feature fusion module and the edge loss function to the model, detailed ablation experiments are conducted. The experiments were carried out on a Linux operating system, implemented using the PyTorch deep learning framework. The server's CPU is an Intel Xeon E5-2620 v4 with a clock speed of 2.1 GHz, and the GPU used is an NVIDIA 2080 with 8GB of memory.

2.4.1 *Experimental data and training*

The algorithms in this paper use the publicly available dataset Underwater-Imagenet [4]. Considering that underwater images typically exhibit a blue or green color bias, while the majority of images in the Underwater-Imagenet dataset display blue-dominated attenuation characteristics, the following strategies are adopted to enhance the diversity of the dataset. First, a color transfer algorithm proposed by Nguyen *et al.* [17] is employed to transform a subset of clear images into underwater-style images with greenish tone degradation, simulating the color distortion typical of underwater environments. Then, the corresponding degraded underwater images from the Underwater-Imagenet dataset are used as guidance maps to perform guided filtering [18] on the color-transferred images, mimicking the blurring effects caused by light scattering during underwater light propagation. The workflow for dataset generation is illustrated in Fig. 2.9.

Using this method, 1645 biased green underwater images were acquired in this paper, and Fig. 2.10 show some of the biased green underwater image datasets obtained using this scheme. Among them, the first row is a clear image, the second row is a biased green underwater image obtained by adopting the dataset generation framework in Fig. 2.9, and the third and fourth rows show the enlarged images of the red-boxed areas in the first and second rows, respectively. It can be observed that blurring is better introduced while changing the image hue using this strategy. Combining the Underwater-Imagenet dataset and filtering it, finally this paper uses 5708 sets of images as the training set and 182 sets of images not involved in training as the test set with reference images.

At the initial stage of model training, the parameters of both the generator and discriminator networks are initialized using a normal distribution with a mean of 0 and a standard deviation of 0.02.

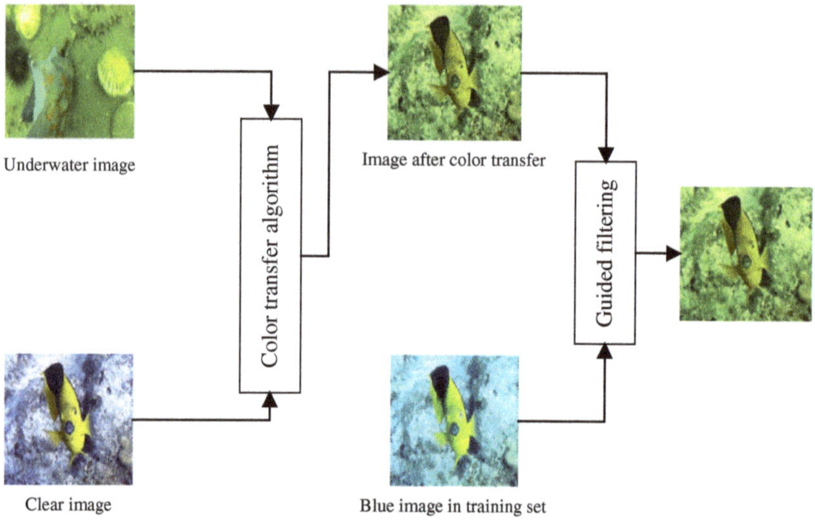

Figure 2.9. Block diagram of green tint data generation.

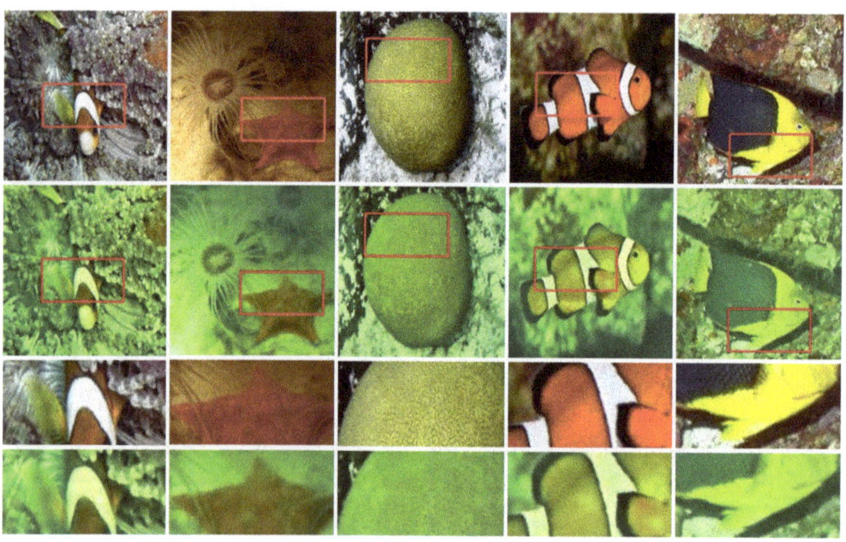

Figure 2.10. Partial greenish data set presentation.

During the training process, the generator and discriminator networks are optimized alternately, where the discriminator is optimized five times for every single optimization of the generator. Additionally, to enhance the performance of the generator, a data augmentation strategy is employed, which involves randomly flipping the training set horizontally and vertically. Both the generator and discriminator networks utilize the Adam optimizer, with the learning rate (lr) set to 0.002, the first momentum term $\beta1$ set to 0.5, and the second-order momentum term $\beta2$ set to 0.999. The learning rate is halved every 80 epochs. The network optimization is performed using mini-batch gradient descent, with a batch size set to 12 and a total of 301 epochs, taking approximately 16.3 hours to complete.

2.4.2 *Experimental results*

In this section, the proposed algorithm is compared with several traditional algorithms and recent deep learning-based methods. The comparison includes algorithms from image enhancement, image restoration, and learning-based approaches, specifically: Contrast Limited Adaptive Histogram Equalization (CLAHE) [19], an underwater image enhancement algorithm based on white balance and image fusion (Fusion) [10], Dark Channel Prior (DCP) [20], an automatic red-channel underwater image restoration algorithm (RedChannel), a generative adversarial network-based underwater image enhancement algorithm (UGAN) [4], and a fast underwater image enhancement algorithm based on generative adversarial network (FUnIE-GAN) [21]. The deep learning-based algorithms are trained using the same training set as in this study, and their network architectures and optimization strategies follow the original papers.

To validate the effectiveness of the proposed algorithm, this paper processes the content from the Underwater-Imagenet test set. Considering the complexity of underwater environments, images with varying degrees of distortion from the test set are selected. The final processing results of each algorithm are illustrated in Fig. 2.11.

As shown in Fig. 2.11, the processed underwater images exhibit different visual effects across various algorithms. The CLAHE algorithm generally addresses the color bias issue in degraded images; however, the enhanced images appear slightly blurred, and artifacts emerge in the edge regions of the enhanced images, as seen in Image3, Image4, and Image6. The DCP algorithm effectively removes the hazy blur in underwater images, but due to the lack of a color correction mechanism, it fails to adequately resolve the color bias issue and may even exacerbate color distortion, as observed

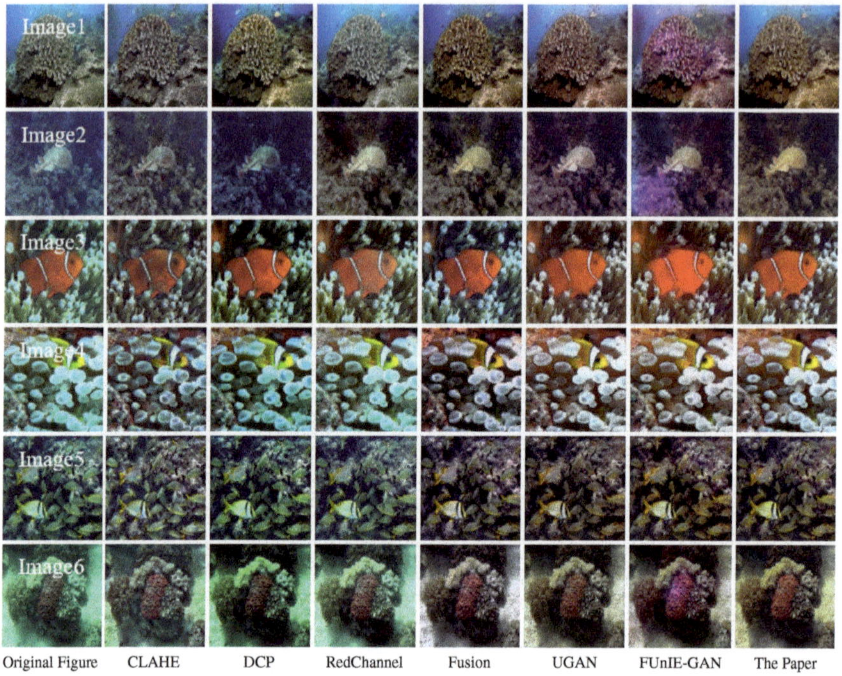

Figure 2.11. Comparison of processing results of each algorithm.

in Image2, Image4, and Image6. The RedChannel algorithm generally corrects the color bias in images, but its performance is less satisfactory when the color distortion is severe, as demonstrated in Image5 and Image6. The Fusion algorithm combines white balance-based contrast enhancement with detail-enhanced images, resulting in noticeable color correction and significant detail features in the enhanced images. However, compared to learning-based methods, some enhanced results exhibit unnatural colors, such as the shadow on the fish surface in Image4, and the color bias in the background region of Image3 remains unresolved. Both the UGAN and FUnIE-GAN algorithms employ an end-to-end single-input model structure, and their test results exhibit localized over-enhancement of red tones, such as in the foreground of Image1 and the background of Image2. The enhanced images lack realism, and the FUnIE-GAN algorithm, due to its lightweight model structure, achieves faster processing at the cost of reduced robustness, resulting in slight purple artifacts in some test images, such as Image1 and Image2. In contrast to the learning-based enhancement algorithms UGAN and FUnIE-GAN, the proposed algorithm effectively suppresses the appearance of artifacts in the scenes, as demonstrated in Image1, Image2, and Image6. Compared to the Fusion algorithm, which performs well among traditional methods, the images enhanced by the proposed algorithm exhibit more natural colors, as seen in Image2, Image3, and Image5. In summary, compared to the aforementioned algorithms, the proposed algorithm utilizes a feature fusion-based generative network structure, which effectively improves the clarity of underwater images with varying degrees of color distortion. The enhanced images display realistic colors and achieve relatively superior visual quality.

To objectively analyze the performance of the proposed algorithm and ensure fairness in the comparative analysis, we did not use reference-based image evaluation metrics. This is because, when the test set data distribution is similar to the training set, deep learning-based methods often achieve higher evaluation metrics, which is unfair to traditional algorithms. Therefore, this paper compares the performance of these algorithms using no-reference image evaluation metrics, including the Underwater Image Quality Measure (UIQM) [22] and the Natural Image Quality Evaluator (NIQE) [23].

The UIQM evaluates the quality of enhanced underwater images by considering the degradation characteristics and imaging features of underwater environments. It combines three metrics: the Underwater Image Colorfulness Measure (UICM), the Underwater Image Sharpness Measure (UISM), and the Underwater Image Contrast Measure (UIConM), through a linear combination. A higher UIQM value indicates better image quality. The calculation formula is as follows:

$$\mathrm{UIQM} = \gamma_1 \times \mathrm{UICM} + \gamma_2 \times \mathrm{UISM} + \gamma_3 \times \mathrm{UIConM} \quad (2.13)$$

where γ_1, γ_2 and γ_3 are the weighting coefficients of the three underwater image attribute metrics, which are set to 0.0282, 0.2953 and 3.5753, respectively, as referenced from the original paper.

The Natural Image Quality Evaluator (NIQE) does not require training on distorted images with human subjective scores. Instead, it extracts features from the Natural Scene Statistics (NSS) model in the spatial domain and models them using a Multivariate Gaussian (MVG) model. The quality of the test image is represented by the distance between the MVG fitting parameters of the NSS features

Table 2.1. Comparison of UIQM metrics for each algorithm.

	CLAHE	UDCP	RedChannel	Fusion	UGAN	FunIEGAN	The paper
Image1	3.297	2.740	3.152	2.600	3.252	3.325	**3.330**
Image2	3.301	2.115	3.397	3.338	3.235	3.208	**3.534**
Image3	3.635	3.044	3.586	3.444	3.527	3.382	**3.703**
Image4	3.524	2.941	3.473	3.290	3.440	3.435	**3.526**
Image5	3.127	2.518	2.866	2.842	3.424	3.353	**3.429**
Image6	3.222	2.284	3.009	3.326	3.346	3.373	**3.387**
mean	3.351	2.607	3.247	3.140	3.371	3.346	**3.485**

Note: The bold font indicates the optimal values in each row.

Table 2.2. Comparison of NIQE metrics for each algorithm.

	CLAHE	UDCP	RedChannel	Fusion	UGAN	FunIEGAN	The paper
Image1	6.899	6.673	6.717	6.755	6.447	7.867	**6.313**
Image2	5.865	5.705	5.770	6.345	4.561	3.640	**3.342**
Image3	4.416	4.162	**4.055**	4.240	7.113	6.004	5.709
Image4	4.663	3.839	4.015	4.672	5.639	4.327	**3.793**
Image5	5.587	5.744	5.471	5.364	7.058	6.033	**5.146**
Image6	**5.921**	8.039	6.342	7.008	6.958	6.679	**6.303**
mean	5.559	5.694	5.395	5.731	6.296	5.758	**5.101**

Note: The bold font indicates the optimal values in each row.

extracted from the image and the parameters of a pre-established model. A lower NIQE value indicates higher image quality.

Tables 2.1 and 2.2 present the numerical results of the two metrics for images processed by various algorithms, with the optimal values highlighted in bold. From the results in the tables, it can be observed that the images enhanced by the proposed algorithm achieve the best UIQM and NIQE evaluation metrics. Compared to the competing algorithms, the UIQM shows an improvement of 0.114 to 0.878, and the NIQE shows a reduction of 0.294 to 1.195. These metric results demonstrate that the proposed algorithm effectively restores the true colors of the images and enhances their contrast and sharpness.

2.4.3 *Ablation experiments*

This subsection investigates the contributions of the feature fusion structure and the edge loss function LE to the overall model. For this purpose, we define two ablated variants: NFEGAN, which is the model without the feature fusion structure and without the edge loss function LE during training, and NEGAN, which is the model with the feature fusion structure but without LE is referred to as NEGAN. This section compares NFEGAN, NEGAN, and the proposed algorithm. Specifically, the generator network without the feature fusion structure only uses a U-Net-based feature extraction network to obtain the degraded underwater image features Fmap_2, and then reconstructs the enhanced image from Fmap_2 through convolutional layers. During training, all models adopt the same initialization methods, hyperparameters, and datasets.

In this phase of the comparison experiment, 182 referenced images that are not involved in training are used as the test set. Two reference image evaluation metrics are used in this experiment to measure the quality of the enhanced images, which are peak signal-to-noise ratio (PSNR) and structural similarity (SSIM) [24]. In addition, we measured the mean square error (MSE) of the enhanced image with respect to the target image to observe the overall pixel difference.

PSNR is defined as the ratio of the energy peak signal to the mean value of the energy difference between the enhanced image and the clear image of the target, and the larger the value of this index indicates that the image has less distortion and higher quality. Its formula is expressed as:

$$\mathrm{MSE} = \frac{1}{mn} \sum_{i=0}^{m-1} \sum_{j=0}^{n-1} \| x(i,j) - y(i,j) \|^2 \tag{2.14}$$

$$\mathrm{PSNR}(x,y) = 10 \log_{10} \left[\frac{\mathrm{MAX}^2}{\mathrm{MSE}(x,y)} \right] \tag{2.15}$$

In this context, m and n represent the number of pixels in the horizontal and vertical direction of the image, respectively, i and j denote the coordinate position of the pixel point in the map, MSE denotes the mean square error of the two images, y is the target clear image, x is the enhanced image, and MAX is the peak energy signal (set to a pixel maximum of 255 for an 8-bit image).

SSIM compares the quality of images in terms of brightness, contrast, and structural differences, with structural difference being the primary influencing factor. In the calculation of the SSIM index, the brightness, contrast, and structural differences of the images are

Table 2.3. Comparison of ablation model result parameters.

	PSNR	SSIM	MSE
NFEGAN	20.279	0.703	0.0119
NEGAN	20.813	0.793	0.0114
Proposed algorithm	**21.279**	**0.803**	**0.0105**

Note: The bold font indicates the optimal values in each column.

estimated using the mean, standard deviation, and covariance of the two images, respectively. The calculation is as follows:

$$\mathrm{SSIM}(y,x)=\frac{(2\mu_y\mu_x+c_1)\,(2\sigma_{yx}+c_2)}{\left(\mu_y^2+\mu_x^2+c_1\right)\left(\sigma_{yx}^2+\sigma_x^2+c_2\right)} \tag{2.16}$$

Here, μ_x and μ_y represent the mean of the generated image x and target image y respectively; σ_x and σ_y represent the variance of x and y respectively; σ_{xy} represents the covariance of x and y; c_1 and c_2 are the constants to avoid the denominator to be zero, which are usually taken to be $c_1 = 6.503$ and $c_2 = 58.523$. Table 2.3 shows the calculation results of the three indexes.

It is derived from the values in Table 2.3 that the PSNR of feature fusion improves by 2.63%, SSIM improves by 12.8%, and MSE decreases by 4.20% compared to no feature fusion structure; on the basis of the feature fusion structure, the use of the edge loss function proposed in this paper leads to an increase in PSNR by 2.24%, an increase in SSIM by 1.26%, and a decrease in MSE by 7.89%. These values show that the feature fusion structure and edge loss function proposed in this paper can indeed enhance the performance of the model and improve the quality of the enhanced image, with the fusion-based structure bringing the greatest enhancement to the whole model.

To provide a more intuitive understanding of the visual improvement brought by feature fusion and edge loss functions, Fig. 2.12 presents the results before and after the ablation of the models and loss functions. From Image1, Image2, and Image3, it can be observed that the generative network with the feature fusion structure demonstrates stronger learning ability, with the enhanced images nearly indistinguishable from the target image. At the same time, it can be seen that removing the color-corrected image features introduces

Figure 2.12. Comparison of ablation experiment results.

color deviation in the results. Furthermore, although the edge loss function shows an improvement in image quality evaluation metrics, this improvement is not perceptible to the human visual system.

In addition, it can be found in the test results that the checkerboard grid effect will occur when there is a large background region with a single color in the underwater image. The reason for this phenomenon is the uneven overlapping during the execution of the deconvolutional operation, especially when the convolutional kernel size is not divisible by the step size, the more likely this problem occurs. Due to the fact that in this paper a convolutional kernel of size 3 with a convolutional step size of 2 is used in the decoder part of U-Net, this problem of uneven overlap occurs during the sampling process. In some of the test results demonstrated in Fig. 2.12, the red box marks the area of checkerboard grid effect. The network structure based on feature fusion can effectively suppress the checkerboard effect and obtain a smoother background. After the above analysis, the effectiveness of the edge loss function and feature fusion structure is concluded.

2.5 Conclusion

This chapter primarily introduces an underwater image enhancement algorithm based on feature fusion generative adversarial networks. First, the basic model structure and mathematical principles of generative adversarial networks are explained. Next, the underwater image enhancement algorithm based on feature fusion generative adversarial networks proposed in this paper is introduced, which includes the improved color correction algorithm, the structure of the feature fusion generative network, the structure of the discriminator network, and the loss functions used during the model training process. Finally, through ablation experiments on the loss functions and models, as well as a comparative analysis with other algorithms, it is concluded that the proposed algorithm effectively improves underwater image quality.

References

[1] Goodfellow IJ, Pouget-Abadie J, Mirza M, *et al.* Generative adversarial networks. arXiv preprint arXiv: 1406.2661, 2014.

[2] Zheng C, Cham TJ, Cai J. Pluralistic image completion. *Proceedings of the IEEE/CVF Conference on Computer Vision and Pattern Recognition.* 2019: 1438–1447.

[3] Li M, Huang H, Ma L, *et al.* Unsupervised image-to-image translation with stacked cycle-consistent adversarial networks. *Proceedings of the European Conference on Computer Vision (ECCV).* 2018: 184–199.

[4] Fabbri C, Jahidul Islam M, Sattar J. Enhancing underwater imagery using generative adversarial networks. *2018 IEEE International Conference on Robotics and Automation (ICRA).* IEEE, New York, 2018: 7159–7165.

[5] Ronneberger O, Fischer P, Brox T. U-net: Convolutional networks for biomedical image segmentation. *International Conference on Medical Image Computing and Computer-assisted Intervention.* Springer, Cham, 2015: 234–241.

[6] Buchsbaum G. A spatial processor model for object colour perception. *Journal of the Franklin Institute*, 1980, 310(1): 1–26.

[7] Land, Edwin H. The retinex theory of color vision. *Scientific American*, 1977, 237(6): 108–129.
[8] Van De Weijer J, Gevers T, Gijsenij A. Edge-based color constancy. *IEEE Transactions on Image Processing*, 2007, 16(9): 2207–2214.
[9] Galdran A, Pardo D, Picón A, *et al.* Automatic red-channel underwater image restoration. *Journal of Visual Communication and Image Representation*. 2015, 26: 132–145.
[10] Ancuti CO, Ancuti C, Vleeschouwer CD, *et al.* Color balance and fusion for underwater image enhancement. *IEEE Transactions on Image Processing*, 2017, 27(1): 379–393.
[11] Mercado MA, Ishii K, Ahn J. Deep-sea image enhancement using 12 multi-scale retinex with reverse color loss for autonomous underwater vehicles. *OCEANS 2017-Anchorage*. IEEE, New York, 2017: 1–6.
[12] Ioffe S, Szegedy C. Batch normalization: Accelerating deep network 15 training by reducing internal covariate shift. *International Conference 16 on Machine Learning*. PMLR, Lille, France, 2015: 448–456.
[13] Isola P, Zhu JY, Zhou TH, and Efros AA. Image-to-image translation with conditional adversarial networks. *Proceedings of IEEE Conference on Computer Vision and Pattern Recognition*. 2017, 1125–1134.
[14] Arjovsky M, Chintala S, Bottou. Wasserstein gan. arXiv preprint arXiv: 1701.07875, 2017, 7.
[15] Gulrajani I, Ahmed F, Arjovsky M, *et al.* Improved training of wasserstein gans. arXiv preprint arXiv: 1704.00028, 2017.
[16] Simonyan K, Zisserman A. Very deep convolutional networks for large-scale image recognition. arXiv preprint arXiv: 1409.1556, 2015.
[17] Nguyen RMH, Kim SJ, Brown MS. Illuminant aware gamut-based color transfer. *Computer Graphics Forum*. 2014, 33(7): 319–328.
[18] He K, Sun J, Tang X. Guided image filtering. *IEEE Transactions on Pattern Analysis and Machine Intelligence*, 2013, 35(6): 1397–1409. USA.
[19] Zuiderveld K. Contrast limited adaptive histogram equalization. *Graphics Gems*, 1994, IV: 474–485.
[20] He K, Sun J, Tang X. Single image haze removal using dark channel prior. *IEEE Transactions on Pattern Analysis and Machine Intelligence*, 2010, 33(12): 2341–2353.
[21] Islam MJ, Xia Y, Sattar J. Fast underwater image enhancement for improved visual perception. *IEEE Robotics and Automation Letters*, 2020, 5(2): 3227–3234.
[22] Panetta K, Gao C, Agaian S. Human-visual-system-inspired underwater image quality measures. *IEEE Journal of Oceanic Engineering*, 2016, 41(3): 541–551.

[23] Mittal A, Soundararajan R, Bovik AC. Making a "completely blind" image quality analyzer. *IEEE Signal Processing Letters*, 2012, 20(3): 209–212.

[24] Wang Z, Bovik AC, Sheikh HR, *et al.* Image quality assessment: From error visibility to structural similarity. *IEEE Transactions on Image Processing*, 2004, 13(4): 600–612.

Chapter 3

ESRGAN-Based Image Super-Resolution Reconstruction Algorithm

3.1 Introduction

Chapter 2 proposed an underwater image enhancement algorithm based on feature fusion generative adversarial networks (GANs), which effectively addresses color distortion while improving image contrast and clarity. However, due to equipment limitations and compression during image acquisition/transmission, underwater images often exhibit low resolution. Such low-resolution images present challenges, including insufficient information content and difficulty in feature extraction. To resolve these issues, this chapter develops an enhanced single-image super-resolution (SISR) algorithm based on ESRGAN [1], with specific improvements to its generator architecture for higher-quality underwater image reconstruction.

3.2 ESRGAN Methodology

Super-resolution image reconstruction remains a persistent research focus in computer vision. Recent advancements in deep learning have propelled learning-based approaches to prominence, particularly with generative adversarial network (GAN)-based algorithms gaining significant traction in super-resolution applications. Ledig *et al.* [2] pioneered this integration through their SRGAN framework, demonstrating enhanced capability for generating photorealistic textures. While effective, this approach sometimes produces artifacts in detailed image regions during high-resolution reconstruction. To mitigate reconstruction artifacts and enhance output quality, Wang *et al.* [1] developed ESRGAN as an enhanced iteration of SRGAN. Their improvements primarily address three critical components: network architecture optimization, adversarial loss function refinement, and perceptual loss function enhancement.

Both ESRGAN and SRGAN utilize the foundational architecture of SRResNet [3], which consists of three primary modules: a shallow feature extraction module, a deep feature extraction module, and a reconstruction module. The process begins with the shallow feature extraction module, which captures the original features of the low-resolution input image. Subsequently, the deep feature extraction module extracts residual information from the low-resolution image. These two sets of features—shallow and deep—are then fused through element-wise summation. Finally, the reconstruction module generates the high-resolution output image. A defining characteristic of the SRResNet architecture is its computational efficiency, as the majority of network operations are performed in the low-resolution feature space, significantly reducing the overall computational load. Figure 3.1 illustrates the basic structure of this network, where the initial convolutional layer (Conv) serves as the shallow feature extraction module, the middle Basic Block functions as the deep feature extraction module, and the upsampling module (Upsampling) combined with the final convolutional layer constitutes the super-resolution reconstruction module.

To further enhance the quality of SRGAN-reconstructed images, ESRGAN introduces two key structural modifications to the generative network: the removal of all batch normalization (BN) layers and the replacement of the residual block (RB) in SRGAN with a novel multilevel Residual-in-Residual Dense Block (RRDB).

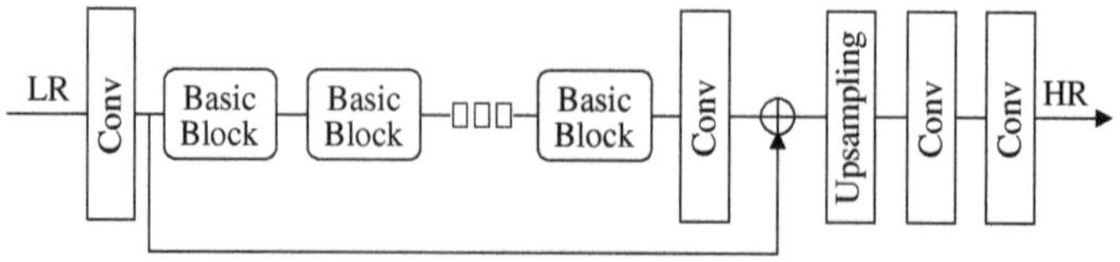

Figure 3.1. SRResNet structure.

The elimination of BN layers has been empirically demonstrated to improve model performance across various peak signal-to-noise ratio (PSNR)-oriented tasks, including image super-resolution [4] and image deblurring [5]. The RRDB architecture integrates multilevel residual connections with dense connectivity, resulting in a deeper and more complex structure compared to the traditional residual connectivity module in SRGAN. This enhanced architecture significantly improves feature representation capabilities, thereby boosting overall model performance. To address potential training instability, a scaling mechanism is implemented: features extracted from the residual path are multiplied by a scaling factor β (where $\beta < 1$) before being integrated into the main pathway. Figure 3.2 illustrates these architectural advancements: (a) depicts the residual module employed in SRGAN's generative network, (b) presents the multilevel RRDB used in ESRGAN, and (c) details the internal structure of the dense block within the RRDB.

In addition to structural enhancements to SRGAN's generator, ESRGAN incorporates a modified adversarial loss function by employing a relativistic average generative adversarial network (RaGAN) [6] discriminator. Unlike traditional GAN discriminators, which focus on distinguishing real from generated data, the relativistic discriminator in RaGAN evaluates the relative realism of real and generated images. Specifically, it predicts the probability that a real

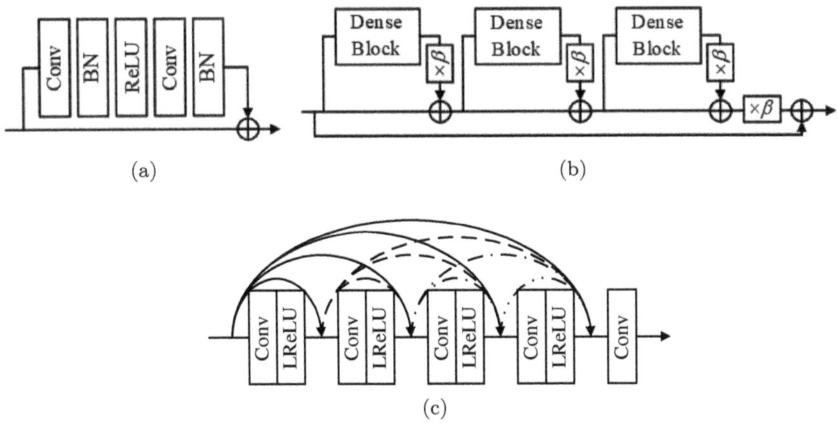

Figure 3.2. Structural improvement diagram of the ESRGAN feature extraction module: (a) the residual block of SRGAN; (b) RRDB; (c) dense connection module.

image appears more realistic and natural compared to a generated one. Furthermore, the RaGAN generator leverages gradients from both real and generated data during training, in contrast to traditional GAN generators, which rely solely on gradients from generated data. The mathematical formulation of the relativistic discriminator is as follows:

$$D_{Ra}(y, G(x)) = \sigma(C(y) - E[C(G(x))]) \to 1 \tag{3.1}$$

$$D_{Ra}(G(x), y) = \sigma(C(G(x)) - E[C(y)]) \to 0 \tag{3.2}$$

where D_{Ra} denotes the relative average discriminant network, x denotes the input low-resolution image, y denotes the target super-resolution image, σ denotes the sigmoid activation function, $G(\cdot)$ denotes the output of the generator, $C(\cdot)$ is the output of the inactivated discriminator, and $E[\cdot]$ denotes the operation of averaging all the data in a small batch. When the real image is more real and natural than the synthetic image, the result of $D_{Ra}(y, x)$ tends to 1, as represented by Eq. (3.1); if the synthetic image is of poorer quality than the real image, the closer the result of $D_{Ra}(x, y)$ is to 0, as shown in Eq. (3.2).

According to the principle of relativistic discriminator, the loss function of the ESRGAN discriminator and generator can be defined as

$$L_D = -E[\log D_{Ra}(y, G(x))] - E[\log(1 - D_{Ra}(G(x), y))] \tag{3.3}$$

$$L_G = -E[\log(1 - D_{Ra}(y, G(x)))] - E[\log(D_{Ra}(G(x), y))] \tag{3.4}$$

where L_D and L_G denote the loss functions of the discriminator and generator, respectively, and D_{Ra} denotes the output of the relative average discriminator, which is calculated as shown in Eqs. (3.1) and (3.2).

In addition, ESRGAN introduces improvements to the perceptual loss function. Building on the concept of perceptual similarity proposed by Johnson *et al.* [7], perceptual loss is defined based on the activation layer of a pre-trained deep network, aiming to enhance image visual quality by minimizing the difference between activated features. In SRGAN, this loss is generalized to improve super-resolution reconstruction by minimizing the distance between high-dimensional features extracted from the activation layer of the VGG19 network. ESRGAN further refines this approach by constructing a more effective perceptual loss that constrains features prior to activation during generator training. This modification addresses two key limitations of SRGAN's perceptual loss: (1) activated features tend to be sparse, particularly in deep networks, resulting in weaker supervision and suboptimal performance; (2) enforcing similarity of activated features can lead to inconsistencies in brightness between reconstructed and target images. By penalizing differences in pre-activated features, ESRGAN's improved perceptual loss provides stronger supervision for both brightness and texture in the reconstructed image. Specifically, ESRGAN employs a pre-trained VGG19 network to construct the perceptual loss, extracting high-level features from the fourth convolutional layer preceding the fifth max-pooling layer. The perceptual loss is mathematically represented as

$$L_{\text{percep}} = E\left[\|\Phi(G(x)) - \Phi(y)\|_2^2\right] \tag{3.5}$$

where $\Phi(\cdot)$ denotes the high-level features extracted by pre-training the VGG19 network.

By improving the above points, ESRGAN successfully improves the blurring problem in the edge region of SRGAN-generated images and enhances the visual effect of the generated super-resolution images.

3.3 Improved ESRGAN for Super-Resolution Reconstruction of Underwater Images

3.3.1 *Generating network structures*

ESRGAN was developed to enhance the visual quality of super-resolution images. To further improve the resolution and texture details of underwater images, this chapter introduces two modifications to the generative network structure of ESRGAN: (1) replacing the original dense connectivity module (DB) with a multi-scale dense connectivity module (MDB); (2) incorporating a channel attention mechanism after the MDB to adaptively adjust the feature responses across different channels. The proposed module, which integrates multi-scale dense connectivity with the attention mechanism, is termed MADB (Multi-scale Attention Dense Block).

Convolutional neural networks (CNNs) extract target features through hierarchical abstraction, with the receptive field being a critical concept in this process. The receptive field refers to the region size in the input image that corresponds to a pixel in the output feature map of a convolutional layer. A small receptive field limits the network to capturing only local features, while an excessively large receptive field may introduce irrelevant information. Multi-scale feature fusion techniques address this by combining features at different scales, enabling effective extraction of object and contextual information, and have been widely applied in image feature extraction [8–10]. To enhance feature utilization and propagation, numerous algorithms have incorporated dense connectivity [11] into CNN architectures. This approach concatenates all preceding layer outputs as inputs to each subsequent convolutional layer, allowing direct access to both gradient and input information throughout the network. This design mitigates the vanishing gradient problem, facilitates training of deeper networks, and improves feature preservation during propagation. Additionally, the dense connection structure reduces parameter count compared to traditional CNNs, thereby helping to prevent overfitting. To further enhance feature representation, attention mechanisms have been extensively integrated into computer vision tasks [12–14]. These mechanisms dynamically assign weights to features based on their importance, emphasizing critical features while suppressing less relevant ones, thereby improving network performance and accuracy. Building on these principles, this chapter proposes multi-scale attention dense block (MADB), a novel module that integrates multi-scale feature fusion, dense connectivity, and attention mechanisms. MADB is designed to effectively learn high-frequency information from low-resolution images. The overall structure of MADB is illustrated in Fig. 3.3(a), while Fig. 3.3(b) details its multi-scale feature extraction component.

Referring to Fig. 3.3(a), assuming that the input feature of MADB is F_0, the feature extraction process of MADB is as follows: firstly, F_0 passes through a multi-scale feature extraction module, whose specific structure is shown in Fig. 3.3(b). This module adopts a parallel multi-branch multi-scale feature fusion structure and uses convolutional layers of size 3 and convolutional layer depths of 1 and 2 to

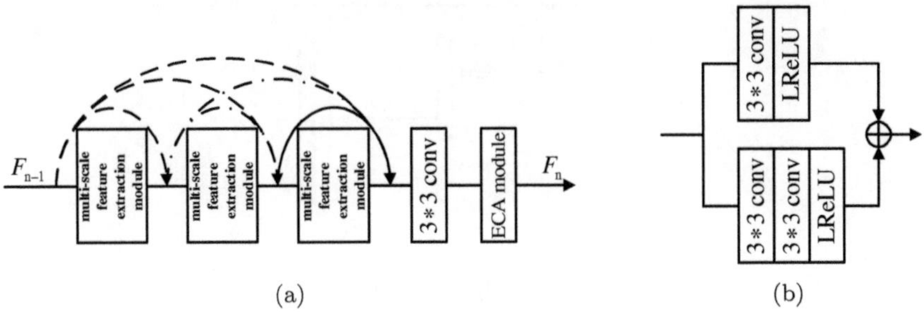

Figure 3.3. This chapter generates the basic modules of the network: (a) multiscale densely connected modules with attention mechanisms; (b) multi-scale feature extraction module.

extract features at different scales. Among them, the receptive field of a single convolutional layer is 3, and the receptive field of two convolutional layers connected in series is 5. The extracted features of different scales are then fused in accordance with the summation of the corresponding elements, and the output is expressed as

$$F_1 = f_{3\times3}(F_0) + f_{3\times3}(f_{3\times3}(F_0)) \tag{3.6}$$

where F_1 denotes the output of the first multiscale feature extraction module and $f_{3\times3}$ denotes the convolution operation with convolution kernel size of 3. Similarly, the output of the two subsequent multiscale feature extraction modules can be expressed as

$$F_2 = f_{3\times3}(C(F_1, F_0)) + f_{3\times3}(f_{3\times3}(C(F_1, F_0))) \tag{3.7}$$

$$F_3 = f_{3\times3}(C(F_2, F_1, F_0)) + f_{3\times3}(f_{3\times3}(C(F_2, F_1, F_0))) \tag{3.8}$$

where F_2 and F_3 denote the outputs of the second and third multiscale feature extraction modules, respectively, and C denotes the feature splicing operation. After the three multi-scale feature extraction modules, a convolutional layer with a convolutional kernel size of 3 is used to achieve the fusion of features of different depths, while feature dimensionality reduction is completed.

To further enhance the expressive power of the deep learning network model, this chapter incorporates an attention mechanism after feature fusion, which improves network performance by adaptively adjusting channel weights and emphasizing critical features. However, while attention mechanisms boost performance, they also increase model complexity. To balance performance and

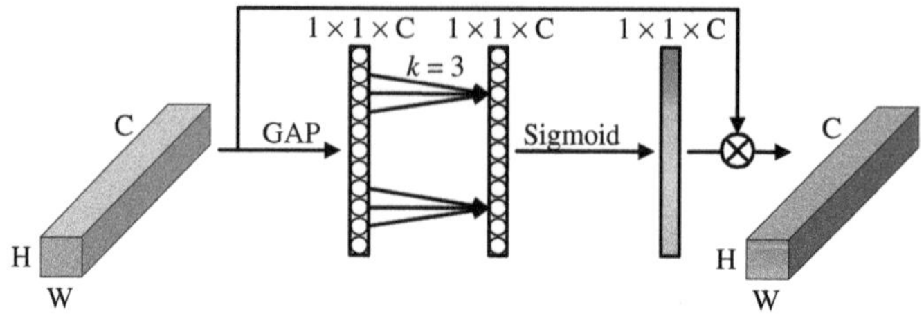

Figure 3.4. ECA module structure.

computational efficiency, we introduce the ECA (Efficient Channel Attention) module [15], a lightweight yet effective channel attention mechanism, following feature fusion. The structure of this module is illustrated in Fig. 3.4. The ECA module employs a local cross-channel interaction strategy that avoids dimensionality reduction, maintaining computational efficiency. Given input features with dimensions H × W × C (height, width, and number of channels, respectively), the ECA module operates as follows: firstly, the global average pooling (GAP) is used independently for each feature channel to obtain the background information of each channel, and its output tensor is 1 × 1 × C; then the cross-channel information interaction is completed by a one-dimensional convolution of the size of k, and the interaction is mapped to each feature channel by the Sigmoid function. The channel information is mapped to the corresponding weights of each feature channel by the Sigmoid function, where the size k of the 1D convolution kernel indicates the range of cross-channel interaction; finally, each channel is multiplied with its weights to obtain the features after adjusting the weights.

At the end of the MADB module, the output of the multiscale features adjusted by the ECA module can be expressed as

$$F_{\text{out}} = ca(f_{3\times 3}(C(F_3, F_2, F_1, F_0))) \tag{3.9}$$

where F_{out} denotes the output of the MADB module and ca denotes the operation of adjusting the feature weights of different channels through the ECA channel attention mechanism.

In terms of overall architecture, the generative network in this chapter retains the same foundational structure as ESRGAN, both being based on the SRResNet framework. The primary enhancement to the generative network lies in the deep residual information extraction module. Notably, this chapter eliminates the use of batch normalization (BN) layers in the network. This decision stems from the fact that BN layers normalize inputs during training using batch-specific mean and variance, while relying on estimated statistics from the entire training set during inference. When the statistical properties of the test and training datasets diverge significantly, BN layers can impair the network's generalization capability and reduce model robustness. Furthermore, removing BN layers decreases computational complexity and memory consumption. Additionally, this chapter adopts the multi-level residual module design from ESRGAN but replaces its dense block with the proposed MADB. The residual structure simplifies the learning process, enhances gradient propagation, and facilitates the training of deeper networks. Figure 3.5 illustrates the multi-level residual MADB module (RR-MADB) introduced in this chapter.

Eventually, the structure of the improved generative network in this chapter is shown in Fig. 3.6. Among them, the input of RR-MADB is 64 channels and the output is 32 channels, and a total of 18 RR-MADB modules are used in the generative network of this chapter. In addition, the up-sampling layer uses the nearest-neighbor interpolation operation, while a convolutional kernel of size 3 is used in the generative network.

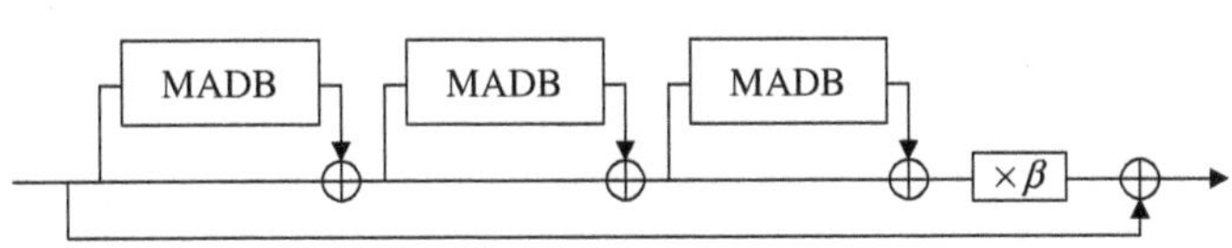

Figure 3.5. Multilevel residual MADB module structure.

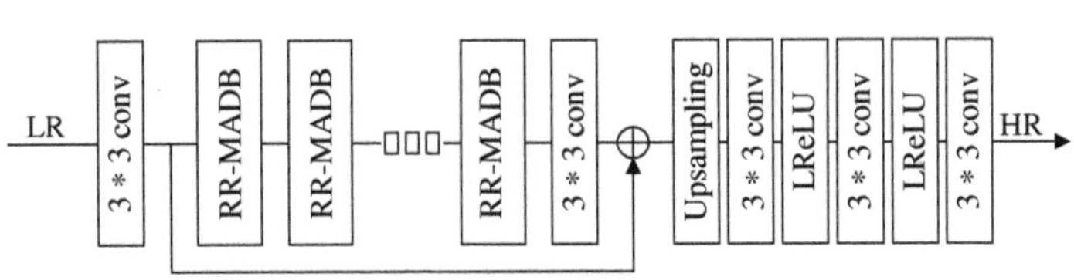

Figure 3.6. Generative network structure of this chapter.

Figure 3.7. Discriminant network structure.

3.3.2 *Discriminant network structure*

To effectively estimate the probability that the target super-resolution image appears more realistic and natural compared to the image generated by the network, we employ the discriminative network structure illustrated in Fig. 3.7 (where c/s denotes the number of convolutional kernels and stride size) during adversarial training. The input to the discriminative network consists of the output image from the generative network and its corresponding target image, while the output represents the probability that the target image is perceived as more realistic and natural than the generated image.

For the design of the discriminative network structure, this chapter adheres to the principles of DCGAN [16], employing the Leaky ReLU (LReLU) activation function and Batch Normalization strategy while avoiding pooling operations. The proposed discriminative network comprises eight convolutional layers, all utilizing 3×3 convolutional kernels. The number of kernels in these layers increases exponentially from 64 to 512. The network alternates between convolutional layers with strides of 1 and 2, ensuring that as the number of features grows exponentially, a stride-2 convolutional layer reduces the image resolution. Finally, the network maps the extracted features to probability values through two fully connected layers (Dense) followed by a Sigmoid activation function.

3.3.3 *Loss function selection*

In order to enhance the quality of the reconstructed image by the generative network, the generative network in this chapter uses a linear combination of multiple loss functions in the form of the following equation:

$$L_G = L_{\text{per}} + \lambda_1 L_{L1} + \lambda_2 L_G^{Ra} \tag{3.10}$$

where L_{per} is the perceptual loss function, L_{L1} is the content loss function, L_G^{Ra} is the adversarial loss function, and λ_1 and λ_2 are the weighting coefficients of each loss function, respectively.

(1) Perceptual loss function: The perceptual loss function is crucial to the performance of the generative network. Unlike the pixel difference-based loss function, the perceptual loss improves the quality of the output image of the generative network by penalizing the differences in the high-dimensional features extracted by the pre-trained network. In this chapter, we choose the pre-trained VGG19 [4] network to construct a more effective perceptual loss function. Specifically, in this chapter, the features extracted from the 4th convolutional layer before the 5th maximum pooling layer of the pre-trained VGG19 are selected to improve the visual perceptual quality of the output image by minimizing the Euclidean distance between the output image of the generative network and the target image features. The perceptual loss function is defined as follows:

$$L_{\text{per}} = E\left[\|\phi(G(x)) - \phi(y)\|_2^2\right] \tag{3.11}$$

where x is a low-resolution underwater image, y is a super-resolution image corresponding to x in the training set, $G(\cdot)$ denotes the output image of the generative network, and $\varphi(\cdot)$ denotes the high-level features extracted through the VGG19 network.

(2) Content loss function: In order to reduce the pixel difference between the output image of the generative network and the information pixel of the real super-resolution image, in this chapter, the pixel-level similarity is improved by reducing the $L1$ distance between the generated image and the real image of the training set, which can be expressed as follows:

$$L_{L1} = E[\|G(x) - y\|_1] \tag{3.12}$$

(3) Adversarial loss function: The adversarial loss in this chapter uses the same relativistic generative adversarial network-based principle as ESRGAN, a discriminator that estimates the probability that the target image is more realistic and natural than the underwater image generated by the generative network. Specifically, in this chapter, the RaGAN adversarial loss function is used to estimate the probability that the real data is more realistic and natural than the synthetic data from an average perspective. The loss function of the discriminative network is defined as

$$L_D = -E[\log D_{Ra}(y, G(x))] - E[\log(1 - D_{Ra}(G(x), y))] \quad (3.13)$$

Accordingly, the adversarial loss function of the generative network in this chapter is defined as

$$L_G = -E[\log(1 - D_{Ra}(y, G(x)))] - E[\log(D_{Ra}(G(x), y))] \quad (3.14)$$

where x denotes the input low-resolution underwater image, y denotes the target high-resolution image corresponding to x, $G(\cdot)$ generates the output image of the network, and $D_{Ra}(\text{input}_1, \text{input}_2)$ denotes the probability that input input_1 is more realistic and natural than input_2.

3.4 Comparison of Experiments and Analysis of Results

This experiment focuses on 2× super-resolution reconstruction of underwater images. To validate the effectiveness of the proposed improvements, the algorithm presented in this chapter is compared with ESRGAN and other representative single-image super-resolution algorithms. The experimental results are analyzed from both subjective and objective perspectives. The implementation is carried out on a Linux operating system using the PyTorch deep learning framework.

3.4.1 *Experimental data and training*

In this experiment, all training datasets utilize the publicly available super-resolution dataset DIV2K [17]. DIV2K comprises 1,000 high-quality 2K resolution images, including 800 training images, 100 validation images, and 100 test images. For testing, the experiment employs the Set5 [18], Set14 [19], BSD100 [20] datasets, along with an underwater image dataset. Set5 contains 5 images of flora and fauna, while Set14 includes 14 such images with richer detail compared to Set5. BSD100 consists of 100 images depicting natural and artificial scenery. These three datasets, known for their diverse content, are widely used for evaluating image super-resolution performance. The underwater image test set comprises 12 underwater scene images, derived from the Underwater-Imagenet test set and enhanced using the algorithm described in Chapter 2. To address limited data availability during network training, data augmentation techniques are applied, including random horizontal or vertical flipping followed by random cropping to produce high-quality 128×128 image patches. Low-resolution images for both training and testing are generated from these randomly cropped patches using Bicubic interpolation implemented via the PIL (Python Image Library) in Python.

The training process in this chapter is divided into two stages. First, a peak signal-to-noise ratio (PSNR)-oriented model is trained using the $L1$ distance between the generator output image and the super-resolution image as the loss function. The initial learning rate is set to 2×10^{-4} and the learning rate is decayed to 0.5 times of the original one every 10^5 iterations. Then, the generator is initialized using the trained PSNR-oriented model. The initial learning rate of the generator and discriminator was set to 1×10^{-4} and the learning rate decayed to 0.5 times the original every 10^5 iterations. The use of pre-training with pixel-by-pixel loss improves the visual performance of the super-resolution images generated by the GAN-based method due to the fact that this strategy avoids the generator from falling into a local optimum, and by initializing the generator with a PSNR-oriented model, the discriminator will receive super-resolution images of relatively high quality instead of the extremely poor-quality images, which facilitates the adversarial training by focusing on the details of the texture. According to the training process in this chapter, two models will be obtained in the end: one focusing on the reduction of pixel variance and focusing on the objective evaluation metric PSNR, and the other focusing on the reduction of perceptual variance and aiming to improve the visual effect of the image.

The model was trained using the Adma optimizer where the first-order momentum term β_1 was set to 0.9 and the second-order momentum term β_2 was set to 0.999. Training was carried out in small batches with the batch size set to 8. The optimization of the generative network was carried out with the weights λ_1 and λ_2 of the loss function set to 1×10^{-2} and 5×10^{-2}, respectively.

3.4.2 *Results*

In this section, the proposed algorithm is compared with several methods, including Bicubic interpolation (Bicubic), FSRCNN [21], and ESRGAN, on the public test sets Set5, Set14, BSD100, and the custom underwater image test set developed in this study. The ESRGAN generative network, which serves as a baseline, employs 23 RRDB modules and contains a total of 16.70 million parameters. Additionally, the PSNR-oriented model trained in the first stage of our training process is included for comparison, denoted as Ours-$L1$.

In this chapter, the peak signal-to-noise ratio (PSNR) is selected as an objective evaluation index of the image, which is calculated as shown in Eq. (3.15):

$$PSNR = 10 \log_{10}\left(\frac{MAX^2}{MSE}\right) \tag{3.15}$$

where MAX denotes the peak energy signal, for digital images, MAX takes the value of 255; MSE denotes the mean square error between the reconstructed image and the target super-resolution image. PSNR evaluates the quality of the reconstructed image by calculating the error between the corresponding pixel points of the two images, and it is most widely used in super-resolution tasks, and a larger value of the metric indicates that the image is less distorted. Table 3.1 lists the results of each super-resolution algorithm on the public test sets Set5, Set14, BSD100 and the underwater image test set.

As shown in the table data, pixel loss-based super-resolution algorithms, such as FSRCNN and Ours-$L1$, achieve high scores on objective evaluation metrics. Specifically, the improved generative network proposed in this chapter attains the highest PSNR score when optimized using a pixel-based loss function. In contrast, the generative network model based on adversarial and perceptual losses

Table 3.1. Comparison of the objective evaluation of 2× super-resolution results of each algorithm.

Test	Bicubic	FSRCNN	ESRGAN	Ours-$L1$	The algorithms in this chapter
Set5	31.787	33.404	32.637	35.758	33.193
Set14	28.298	29.487	28.787	31.387	29.481
BSD100	26.725	26.763	25.801	26.964	25.953
Underwater image	30.288	32.496	29.047	32.751	29.217

yields relatively lower PSNR values. Notably, when the network structure remains unchanged, Ours-$L1$ consistently outperforms the proposed algorithm in terms of objective evaluation metrics. However, loss functions defined by pixel differences exhibit limited capability in capturing texture details. Networks optimized with such loss functions struggle to recover lost high-frequency information, often resulting in reconstructed images that appear overly smoothed in edge regions, leading to degraded visual quality [2].

To provide a more intuitive assessment of the effectiveness of the improved ESRGAN-based super-resolution reconstruction algorithm for underwater images proposed in this chapter, as well as the limitations of using pixel differences as the loss function, Fig. 3.8 presents the 2× super-resolution results of each algorithm. The left column displays the low-resolution input images, while the corresponding right columns show the super-resolution results generated by each algorithm, highlighted with blue and green boxes, respectively.

From Fig. 3.8, it is evident that the super-resolution images generated by the Bicubic algorithm exhibit overly smooth edge regions, failing to produce sharp edges and resulting in a blurred appearance that diminishes visual quality. In contrast, learning-based methods achieve superior reconstruction quality compared to interpolation-based algorithms. Specifically, the FSRCNN algorithm produces overall better results than Bicubic by optimizing the network model with a pixel difference-based loss function. Although FSRCNN achieves higher PSNR metrics in some test cases, the resulting super-resolution images still display edge blurring, as seen in the fish tail region (blue box) and fish head region (green box) of Image1, as well as the fish head region (blue box) of Image3.

Ours-$L1$, which also employs pixel differences as the loss function, delivers improved reconstruction results with clearer textures, significantly enhancing visual quality compared to Bicubic and FSRCNN. However, this algorithm exhibits slight edge blurring in regions with dense or less prominent details in low-resolution underwater images, such as the turbid region (blue box) in Image2, the stone region (green box) in Image3, and the coral region (green box) in Image4, where edge regions appear smooth and textures are less distinct. Both ESRGAN and the proposed algorithm utilize a generative network optimized by adversarial and perceptual losses, effectively suppressing edge blurring and producing super-resolution images with

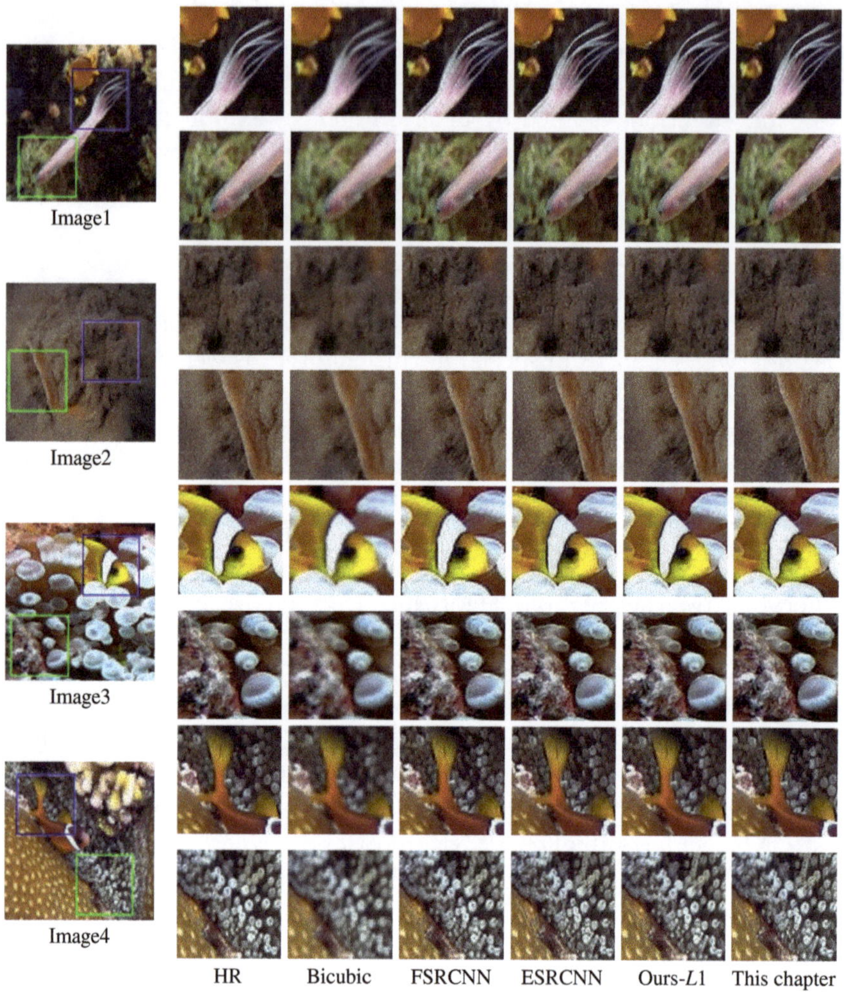

Figure 3.8. Display of 2× super-resolution reconstruction results for each algorithm.

sharp edges. In several cases, the proposed algorithm achieves higher-quality reconstructions. For instance, in the fish tail region (blue box) of Image1, ESRGAN introduces slight artifacts, while the proposed algorithm generates clearer edges. Similarly, in the green box region of Image2, ESRGAN results in mild edge blurring, whereas the proposed algorithm produces images with sharpened edges.

Based on the above analysis, the proposed algorithm demonstrates significant improvements in reconstruction quality compared to Bicubic and FSRCNN, providing richer detail and substantially enhancing visual effects. Relative to ESRGAN, the proposed algorithm achieves a 0.17 dB increase in the objective evaluation metric PSNR and delivers superior visual quality in certain test cases. Notably, the total parameters of the improved generative network are approximately 15.66 M, representing a 6.79% reduction compared to ESRGAN. This improvement in reconstructed image quality with fewer parameters underscores the effectiveness of the proposed enhancements.

3.5 Conclusion

This chapter focuses on the enhanced ESRGAN-based super-resolution reconstruction algorithm tailored for underwater images. First, the super-resolution algorithms SRGAN and ESRGAN, both based on generative adversarial networks, are described, along with the key improvements ESRGAN introduces over SRGAN. Next, the proposed ESRGAN-based super-resolution algorithm for underwater images is presented, detailing the architecture and functionality of both the generative and discriminative networks, as well as the loss function employed during model training. Finally, the proposed algorithm is compared with other representative super-resolution methods to demonstrate the effectiveness of the introduced improvements.

References

[1] Wang X, Yu K, Wu S, *et al.* Esrgan: Enhanced super-resolution generative adversarial networks. *Proceedings of the European Conference on Computer Vision (ECCV) Workshops.* 2018.

[2] Ledig C, Theis L, Huszar F, *et al.* Photo-realistic single image super-resolution using a generative adversarial network. *Proceedings of the IEEE Conference on Computer Vision and Pattern Recognition.* 2017: 4681–4690.

[3] Shi W, Caballero J, Theis L, *et al.* Is the deconvolution layer the same as a convolutional layer? arXiv preprint arXiv: 1609.07009, 2016.

[4] Lim B, Son S, Kim H, *et al.* Enhanced deep residual networks for single image super-resolution. *Proceedings of the IEEE Conference on Computer Vision and Pattern Recognition Workshops.* 2017: 136–144.
[5] Nah S, Kim TH, Lee KM. Deep Multi-scale convolutional neural network for dynamic scene deblurring. *Proceedings of the IEEE Conference on Computer Vision and Pattern Recognition.* 2017: 3883–3891.
[6] Jolicoeur-Martineau A. The relativistic discriminator: A key element missing from standard GAN. arXiv preprint arXiv:1807.00734, 2018.
[7] Johnson J, Alahi A, Fei-Fei L. Perceptual losses for real-time style transfer and super-resolution. *European Conference on Computer Vision.* Springer, Cham, 2016: 694–711.
[8] Guo J, Guo H, Guo C. Single image rain removal based on multi-scale convolutional neural network. *Journal of Harbin Institute of Technology*, 2018, 50(3): 191–197.
[9] Jiang K, Wang Z, Yi P, *et al.* Multi-scale progressive fusion network for single image deraining. *Proceedings of the IEEE/CVF Conference on Computer Vision and Pattern Recognition*, 2020: 8346–8355.
[10] Shao MW, Li L, Meng DY, *et al.* Uncertainty guided multi-scale attention network for raindrop removal from a single image. *IEEE Transactions on Image Processing*, 2021, 30: 4828–4839.
[11] Huang G, Liu Z, Van Der Maaten L, *et al.* Densely connected convolutional networks. *Proceedings of the IEEE Conference on Computer Vision and Pattern Recognition.* 2017: 4700–4708.
[12] Qian R, Tan RT, Yang W, *et al.* Attentive generative adversarial network for raindrop removal from a single image. *Proceedings of the IEEE Conference on Computer Vision and Pattern Recognition.* 2018: 2482–2491.
[13] Liu X, Ma Y, Shi Z, *et al.* Griddehazenet: Attention-based multi-scale network for image dehazing. *Proceedings of the IEEE/CVF International Conference on Computer Vision.* 2019: 7314–7323.
[14] Fu J, Liu J, Tian H, *et al.* Dual attention network for scene segmentation. *Proceedings of the IEEE/CVF Conference on Computer Vision and Pattern Recognition.* 2019: 3146–3154.
[15] Wang Q, Wu B, Zhu P, *et al.* ECA-Net: Efficient channel attention for deep convolutional neural networks. *Proceedings of the IEEE/CVF Conference on Computer Vision and Pattern Recognition (CVPR).* 2020: 11531–11539.
[16] Radford A, Metz L, Chintala S. Unsupervised representation learning with deep convolutional generative adversarial networks. arXiv preprint arXiv: 1511.06434, 2015.

[17] Agustsson E, Timofte R. Ntire 2017 challenge on single image super-resolution: Dataset and study. *Proceedings of the IEEE Conference on Computer Vision and Pattern Recognition Workshops.* 2017: 126–135.

[18] Bevilacqua M, Roumy A, Guillemot C, *et al.* Low-complexity single-image super-resolution based on nonnegative neighbor embedding. *Proceedings of the British Machine Vision Conference 2012.* 2012.

[19] Zeyde R, Elad M, Protter M. On single image scale-up using sparse-representations. *International Conference on Curves and Surfaces.* Springer, Berlin, Heidelberg, 2010: 711–730.

[20] Martin D, Fowlkes C, Tal D, *et al.* A database of human segmented natural images and its application to evaluating segmentation algorithms and measuring ecological statistics. *Proceedings Eighth IEEE International Conference on Computer Vision (ICCV).* 2001, 2: 416–423.

[21] Dong C, Loy C, Tang X. Accelerating the super-resolution convolutional neural network. *European Conference on Computer Vision.* Springer, Cham, 2016: 391–407.

Chapter 4

The Image Target Segmentation Algorithm Based on a Nested U-Net

4.1 Introduction

The previous two chapters, which are based on the improved PCNN model, effectively address challenges such as noise interference and adaptive segmentation in crack detection. However, the PCNN remains a traditional neural network approach, which limits its ability to handle large volumes of crack data, and its processing speed does not meet the required performance standards. In conventional pavement crack detection algorithms, crack image data is typically collected and processed offline in the backend. With increasing demands for both accuracy and real-time performance in certain pavement detection systems, the fast and accurate detection of pavement cracks has become crucial for pavement maintenance. In recent years, deep learning has demonstrated outstanding performance in image recognition tasks. Although deep learning techniques initially require significant time and resources for training, they offer faster processing and superior recognition performance compared to traditional methods in practical detection scenarios. These techniques are capable of real-time detection while simultaneously collecting crack data in real-world environments, making them well-suited for the rapid processing of large datasets of crack images.

Reference [1] proposed a semantic segmentation method for concrete crack images based on a deep fully convolutional network

(FCN), achieving an average precision of 90%. The cracks were reasonably detected, and the crack density was correctly evaluated, although there were many noisy crack-like features. Unet [2] is an improved network based on the FCN model, without fully connected layers, and is capable of segmenting images of arbitrary sizes. Unet was initially proposed for medical image segmentation, such as for liver and eyeball images. We applied the Unet model to crack image segmentation and proposed a new nested Unet convolutional neural network model for crack segmentation combined with an attention mechanism (Att_Nested_Unet). The nested Unet uses long and short connections to better fuse features from different levels, effectively preserving the detailed features of cracks. However, there is often a significant amount of noise in crack images, so we introduced the attention mechanism to suppress irrelevant regions in crack images. The proposed Att_Nested_Unet model was evaluated on a dataset of 9,990 different types of crack images. Both subjective experimental results and objective performance metrics indicate that this method outperforms Unet++, Att_Unet, and Unet in crack image segmentation, improving the accuracy of crack segmentation, eliminating noise, and preserving the texture details of cracks. It achieves fast and accurate detection on large-scale crack datasets.

4.2 Convolutional Neural Network-Related Technologies

With the advent of the AI era, the exceptional performance of deep learning is increasingly being demonstrated across various fields, including image classification, object detection, and image segmentation. Deep learning models typically consist of numerous parameters and complex architectures, with convolutional neural networks (CNNs) serving as a prominent example and one of the most widely utilized models. CNNs are designed to share weights and operate on local regions, which significantly reduces the number of parameters in comparison to other models. As illustrated in Fig. 4.1, the general structure of a CNN comprises an input layer, an output layer, and intermediate layers. The intermediate layers, which are the core of the CNN, consist of convolutional layers, pooling layers, and fully connected layers. The primary function of these intermediate layers is to extract high-dimensional features from the input image.

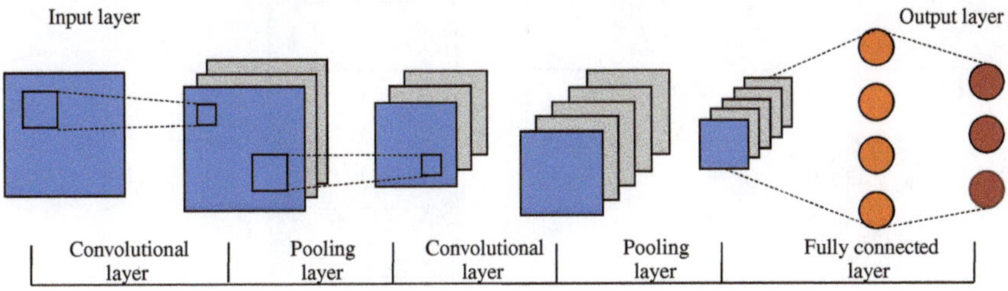

Figure 4.1. General structure of a convolutional neural network.

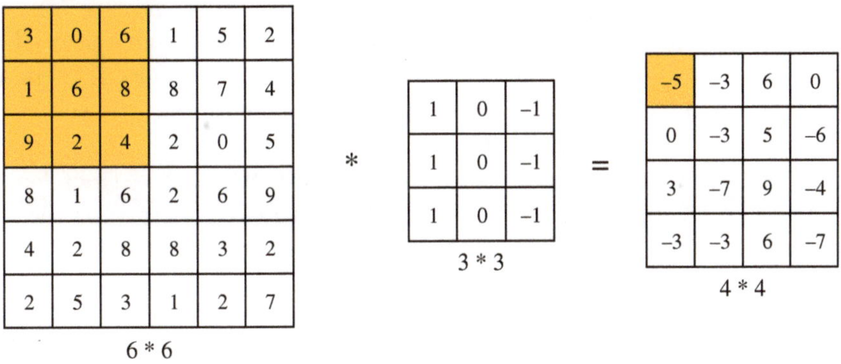

Figure 4.2. Convolution operation.

The convolution layer in a CNN involves the process of convolution operations. The main procedure of the convolution operation is to use a convolution kernel to multiply the pixels within the neighborhood of a certain point in the input image, and the sum of the products is used as the pixel value for that position in the output image, as shown in Fig. 4.2. Several concepts are involved here: the input image size n, the filter size k, the stride s, and the padding size p. The output size after convolving the image with the filter is as follows $\left\lfloor \frac{n+2p-k}{s} \right\rfloor + 1$. In a convolutional neural network, the parameters at each position of the convolution kernel are not preset but are updated during the training process through back-propagation.

The role of the pooling layer is to remove redundant information, simplify the model, and improve computational speed. As shown in Fig. 4.3, there are mainly two types of pooling: max-pooling and mean-pooling. As the names suggest, max-pooling selects the maximum pixel value within the region, while mean-pooling calculates

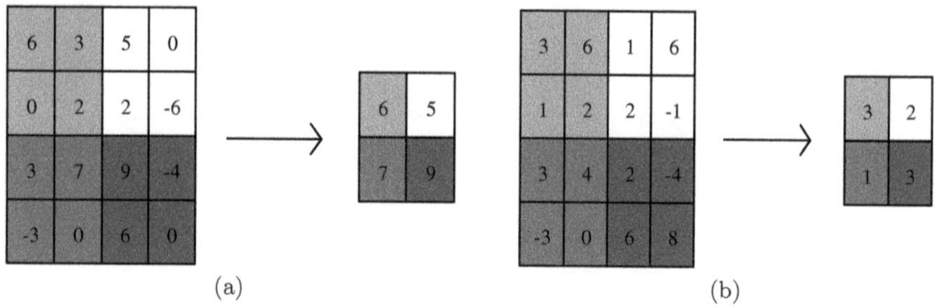

Figure 4.3. Pooling operation. (a) Max-pooling, (b) Mean-pooling.

the average value of the pixels in the neighborhood. From the pooling operation, we can see that the specific position of the local region does not affect the result. This rotational, translational, and scaling invariance is an important characteristic of CNNs.

The primary function of convolution in a CNN is to extract features from an image. In image recognition tasks, the extracted local features (feature maps) are passed to the fully connected layers to be combined and produce the final classification or recognition result. However, in segmentation tasks, the spatial structural characteristics of the feature maps cannot be ignored, which is why fully connected layers are not suitable for tasks that require finding targets based on spatial location.

4.3 Fully Convolutional Neural Network (FCN)

When traditional CNNs handle image semantic segmentation tasks, a common approach is to select a small patch of the image as the input to the CNN. This method presents the following issues: (1) High storage overhead: Since every pixel must be traversed and the image patch centered around each pixel is used as input, if the patch size is $15 * 15$, the storage space increases to 225 times that of the original image. (2) Low computational efficiency: As the sliding window traverses neighboring pixels, many pixels within the window are repeated, resulting in a significant amount of redundancy in the convolution operation. (3) Limited receptive field size: The sliding window's size, often referred to as the receptive field, restricts classification performance. Typically, the sliding window size is chosen to be $15 * 15$ or $25 * 25$, which is much smaller than the original

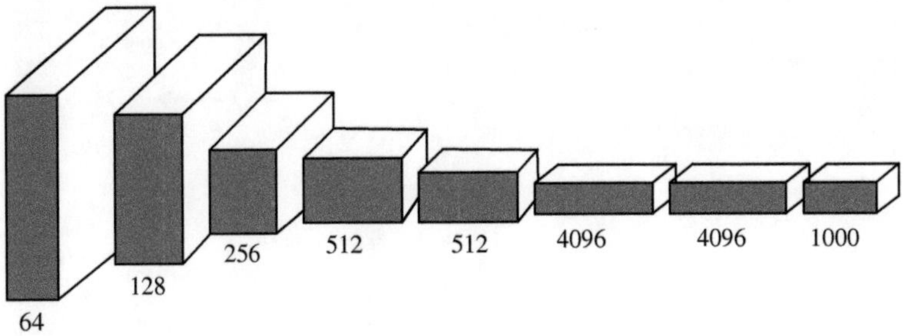

Figure 4.4. Convolution structure in FCN.

image and thus only captures local features. As a result, CNNs face significant limitations in semantic segmentation. To address these problems, Jonathan Long proposed the concept of Fully Convolutional Networks (FCN) [3], which is an end-to-end, point-to-point network capable of making pixel-level predictions.

In image semantic segmentation tasks, the final output needs to be a two-dimensional segmentation map, whereas in traditional CNNs, the fully connected layers output the probability values for different categories. Therefore, in FCN, the fully connected layers of the CNN are discarded. FCN uses the VGG network as a pre-trained model to perform multiple down-samplings to extract features, and the last three fully connected layers are replaced with convolutional layers, as shown in Fig. 4.4. The VGG network is a classic model in traditional CNNs, consisting of convolutional layers and fully connected layers. Layers 1 to 5 are convolutional layers, while the final three layers (layers 6 to 8) are fully connected layers, represented by one-dimensional vectors with lengths of 4096, 4096, and 1000, respectively. The values in these one-dimensional vectors correspond to the probability of each class. In FCN, the last three fully connected layers are replaced with convolutional layers, transforming the one-dimensional vectors into two-dimensional ones while keeping their length unchanged. The corresponding sizes of the convolution kernels are (1,1,4096), (1,1,4096), and (1,1,1000). Since the FCN model is entirely composed of convolutional structures without fully connected layers, it can accept input images of any size.

As the pioneering work in image semantic segmentation, the FCN model structure is mainly composed of three parts: convolutional structure, deconvolutional structure, and skip connection structure,

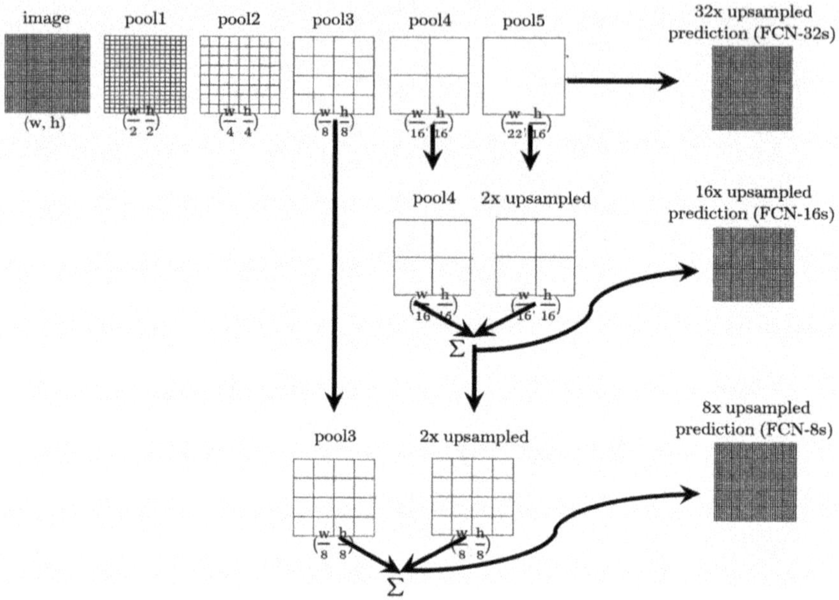

Figure 4.5. FCN network model.

as shown in Fig. 4.5. The convolutional structure typically performs down-sampling on the input image to extract high-dimensional features. During down-sampling, the image size is gradually reduced, with each of the first five layers applying convolution and pooling in sequence, halving the image size at each layer. By the fifth layer, the image size is reduced to 1/32 of the original. The last three layers maintain the same size, followed by a deconvolution operation that up-samples the output from the fifth layer back to the original image size for output prediction, producing the segmentation map, which is referred to as the FCN-32s model. At this point, the prediction accuracy of the model is still not precise enough, and some detailed information is lost. To achieve a more accurate prediction segmentation map, the output from the earlier layers can be skip-connected with the up-sampled output of the fifth layer, resulting in FCN-16s and FCN-8s models. Skip connections incorporate feature information from different levels, making the results more precise.

In this paper, the FCN model was first tested on a dataset of 525 backpack images to evaluate the segmentation performance of the algorithm, and then the model was transferred to a dataset of 1,740

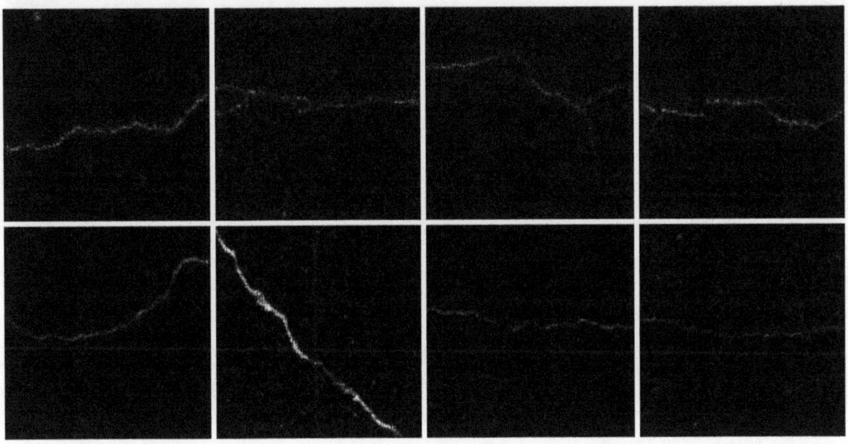

Figure 4.6. FCN performance on crack image.

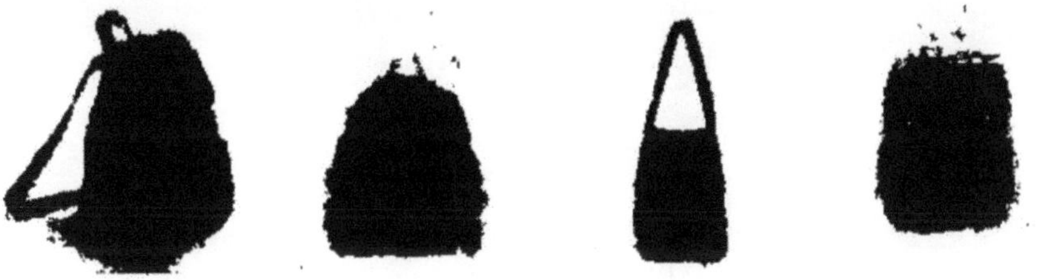

Figure 4.7. FCN performance on backpack image.

crack images. As shown in Fig. 4.6, the performance of FCN on crack images was poor. The segmentation results were still not detailed enough. Although FCN classifies each pixel, it does not consider the relationships between pixels. From Fig. 4.7, we can see that FCN is suitable for classifying large regions of an image, but the segmentation results remain relatively blurry, losing the edge detail information in the image. Since the target cracks in crack images are thin and elongated, the segmentation effect is even less pronounced.

4.4 U-net Model

Although FCN produces coarse segmentation results, it holds significant importance as the pioneer of semantic segmentation, and researchers have conducted extensive studies based on it. Unet is a

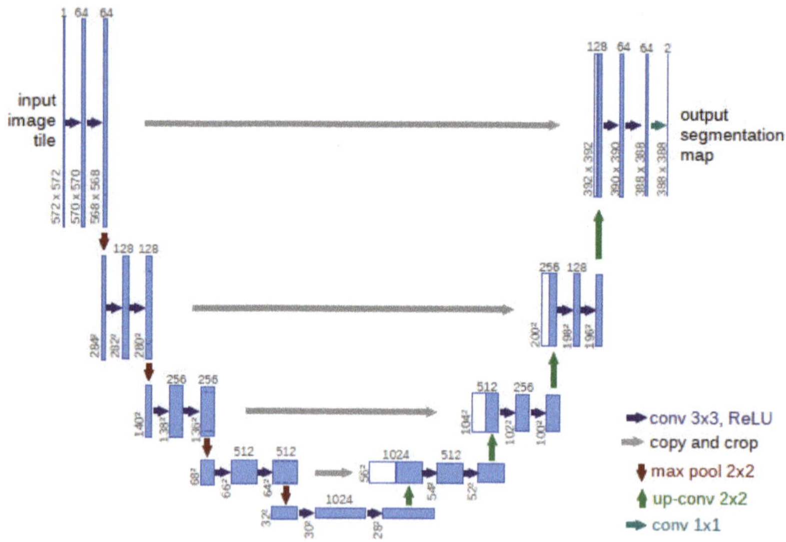

Figure 4.8. Unet model.

medical image segmentation model based on the FCN model, with its network consisting of two parts in a U-shape, hence it is called the Unet network, as shown in Fig. 4.8. Unet also includes the three components from FCN: the convolutional structure, deconvolutional structure, and skip connection, but Unet uses a different feature fusion method in the skip connections compared to FCN. In the FCN model, the next layer's upsampled feature map is added to the previous layer's feature map, whereas in the Unet model, features of the same dimensions from different layers are concatenated. In the Unet model, the down-sampling process is actually the process of extracting multi-scale features from the image, while the up-sampling part fuses these multi-scale features to restore the image's detailed features. In medical imaging, high-resolution information is needed to segment complex areas such as boundaries, and the segmentation targets, like human organs, are relatively fixed in position and semantically simple. Unet, by combining deep and shallow information, has been widely applied in medical image segmentation. However, crack images differ significantly from medical images in terms of their characteristics. The following section will experiment with applying crack images to the Unet model and propose an improved Unet model for crack segmentation.

4.5 Crack Image Segmentation Model Att_Nested_Unet

4.5.1 *Related research*

The Unet model was first proposed by Ronneberger for use in medical image segmentation. The network consists of a contraction path on the left, composed of convolutional and pooling layers, and an expansion path on the right, composed of convolutional and deconvolutional layers. Its most notable feature is the use of skip connections to fuse deep and shallow features. Li *et al.* [4] proposed DenseNet, which directly connects each layer with the same feature map size, promoting feature propagation and alleviating the problem of vanishing gradients. Inspired by this, Zhou *et al.* [5] proposed Unet++. Since Unet models of different depths perform differently on various datasets, Zhou combined multiple layers of Unet, using both long and short connections to capture features at different levels, thus achieving excellent performance. Although these models have shown good results in medical imaging, their effectiveness for complex crack images remains to be tested due to the interference from lighting conditions, imaging equipment, and noise. In medical image lesion detection tasks, the target areas are often localized, while in crack images, the cracks are distributed widely and exhibit complex, varied shapes.

The attention mechanism has been widely applied in image processing and natural language processing tasks. Its essence lies in weighted summation, assigning larger weights to key regions and smaller weights to irrelevant ones. In crack images, our focus is on the cracks, while noise and background, as irrelevant regions, should be suppressed. Therefore, we introduce the self-attention mechanism. Contextual information is crucial for visual tasks such as semantic segmentation and object detection, and the self-attention mechanism provides an effective way to capture global contextual information. In the literature [6] significant progress has been made in sequence models. Danet [7] adopts both spatial and channel attention mechanisms and then fuses the features before feeding them into the segmentation network, achieving great results. In literature [8] an attention gate (AG) was introduced to focus on medical structures of different shapes and sizes, improving the model's prediction accuracy.

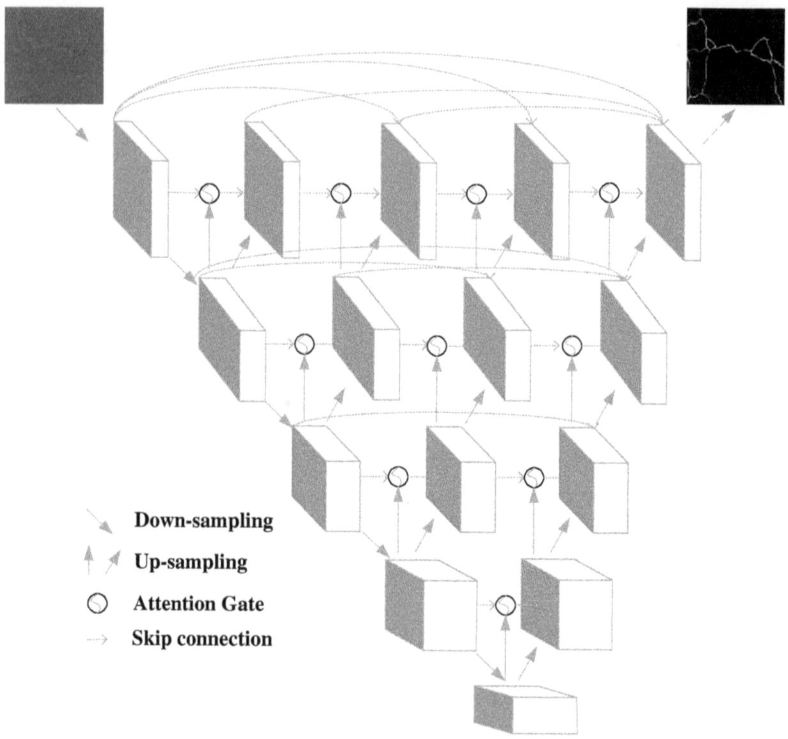

Figure 4.9. Att_Nested_Unet network model.

4.5.2 *Att_Nested_Unet algorithm*

In this paper, we propose a new nested Unet crack segmentation model combined with a self-attention mechanism, as shown in Fig. 4.9. The model is divided into three main parts: down-sampling, attention module, and skip connections. The down-sampling process is as follows: the RGB three-channel crack image is used as the input to the entire model, and a combination of a $3 * 3$ convolutional layer, batch normalization layer, and ReLU activation function is applied twice before performing max-pooling to move to the next layer. Each subsequent layer performs the same operation, doubling the size of the feature maps each time. During the down-sampling process, the size of the feature maps progressively increases. The low-resolution information obtained after multiple down-sampling steps provides contextual semantic information about the segmentation

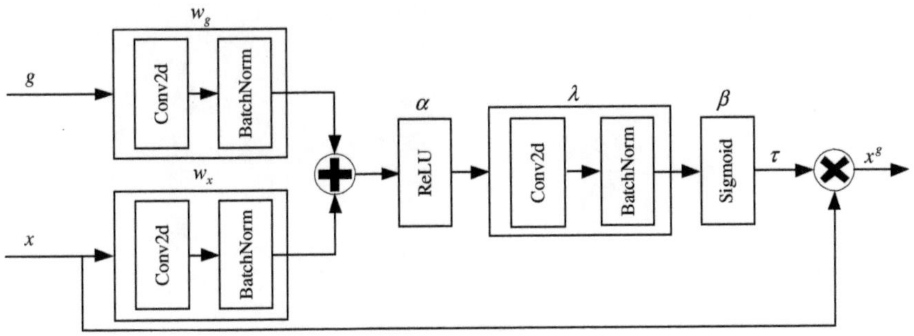

Figure 4.10. Attention module.

target within the entire image. After up-sampling using bilinear interpolation, the feature maps at the same scale are concatenated to fuse the information. After each concatenation, a combination of a 3 ∗ 3 convolutional layer, batch normalization layer, and ReLU activation function is applied twice, and the number of feature maps is halved.

The attention module is shown in Fig. 4.10, with the formula as follows:

$$\tau_i^l = \beta(\lambda^T(\alpha(w_g^T g_i + w_g^T x_i^l))) \tag{4.1}$$

$$\overline{x}_i^l = \tau_i^l \bullet x_i^l \tag{4.2}$$

where $w_x \in \mathbb{R}^{F_l \times F_{\text{int}}}$, $w_g \in \mathbb{R}^{F_g \times F_{\text{int}}}$, $\lambda \in \mathbb{R}^{F_{\text{int}} \times 1}$, α is the ReLU activation function, and β represents the Sigmoid activation function, F_l indicates the number of feature maps in layer l. In this paper, the sizes of F_l and F_g are the same. The attention coefficient τ_i^l represents the weight of each pixel i, $\tau_i^l \in [0, 1]$, suppresses the feature response of irrelevant regions, activating only the response of specific regions. The gating signal g_i is a higher-level feature response that contains richer information about the target region. By adding the gating signal g_i to the multi-scale information of x_i, the attention coefficient for the target region is trained to tend toward 1. Finally, by multiplying x_i by the attention coefficient, the attention of x_i is focused on the target region.

Unlike the skip connections in Unet, the nested Unet model can be viewed as a nested combination of four Unet models. Through long and short connections, the features from each preceding layer are effectively fused. Taking a two-layer nested Unet model as an

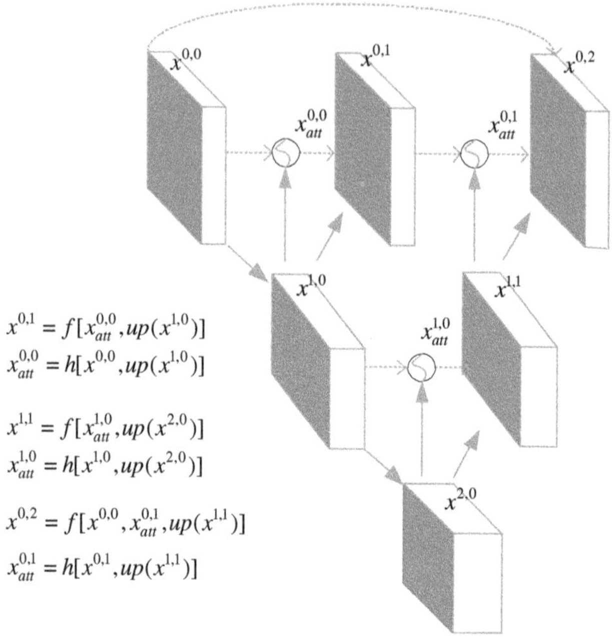

Figure 4.11. Skip connections.

example, as shown in Fig. 4.11, $h[\bullet]$ represents the attention mechanism, and $f[\bullet]$ represents the concatenation operation. After performing max pooling, a $3 * 3$ convolutional layer, batch normalization layer, and ReLU activation function are applied twice to obtain $x^{1,0}$.

After upsampling $x^{1,0}$, $up(x^{1,0})$ is obtained it is first combined with $x^{0,0}$ and passed into the attention mechanism model to obtain. Then, $up(x^{1,0})$ is concatenated with $x_{att}^{0,0}$. After concatenation, a combination of a $3 * 3$ convolutional layer, batch normalization layer, and ReLU activation function is applied twice to fuse the feature information at the same scale, resulting in $x^{0,1}$. Similar operations are performed to obtain the outputs of each Unet layer: $x^{0,2}$, $x^{0,3}$ and $x^{0,4}$. Finally, after $x^{0,1}$, $x^{0,2}$, $x^{0,3}$ and $x^{0,4}$, a $1 * 1$ convolution kernel is applied, followed by summation and averaging.

Table 4.1 shows the structural properties of each unit module in the Att_Nested_Unet algorithm. The input crack image has a size of $128 \times 128 \times 3$, and in the downsampling module, the output sizes for layers $x^{0,0}$, $x^{1,0}$, $x^{2,0}$, $x^{3,0}$, and $x^{4,0}$ are $128 \times 128 \times 64$, $64 \times 64 \times 128$, $32 \times 32 \times 256$, $16 \times 16 \times 512$, and $8 \times 8 \times 1024$, respectively. It can

Table 4.1. Structure of Att_Nested_Unet.

Unit layer	Type	Input size	Number	Convolutional kernel size	Pad	Output size
Downsampling multi-scale feature extraction	Convolution	128 × 128 × 3	64	3 × 3 × 2	1	128 × 128 × 64
	Pooling	128 × 128 × 64	–	2 × 2	0	64 × 64 × 64
	Convolution	64 × 64 × 64	128	3 × 3 × 2	1	64 × 64 × 128
	Pooling	64 × 64 × 128	–	2 × 2	0	32 × 32 × 128
	Convolution	32 × 32 × 128	256	3 × 3 × 2	1	32 × 32 × 256
	Pooling	32 × 32 × 256	–	2 × 2	0	16 × 16 × 256
	Convolution	16 × 16 × 256	512	3 × 3 × 2	1	16 × 16 × 512
	Pooling	16 × 16 × 512	–	2 × 2	0	8 × 8 × 512
	Convolution	8 × 8 × 512	1024	3 × 3 × 2	1	8 × 8 × 1024
Attention module (one example shown)	Upsampling	64 × 64 × 128	–	–	–	128 × 128 × 64
	Convolutional attention	128 × 128× 64	32	1 × 1× 1	0	128 × 128 × 32
	Convolution	128 × 128 × 64	32	1 × 1 × 1	0	128 × 128 × 32
	Summation	128 × 128 × 32 128 × 128 × 32		–		128 × 128 × 32
	Convolution	128 × 128 × 32	1	1 × 1 × 1	0	128 × 128 × 1
	Multiplication	128 × 128 × 64 128 × 128 × 1		–		128 × 128 × 64
Multi-scale feature fusion module (one example shown)	Concatenation	128 × 128 × 64 128 × 128 × 64		–		128 × 128 × 128
	Convolution	128 × 128 × 128	64	3 × 3 × 2	1	128 × 128 × 64

be seen that the image size is halved with each downsampling, while the number of channels doubles. As the image resolution decreases, higher-dimensional features are extracted. From Fig. 4.9, we can see that the attention mechanism module is used in 10 places. Taking $x^{0,0}$ and $up(x^{1,0})$ as examples, $up(x^{1,0})$ has a size of $128 \times 128 \times 64$, and $x^{0,0}$ also has a size of $128 \times 128 \times 64$. After being input into the attention module, the output $x_{\text{att}}^{0,0}$ has a size of $128 \times 128 \times 64$. It can be observed that the attention module does not change the image resolution but is instead a process of feature integration. The subsequent feature fusion module concatenates the output $x_{\text{att}}^{0,0}$ from the attention module with the upsampled $\text{up}(x^{1,0})$, doubling the number of channels to $128 \times 128 \times 128$. Finally, after convolution, the number of channels is reduced, and the final output from the feature fusion module $x^{0,1}$ has a size of $128 \times 128 \times 128$. This stage is a process of feature fusion. The other feature points in Fig. 4.9 are processed in the same way as these three parts.

4.5.3 *Experiments and results*

(1) Dataset: Due to the lack of a standardized crack image dataset, we expanded the limited crack data obtained online through data augmentation. The dataset includes a total of 9,990 RGB crack images with a resolution of $480 * 320$, divided into a training set and a test set. The training set contains 8,700 images, while the test set contains 1,290 images. During training, 1,305 images were randomly selected from the training set as a validation set to assess whether the model was overfitting and to validate the model's generalization ability. Figure 4.12 shows the performance of different algorithms during the training and validation process.

(2) Loss Function: Crack image segmentation is essentially a binary classification problem at the pixel level. For binary classification tasks, the binary cross-entropy loss function (binary_cross_entropy_with_logits) is commonly used. In medical image segmentation, the Dice coefficient loss function (Dice loss) is often employed, with the introduction of a smoothing factor S.

$$\text{bce} = -\frac{1}{2}(Y \times \log(\text{sigmoid}(X)) + (1 - Y) \times \log(1 - \text{sigmoid}(X))) \tag{4.3}$$

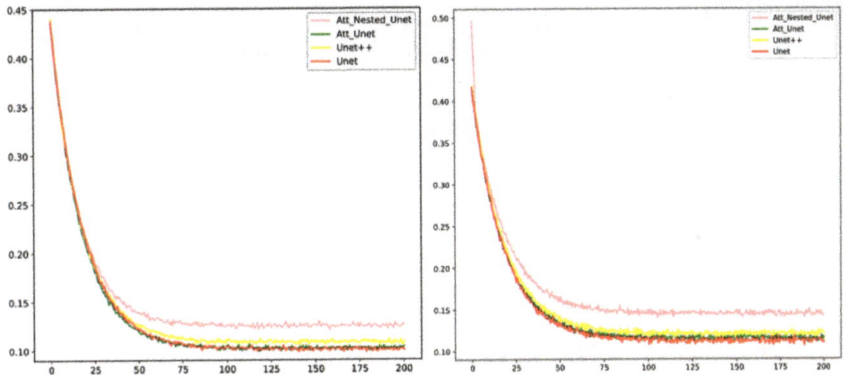

Figure 4.12. Loss curves of different algorithms on training and validation sets.

$$\text{Dice} = 1 - \frac{2|X \cap Y|}{|X| + |Y| + S} \tag{4.4}$$

In the formula, X represents the predicted image, Y represents the label image, and $S = 1$.

The two loss functions are suited for different sample data scenarios. In this paper, we effectively combine both loss functions, as shown in the following equation:

$$\text{loss} = w * \text{bce} + (1 - w) * \text{Dice} \tag{4.5}$$

w represents the coefficient that balances the two loss functions, and here w is set to 0.5.

(3) Hyperparameters:

(1) Learning rate (lr): Initialized to 0.001
(2) Momentum: 0.9
(3) Cosine annealing is used to adjust the learning rate
(4) Batch size: 4
(5) Optimizer: Stochastic Gradient Descent (SGD)

(4) Experimental results: To compare with other methods, different evaluation metrics were used: the Dice coefficient (commonly used in medical imaging), Accuracy, Recall, Precision, and F1 score.

$$s = \frac{2|X \cap Y|}{|X| + |Y|} \tag{4.6}$$

$$Acc = \frac{TP + TN}{TP + TN + FP + FN} \tag{4.7}$$

$$\text{Re call} = \frac{TP}{TP + FN} \tag{4.8}$$

$$\text{Pr ecision} = \frac{TP}{TP + FP} \tag{4.9}$$

$$F1 = 2 \bullet \frac{\text{precision} \bullet \text{recall}}{\text{precision} + \text{recall}} \tag{4.10}$$

In this study, TP (True Positive) represents the number of crack pixels correctly predicted as crack pixels, TN (True Negative) represents the number of non-crack pixels correctly predicted as non-crack pixels, FP (False Positive) represents the number of non-crack pixels incorrectly predicted as crack pixels, and FN (False Negative) represents the number of crack pixels incorrectly predicted as non-crack pixels.

We performed qualitative and quantitative experiments and analyses using a dataset of 9,990 crack images. The proposed algorithm was trained and tested in a software environment of Ubuntu 5.3.1, Python 3.6, and PyTorch 1.2.0, on a GeForce RTX 2080 GPU with 8GB of memory. Due to hardware limitations and model size, the data type was set to "half," and the training time was approximately 18 hours. The testing phase used a test set of 1,290 crack images, with each image taking around 0.5 seconds to process. As shown in Fig. 4.13, the comparison results between the proposed algorithm and Unet++, Att_Unet, and Unet are presented. From left to right are the original image, label, Att_Nested_Unet segmentation result, Unet++ segmentation result, Att_Unet segmentation result, and Unet segmentation result. To improve visibility, the label and final segmentation images were converted to RGB format. From a subjective perspective, the proposed algorithm is more accurate in crack segmentation compared to the other algorithms, preserving crack details more completely, reducing noise, and detecting fewer incorrect pixels. For complex network-like cracks, which tend to lose detail, such as in the 2nd and 3rd rows of Fig. 4.13, Unet++, Att_Unet, and Unet show more crack breakage and missed detection in the detailed crack regions. In contrast, the proposed algorithm retains the crack regions more completely.

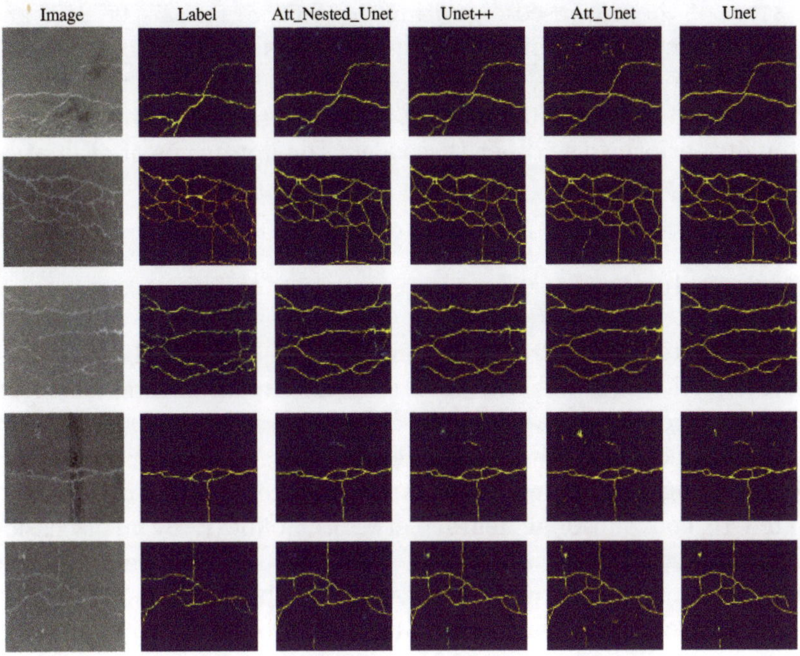

Figure 4.13. Experimental results of different algorithms.

Table 4.2. Evaluation metrics of different algorithms.

Metric	Att_Nested_Unet	Unet^{++}	Att_Unet Gray	Unet
Dice	**0.6656**	0.6614	0.6299	0.6652
Acc	**0.9827**	0.9823	0.9801	0.9823
Recall	0.6129	0.6212	0.6344	**0.6364**
Precision	**0.7810**	0.7611	0.6751	0.7493
F1	**0.6656**	0.6614	0.6299	0.6652

Note: The bold font indicates the optimal value in each row.

For the crack images in the 1st, 4th, and 5th rows of Fig. 4.13, the proposed algorithm has less noise interference in the non-crack areas compared to the other three algorithms. To further verify the reliability of the proposed algorithm, a quantitative analysis was conducted on the test set of 1,290 images, and the evaluation results are shown in Table 4.2, with the best results highlighted in bold. From the evaluation metrics, the average Dice coefficient, accuracy, precision, and

F1 score of the proposed algorithm are 0.6656, 0.9827, 0.7810, and 0.6656, respectively, which are improvements of 0.42%, 0.04%, 2%, and 0.4% over Unet++, 4%, 0.2%, 10%, and 4% over Att_Unet, and 0.04%, 0.04%, 3%, and 0.04% over Unet. Overall, the proposed algorithm outperforms the other three algorithms in terms of evaluation metrics.

4.6 Conclusion

In this chapter, we address the limitations of traditional methods in crack detection systems with high real-time requirements, which are unable to process large-scale crack detection effectively. To achieve faster and more accurate segmentation of crack images, we employ deep learning techniques. First, we introduce relevant technologies related to convolutional neural networks, followed by a discussion of the structural characteristics of fully convolutional networks and their performance on crack datasets. Finally, building upon the medical image segmentation model Unet, we propose a novel network architecture called Att_Nested_Unet. This model retains the design philosophy of Unet while incorporating the nested Unet++ architecture and embedding an attention mechanism into each layer of the Unet model. Through training on a dataset of 8,700 crack images and validation on a test set of 1,290 crack images, the Att_Nested_Unet model demonstrates superior performance compared to Unet++, Att_Unet, and Unet, both in subjective visual quality and objective performance metrics. The model effectively detects cracks across a variety of shapes and background conditions.

References

[1] Cao VD, Le DA. Autonomous concrete crack detection using deep fully convolutional neural network. *Automation in Construction*, 2018, 99: 52–58.

[2] Ronneberger O, Fischer P, Brox T. U-Net: Convolutional Networks for Biomedical Image Segmentation. *Medical Image Computingand Computer-Assisted Intervention: 9351*. Springer, Cham, 2015: 234–241.

[3] Long J, Shelhamer E, Darrell T. Fully convolutional networks for semantic segmentation. *IEEE Transactions on Pattern Analysis & Machine Intelligence*, 2014, 39(4): 640–651.

[4] Huang G, Liu Z, Maaten L V D, *et al.* Densely connected convolutional networks. In *Proceedings of the IEEE Conference on Computer Vision and Pattern Recognition*, 2017, 1: 3.

[5] Zhou Z, Rahman Siddiquee M M, Tajbakhsh N, *et al.* U-Net++: A nested U-Net architecture for medical image segmentation. In *Proceedings of the International Workshop on Deep Learning in Medical Image Analysis*, 2018: 3–11.

[6] Vaswani A, Shazeer N, Parmar N, *et al.* Attention is all you need. *Advances in Neural Information Processing Systems*. 2017: 30.

[7] Fu J, Liu J, Tian H, *et al.* Dual attention network for scene segmentation. In *Proceedings of the IEEE Conference on Computer Vision and Pattern Recognition*, 2019.

[8] Oktay O, Schlemper J, Folgoc L L, *et al.* Attention U-Net: Learning where to look for the pancreas. *1st Conference on Medical Imaging with Deep Learning*, 2018.

Chapter 5

Underwater Dam Crack Image Segmentation Algorithm Based on Adversarial Transfer Learning

5.1 Introduction

Underwater dams and hydraulic structures are frequently threatened by structural cracks, necessitating periodic inspection and repair to ensure operational integrity. Visual inspection via submersible robots has become the mainstream method for autonomous monitoring of submerged infrastructure. However, complex underwater environments (e.g., high turbidity and light attenuation) and limited availability of annotated underwater crack image datasets restrict the applicability of existing morphology-based algorithms and supervised learning models for underwater crack detection.

To address these challenges, this study proposes a deep adversarial transfer learning-based method for underwater dam crack detection. The framework employs multi-stage adversarial transfer learning to achieve unsupervised domain adaptation of underwater crack features, effectively transferring extracted terrestrial crack image features to underwater crack segmentation while maintaining detection accuracy.

With the continuous progress of technology, the construction of water conservancy and hydropower projects has achieved substantial development [1]. Embankment dams, as critical infrastructure in hydraulic engineering, play a pivotal role in agricultural irrigation, hydroelectric power generation, and flood disaster prevention [2]. However, dam cracks pose a significant threat to the normal operation of embankment systems. The existence of cracks compromises dam strength and service life, potentially leading to seepage and breaching failures [3,4]. These cracks not only manifest on the dam surface but also propagate internally, with their disaster-inducing effects being unpredictable; they constitute a primary factor in triggering emergencies, exacerbating hazards, and inducing catastrophic incidents [5]. Timely and accurate detection and identification of dam cracks are essential for diagnosing risks, implementing reinforcement measures, and ensuring the operational integrity of embankment systems.

Traditional manual inspection methods, characterized by low speed, limited accuracy, and susceptibility to inspector subjectivity, have been gradually replaced by submersible robot-based visual detection techniques [6]. These techniques now represent one of the most critical non-destructive testing methods in structural crack detection for hydraulic infrastructure [7]. For dam crack inspection, the predominant approach involves deploying submersible robots to capture underwater imagery, followed by crack image processing and analysis to determine crack type, location, and dimensions. This workflow provides actionable guidance for dam health diagnostics and reinforcement planning [8,9].

Crack image segmentation algorithms can be categorized into morphology-based methods and deep learning-based methods [10]. The former refers to algorithms developed prior to the widespread adoption of deep learning, which utilize knowledge from digital image processing, topology, and mathematics to achieve image segmentation [11]. These methods are susceptible to image quality degradation, noise interference, and require stringent operational conditions, resulting in limited applicability and inferior segmentation performance compared to deep learning approaches.

5.2 Related Work

5.2.1 *Crack image segmentation*

With the continuous development of deep learning, more and more researchers choose to apply it to the task of crack image segmentation [12]. Because of its complex texture features, cracks put forward higher requirements for the segmentation performance of the model. At present, fully convolutional network (FCN) and its variants are widely used in the field of fracture image segmentation [13]. In 2015, FCN was proposed by Jonathan Long *et al.* [14]. The network consists of an encoder subnetwork and a decoder subnetwork. The encoder sub-network is used to extract image features, and the decoder sub-network is responsible for classifying the pixels of the image. The decoder sub-network limited by FCN is too simple, and its segmentation effect is not ideal, and misjudgment often occurs.

OlafRonneberger et al proposed the Unet network [15] on the basis of FCN, which realizes semantic fusion of features of different layers of medical images through skip connection. Similar to SegNet network [16], it uses the index generated by encoder network pooling operation to achieve image semantic feature fusion. Compared with FCN, these improved algorithms change the network into a symmetrical structure, enrich the semantic features of decoder output, and effectively improve the image segmentation accuracy.

Although U-net and SegNet were not proposed to solve the problem of crack image segmentation, their effectiveness has been proven. Huyan Ju *et al.* [17] proposed an improved road crack image segmentation network, Crack-net, based on U-net. With padding, the scheme can keep the size of the feature map unchanged. Jierong Cheng *et al.* [18] based on the classical U-net a pixel level of road crack image segmentation scheme, by introducing a loss function based on distance transform, Achieves outstanding pixel-level accuracy is achieved. Shengyuan Li *et al.* [19] proposed a new crack detection algorithm for concrete structures by integrating DenseBlock on the basis of SegNet. Qin Zou *et al.* [20] applied multi-scale and cross-layer fusion to SegNet network and proposed a crack detection algorithm named Deep Crack.

Although these methods can effectively improve the segmentation accuracy of surface crack images, there are still some problems in applying them directly to underwater crack image segmentation tasks. Since these methods are supervised learning methods, their model training requires a large amount of labeled data. In view of the difficulty of acquiring underwater crack image and the time consuming of data set annotation, it is difficult to implement supervised learning for underwater crack image segmentation.

5.2.2 *Underwater crack image segmentation*

Underwater crack images are different from surface crack images. Due to the limitation of image acquisition system, most underwater images have poor quality [21]. Underwater crack images have low contrast, less information, and a lot of random noise and black spots, which bring great difficulties to crack feature extraction and image segmentation [22]. Conventional methods to process underwater crack images are as follows: first, the original image is enhanced, then the enhanced image is segmented. Ma Jinxiang *et al.* [23] proposed an adaptive enhancement algorithm for dam underwater crack images based on improved dark channel prior, which can effectively suppress the noise of underwater images and increase the clarity of images. Chen Wenjing [24] proposed a Retinex algorithm based on guided filtering, which could effectively retain the edge information of the underwater image while filtering it. CongpingChen *et al.* [25] proposed a new algorithm for dam image crack detection. This algorithm converts 2D crack images into 3D spatial surfaces according to pixel intensity, and detects cracks by analyzing curvature features. Although these algorithms have improved the detection effect of underwater crack images to a certain extent, the accuracy still needs to be improved.

Image enhancement combined with morphology is the most common method to solve the problem of underwater crack image segmentation, but the segmentation performance of this method is greatly affected by the image enhancement effect, and the adaptability is poor. Therefore, this paper hopes to realize underwater crack image segmentation by deep learning method to improve the adaptability and segmentation accuracy of the algorithm. Currently, there are few open source data sets of underwater fracture images. However, deep learning has high requirements on data sets, and insufficient data sets may lead to inadequate model training, and eventually poor segmentation effect of underwater crack images. Therefore, the problem of insufficient underwater samples should be considered when deep learning method is used to process underwater crack image segmentation.

5.2.3 *Transfer learning*

Since the direct use of supervised learning methods to deal with various learning tasks often faces the problem of insufficient data samples, researchers have proposed some solutions, such as semi-supervised learning, small sample learning and transfer learning. Semi-supervised learning [26] extracts and learns the features of labeled data and unlabeled data with the same distribution to reduce the demand for sample label quantity. The performance of the model is guaranteed. Small sample learning [27] is a kind of transfer learning. By further training the pre-trained model on a small amount of labeled target domain data, the learning of specific tasks in the target domain is realized. Transfer learning [28] is a widely applied learning method, which can apply the prior knowledge learned during the pre-training of the model on the source domain to the learning task of the target domain, effectively shorten the training time and ensure the accuracy of the model. Compared with semi-supervised learning, its advantage is that the data distribution of labeled source domain data and unlabeled target domain data can be inconsistent.

After years of development, transfer learning has evolved into many branches. Deep transfer learning has achieved satisfactory results in many fields such as image classification [29] and semantic segmentation [30]. Transfer learning can be broadly divided into two categories: domain adaptation and domain generalization. The difference between the two is that in the training process, domain adaptive can access both labeled source domain data and unlabeled target domain data, while domain generalization can only access source domain data [31]. Considering that a certain number of labeled open source surface crack images can be obtained during the experiment, as well as unlabeled underwater crack images required by the experiment, this paper decides to adopt the domain adaptive method.

The purpose of domain adaptive is to map source domain data and target domain data with different distributions into the same feature space, and to find a measurement criterion to make their "distance" in this space as close as possible [32]. In this case, the network model trained on the source domain data can be directly applied to the target domain data, and the ideal result is obtained.

EricTzeng *et al.* [33] introduced domain adaptive into the semantic segmentation task and constrained CNN by applying adversarial learning on the feature representation layer of the full convolutional network. Although this method can achieve pixel-level domain adaptation, the segmentation accuracy is not ideal, because the scheme ignores the spatial and local information necessary for semantic segmentation. Inspired by Yi-HsuanTsai *et al.* [34], this paper improves the discriminator network and changes it to a multi-level architecture. By classifying the abstract high-dimensional features and the output spatial information containing rich structural information, the segmentation accuracy of the image can be effectively improved, and the pixel-level domain adaptive in the output space can be realized.

5.3 Proposed Method

5.3.1 *Network model*

In this paper, an image segmentation method for underwater fractures based on adversarial transfer learning is proposed. As shown in Fig. 5.1, the network is mainly composed of two parts: the crack image segmentation network G and the discriminator network D_i, where i represents the level of the multilevel discriminator. The data involved in model training consists of two parts: source domain data I_s and target domain data I_t. Where I_s is a labeled surface crack image, while I_t is an unlabeled underwater crack image.

Segmentation network: In order to obtain high quality fracture image segmentation results, it is necessary to select an excellent baseline model. In this paper, Unet framework is used as the baseline model, which is an encoder-decoder structure image segmentation model. The encoder subnetwork is responsible for extracting the abstract features of the crack image, and the decoder subnetwork

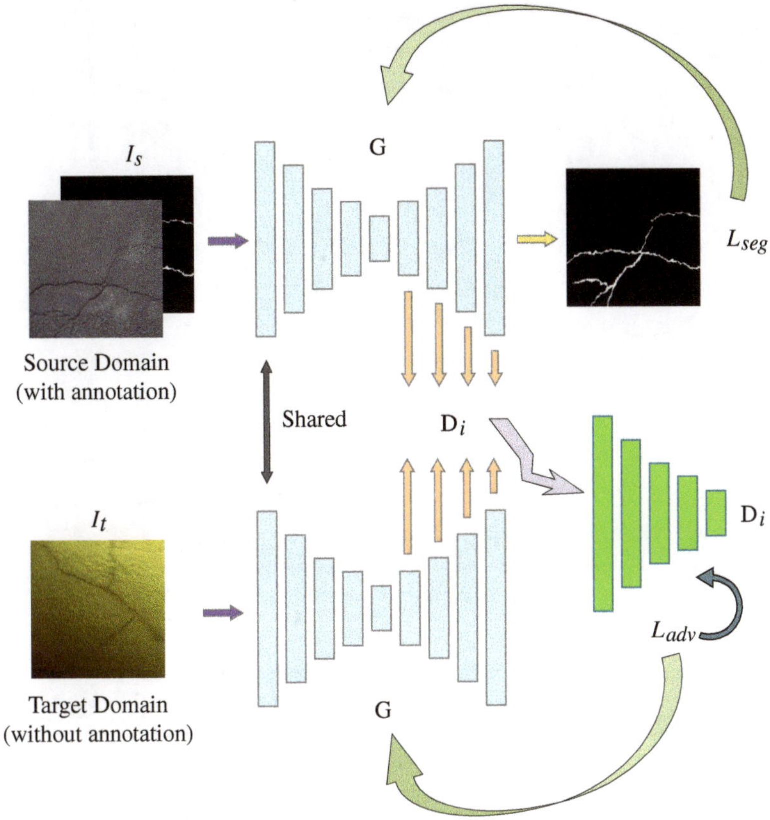

Figure 5.1. Model framework.

is responsible for predicting the segmentation results of the crack image according to the extracted abstract features.

As shown in Fig. 5.2, in order to further improve the segmentation accuracy of crack images and eliminate the influence of noise on segmentation results, this paper integrates an attention mechanism into the jump connection path of Unet. The module input is the upsampled result of the encoder output of the current layer and the decoder output of the next layer. Figure 5.3 shows the module details, where x^l is the output of the layer l encoder and g^l is the upsampled output of the layer $l-1$ decoder. By adding the features of module input extracted by convolutional networks and further training, the model can generate an attention coefficient $\tau \in [0, 1]$. This coefficient

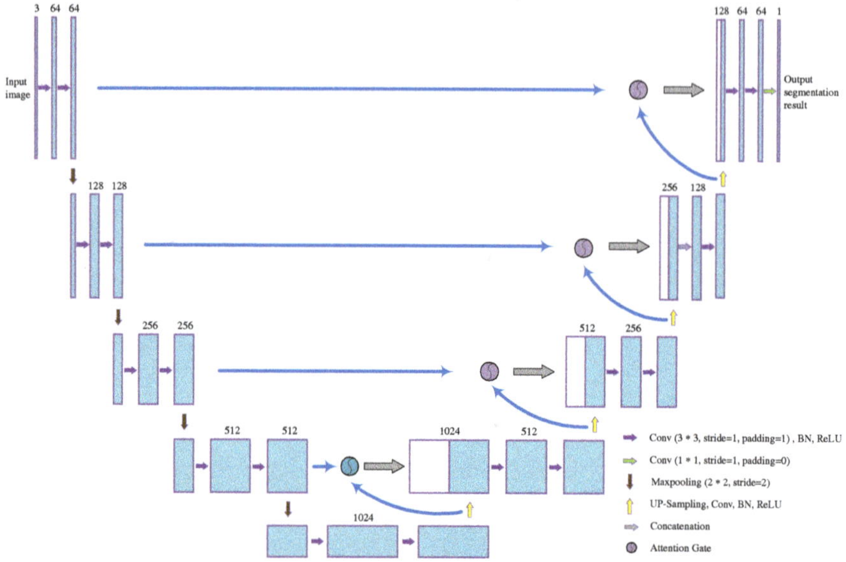

Figure 5.2. Splitting the network.

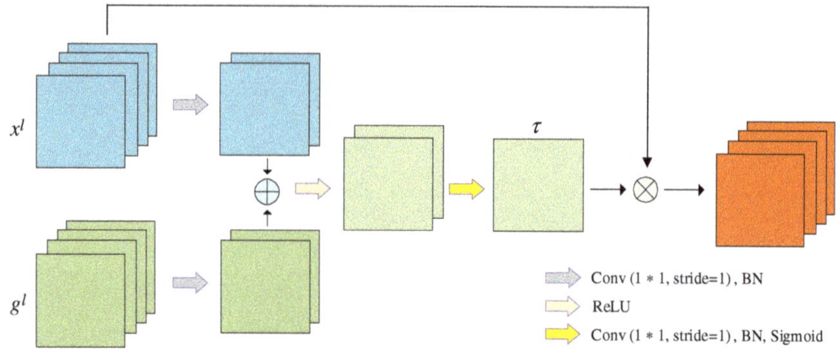

Figure 5.3. Attention module.

is a high-order feature feedback that assigns a higher weight to the target region (cracked pixels) and a lower weight to the irrelevant region (background noise). By multiplying the attention coefficient τ with the output x^l of the encoder, the noise of irrelevant regions in the crack image can be effectively eliminated, and the model can focus on the segmentation target (crack) itself.

Discriminator network: The domain discriminator used in this paper is a full convolutional network, and the difference between it and the domain discriminator used in the classification task is that the full connection layer is abandoned, which can better retain the spatial information of the crack image. The network consists of five convolutional layers. The number of channels in each layer is $\{64, 128, 256, 512, 1\}$, the convolution kernel size is $3 * 3$, the step size is 2, and the padding is 1. In addition, with the exception of the last convolution layer, each four convolution layer is followed by a BatachNorm layer and LeakyReLU with a negative slope of 0.2.

In order to better constrain the segmentation network, the discriminator used in this paper is multi-level, and each discriminator will accept the output of the decoder of the corresponding layer of the segmentation network as input. The decoder of the split network has four layers, the first three layers output high-dimensional features, and the last layer (output space) outputs predictive results. Because the high-dimensional features of the output are activated by ReLU, they can be directly fed into the discriminator of the corresponding level. The output of the output space is a convolutional output, which requires a Sigmoid activation before it can be sent to the discriminator of its corresponding level.

5.3.2 *Adversarial transfer learning*

In the forward propagation process of model training, the segmentation network G extracts the feature F of source domain image I_s and target domain image I_t, and predicts the segmentation result P of the image. In this paper, F_s and F_t are used to represent the extracted source domain image features and target domain image features respectively, while P_s and P_t are used to represent the predicted source domain image segmentation results and target domain image segmentation results. Because the model is expected to achieve similar segmentation performance in the target domain as in the source domain, the "distance" between the target domain and the source domain needs to be reduced.

The method adopted in this paper is to constrain the segmentation network by domain discriminator to extract the uniformly distributed abstract features from the source domain data and the target domain data. Specific scheme: During model training, the abstract feature F extracted and the predicted segmentation result P are taken as the input of the corresponding level of the multi-level discriminator D_i, and the input of the domain discriminator is judged whether it is from the source domain or the target domain. If the domain discriminator cannot distinguish the data source, it means that the extracted feature is the common feature of the source domain image and the target domain image (that is, the crack feature). By backpropagating the adversarial loss on the target domain from the domain discriminator to the segmentation network, the segmentation network can generate similar prediction on the target domain and the distribution of segmentation results on the source domain, so as to realize the domain adaptive segmentation of the crack image semantic segmentation.

5.3.3 *Loss function*

The loss function L of the network framework proposed in this paper consists of two parts: crack image segmentation loss L_{seg} and adversarial loss L_{adv}.

$$L(I_s, I_t) = L_{\text{seg}}(I_s) + L_{\text{adv}}(I_t) \tag{5.1}$$

Segmentation loss: Crack image segmentation is essentially a binary classification task. In this paper, binary cross entropy loss function (BCELoss) is used to regularize the segmentation network to achieve supervised learning of crack image segmentation in the source domain. In addition, in view of the imbalance between the number of cracked pixels and the number of background pixels in the crack image, Dice loss is introduced in this paper.

$$L_{\text{seg}}(I_s) = \lambda_{\text{bce}} L_{\text{bce}}(P_s, G_s) + (1 - \lambda_{\text{bce}}) L_{\text{dice}}(P_s, G_s) \tag{5.2}$$

$$L_{\text{bce}}(P_s, G_s) = -\frac{1}{N}\sum_{i}^{N}[G_s^i \log(P_s^i) + (1 - G_s^i)(1 - \log(P_s^i))] \tag{5.3}$$

$$L_{\text{dice}}(P_s, G_s) = 1 - \tfrac{1|P_s \cap G_s| + \varepsilon}{|P_s| + |G_s| + \varepsilon} \tag{5.4}$$

where, P_s, G_s are the predicted value and the ground real value of the source domain image segmentation results respectively. N is the total number of pixels of the crack image, P_s^i is the prediction probability of the crack pixel i, and G_s^i is the label value of the pixel i. If the pixel point is a crack pixel, G_s^i is 1, otherwise it is 0. λ_{bce} is the equilibrium coefficient, which is used to balance the cross entropy loss and Dice loss, 0.5 is used here. ε is the smoothing coefficient, used to prevent the numerator or denominator from being 0, where 1 is used.

Adversarial loss: The discriminator network used in this paper is a multi-level architecture, and the input of each discriminator is the prediction node of the output space results and the high-dimensional features extracted by the segmentation network. Since domain classification is a binary classification problem, binary cross entropy loss is used as the domain classification loss function. Judy Hoffman *et al.* pointed out that in the adaptive semantic segmentation task of images, it is easier to realize domain adaptation in the output space than in the feature space. Therefore, this paper assigns different weight coefficients to the output space domain discriminator and the feature space domain discriminator.

$$L_{\text{adv}} = \lambda_{\text{out}} L_{\text{out}}(D, D_1) + \lambda_{\text{feature}} \sum_{i=1}^{3} L_{\text{feature}}(D_p, D_1) \tag{5.5}$$

Where, λ_{out}, λ_{feature} are the weight coefficients of output spatial domain discriminator loss L_{out} and feature spatial domain discriminator loss L_{feature}, respectively. λ_{out} is 0.001, and λ_{feature} is 0.0002. D_p is the predicted value of the classification result of the input image feature domain, and D_l is the domain label of the image. The source domain tag D_l^s is 0, and the target domain tag D_l^t is 1.

The adversarial learning of the model needs to go through several iterations, each iteration consists of two steps: training the segmentation network and training the discriminator network. In order to realize the domain adaptive of the segmentation network and make the segmentation network extract similar features in the source domain and the target domain, it is necessary to maximize the probability of the target domain being judged as the source domain to fool the discriminator.

$$\max_{D} \min_{G} L_{\text{adv}}(I_s, I_t) \tag{5.6}$$

Specific scheme: When training segmentation network, the target domain label D_l^t is set to 1 and the gradient is calculated; In this case, the source domain data does not participate in the domain adversarial training (does not calculate the gradient); When training the discriminator network, the source domain tag D_l^t is set to 1 and the target domain tag D_l^s is set to 0.

5.4 Experiment and Results

5.4.1 *Datasets*

The data set used in this experiment consists of two parts: surface crack image data set and underwater crack image data set. Among them, the ground crack image dataset is a mixture of multiple open source tagged ground crack image datasets. It mainly includes CrackTree260 [20], CRKWH100 [20], Stone311 [20], CrackForest [35], CRACK500 [36], DeepCrack [37], and UAV75 [38]. The open source dataset contains 1,905 images of cracks in the ground. In view of the large amount of labeled data required for model training, this paper expanded the original data set by flipping, cropping, scaling, rotating and other operations, and obtained 11298 $448 * 448$ ground crack images. These labeled ground crack images are used as source domain data to participate in model training.

The underwater crack images used in the experiment were captured by underwater cameras in the dam field, which mainly included two parts: unlabeled target domain data and labeled verification set data. In total, the camera obtained 1,128 valid raw images of underwater fractures. Through data expansion, a total of 6168 unlabeled underwater crack images of $448 * 448$ were obtained, which were used as target domain data to participate in model training. In addition, 250 original underwater fracture images were labeled in this paper, and a total of 1200 $448 * 448$ labeled underwater fracture images were obtained through data expansion, which were used as validation sets to test the validity of the model.

5.4.2 *Training strategy*

The model proposed in this paper was trained and tested in Ubuntu18.04.06+Python3.8.3+Pytorch1.7.0 software environment. In addition, a GeForceRTX3070 with 8 gigabytes of memory was used for gradient calculations. In order to shorten the training time, the model is pre-trained on the source domain data before the implementation of adversarial transfer learning, which can speed up the convergence of the model.

Table 5.1. Hyperparameters used in model training.

Training mode		Pre-training	Adversarial transfer learning
Batch size		4	2
Split network	Initial learning rate	0.001 (Cosine annealing)	0.0005 (Cosine annealing)
	Optimizer	SGD (momentum = 0.9)	Adam
Discriminator network	Initial learning rate	\	0.00005
	Optimizer	\	Adam

Note: The backslash (\) in the Pre-training column for the discriminator network indicates that the discriminator is not used or trained during the pre-training phase, where only the split network is trained. The discriminator is only activated and trained in the subsequent adversarial transfer learning stage, so no corresponding hyperparameters are required for it in pre-training.

In order to better realize the domain adaptive of crack image segmentation, the model loads the same number of source domain images and target domain images to participate in training, so as to ensure the balance of source domain data and target domain data in each training batch. Take source domain images into account. The number is greater than the target domain image (underwater crack image), and loading images sequentially may lead to the waste of part of the source domain data. In order to make full use of source domain images, each epoch of the model will randomly extract the same number of source domain images as the target domain images to participate in training.

The hyperparameters used in model training are shown in Table 5.1. The cosine annealing function is used to dynamically adjust the learning rate during training. It should be noted that although the Batch size in the process of adversarial transfer learning is 2, the number of images loaded by the model in actual training is 4. Among them, two are source domain images, while the other two are target domain images.

5.4.3 *Experimental results*

In order to verify the effectiveness of the algorithm proposed in this paper, we compared it with other algorithms, and the comparison

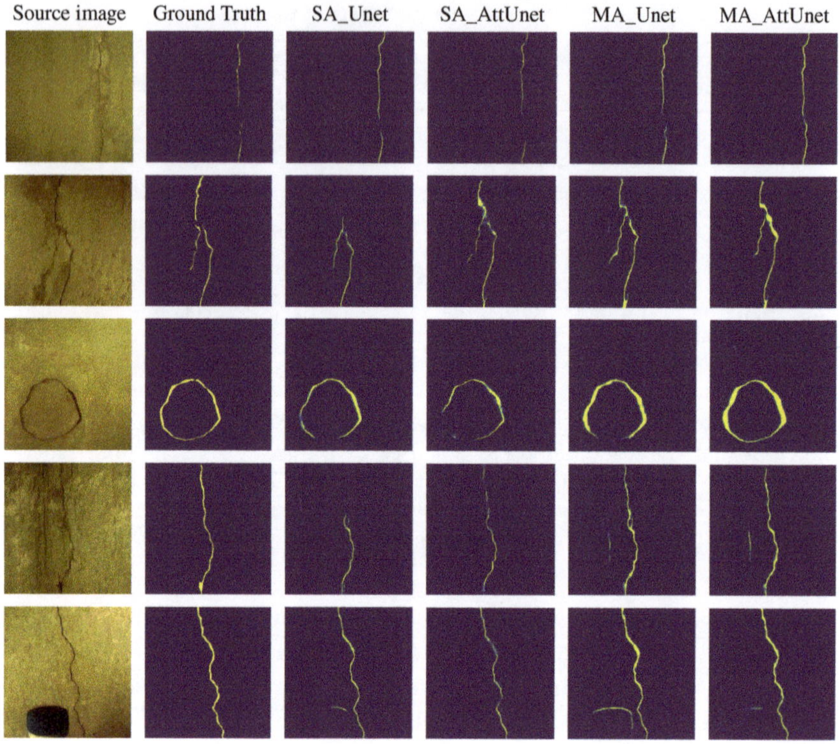

Figure 5.4. Setting point-to-line intersection parameters.

results are shown in Fig. 5.4. In order to better show the segmentation performance of the model, we convert the ground real values and segmentation results into heat maps.

Figure 5.4 shows, from left to right, the original image, ground reality values, UNET-based single-level adversarial transfer learning segmentation results (SA_Unet), and Unet combined with attention mechanism single-level adversarial transfer learning segmentation results (SA_AttUnet). Multilevel adversarial transfer learning segmentation results based on Unet (MA_Unet) and multilevel adversarial transfer learning segmentation results combined with Unet (MA_AttUnet). Among them, single-level adversarial transfer learning uses only one domain discriminator, whose input is the prediction result of the output space. Multilevel adversarial transfer learning uses multiple domain discriminators whose inputs are the prediction results of the output space and the high-dimensional features of the decoder output.

The experimental results show that compared with single-level adversarial transfer learning, multi-level adversarial transfer learning can retain more details of crack image without missing detection. By comparing the fifth and sixth columns in Fig. 5.3, it can be found that adding attention mechanism to the jump path of Unet can effectively improve the anti-noise performance of the model, avoid the occurrence of false detection, and thus improve the segmentation accuracy of the crack image.

5.4.4 *Evaluation indicators*

In order to better compare with other methods, this paper introduces some commonly used image segmentation performance evaluation indexes: Pixel accuracy (piexlaccuracy, PA), occurring simultaneously than (IntersectionOverUnion, IoU), Dice coefficient (Dice), the Recall rate (Recall), Precision (Precision), and F1. The corresponding formula is as follows:

$$\mathrm{PA} = \frac{TP + TN}{TP + TN + FP + FN} \tag{5.7}$$

$$\mathrm{Dice} = \frac{2|P \cap G|}{|P| + |G|} = \frac{2TP}{2TP + FP + FN} \tag{5.8}$$

$$\mathrm{loU} = \frac{|P \cap G|}{|P \cup G|} = \frac{TP}{TP + FP + FN} \tag{5.9}$$

$$\mathrm{Recall} = \frac{TP}{TP + FN} \tag{5.10}$$

$$\mathrm{Precision} = \frac{TP}{TP + FP} \tag{5.11}$$

$$F1 = 2 * \frac{\mathrm{Precision} * \mathrm{Recall}}{\mathrm{Precision} + \mathrm{Recall}} \tag{5.12}$$

where, P is the segmentation result predicted by the model, and G is the ground real value. TP, TN, FP and FN are true positive, true negative, false positive and false negative, respectively.

In order to verify the effectiveness of the proposed algorithm, it was tested on a labeled data set of 1200 underwater crack images,

Table 5.2. Evaluation indexes of different algorithms.

		Algorithms			
Metrics	UpperBound	MA_Unet	MA_AttUnet	MA_Unet	MA_AttUnet
PA	0.9232	**0.9838**	0.9800	0.9806	0.9680
Dice	0.4199	0.2962	0.2970	0.2728	**0.3025**
IoU	0.3014	0.2043	0.2043	0.1802	**0.2081**
Recall	0.6197	**0.4279**	0.3828	0.3628	0.3895
Precision	0.5088	0.4677	**0.4957**	0.4455	0.4774
F1	0.4202	0.3000	0.2980	0.2734	**0.3032**

Note: The bold font indicates the optimal values in each row.

and the test results are shown in Table 5.2. In order to show the segmentation performance of the model more clearly, it is also tested on the source domain data, and the test results are used as the upper limit of the segmentation performance of the model.

As can be seen from Table 5.2, the Unet model based on multilevel adversarial transfer learning combined with attention mechanism (MA_AttUnet) has achieved the best score on a number of indicators. Although the model is not optimal on some indicators, the gap between them is not obvious. It should be noted that although the transfer learning algorithm achieves a score above the upper limit in pixel accuracy (PA), it does not mean that the segmentation performance of the model exceeds the upper limit, but there is a problem of missing detection, which is also the future research direction.

5.5 Conclusion

Aiming at the problems faced by the underwater crack image segmentation task that the available dataset is small, manual labeling is time-consuming and laborious, and it is difficult to realize supervised learning. In this paper, an unsupervised domain adaptive scheme is proposed to apply the features extracted from the source domain (labeled ground crack fissure images) to the underwater crack image segmentation task by constructing a multilevel feature adversarial network, which effectively alleviates the demand for the underwater labeled dataset and ensures the segmentation accuracy to a certain

extent. However, due to the reason that the ground crack image types are not rich enough, there is still room for further improvement of the model, which is also a future research direction.

References

[1] Ministry of Water Resources, People's Republic of China. 2019 National Water Resources Development Statistical Bulletin. 2021. Ministry of Water Resources, People's Republic of China. 2019 Statistic bulletin on China water activities. 2021.

[2] Huang L, Li X, Fang H, *et al.* Balancing social, economic and ecological benefits of reservoir operation during the flood season: A case study of the Three Gorges Project, China. *Journal of Hydrology*, 2019, 572: 422–434.

[3] Lin P, Guan J, Peng H, *et al.* Horizontal cracking and crack repair analysis of a super high arch dam based on fracture toughness. *Engineering Failure Analysis*, 2019, 97: 72–90.

[4] Tang J, Mao Y, Wang J, *et al.* Multi-task enhanced dam crack image detection based on faster R-CNN. *2019 IEEE 4th International Conference on Image, Vision and Computing (ICIVC)*. IEEE, New York, 2019: 336–340.

[5] Fan X, Wu J, Shi P, *et al.* A novel automatic dam crack detection algorithm based on local-global clustering. *Multimedia Tools and Applications*, 2018, 77(20): 26581–26599.

[6] Feng C, Zhang H, Wang H, *et al.* Automatic pixel-level crack detection on dam surface using deep convolutional network. *Sensors*, 2020, 20(7): 2069.

[7] Li L, Zhang H, Pang J, *et al.* Dam surface crack detection based on deep learning. *Proceedings of the 2019 International Conference on Robotics, Intelligent Control and Artificial Intelligence*, 2019: 738–743.

[8] Tan J, Wang M, Tian J, *et al.* Research on dam leakage detection based on visual and acoustic integration: A case study of CFRD. *IOP Conference Series: Earth and Environmental Science*, 2020, 525(1): 012053.

[9] Hirai H, Ishii K. Development of dam inspection underwater robot. *Journal of Robotics, Networking and Artificial Life*, 2019, 6(1): 18–22.

[10] Wang W, Wang M, Li H, *et al.* Pavement crack image acquisition methods and crack extraction algorithms: A review. *Journal of Traffic and Transportation Engineering* (English Edition), 2019, 6(6): 535–556.

[11] Cao W, Liu Q, He Z. Review of pavement defect detection methods. *IEEE Access*, 2020, 8: 14531–14544.

[12] Kang D, Benipal SS, Gopal DL, *et al.* Hybrid pixel-level concrete crack segmentation and quantification across complex backgrounds using deep learning. *Automation in Construction*, 2020, 118: 103291.

[13] Dung CV. Autonomous concrete crack detection using deep fully convolutional neural network. *Automation in Construction*, 2019, 99: 52–58.

[14] Long J, Shelhamer E, Darrell T. Fully convolutional networks for semantic segmentation. *Proceedings of the IEEE Conference on Computer Vision and Pattern Recognition.* 2015: 3431–3440.

[15] Ronneberger O, Fischer P, Brox T. U-net: Convolutional networks for biomedical image segmentation. *International Conference on Medical Image Computing and Computer-Assisted Intervention.* Springer, Cham, 2015: 234–241.

[16] Badrinarayanan V, Kendall A, Cipolla R. Segnet: A deep convolutional encoder-decoder architecture for image segmentation. *IEEE Transactions on Pattern Analysis and Machine Intelligence*, 2017, 39(12): 2481–2495.

[17] Huyan J, Li W, Tighe S, *et al.* CrackU-net: A novel deep convolutional neural network for pixelwise pavement crack detection. *Structural Control and Health Monitoring*, 2020, 27(8): e2551.

[18] Cheng J, Xiong W, Chen W, Gu Y, Li Y. Pixel-level crack detection using U-Net. *TENCON 2018 — 2018 IEEE Region 10 Conference*, Jeju, Korea (South), 2018: 0462–0466.

[19] Li S, Zhao X. Automatic crack detection and measurement of concrete structure using convolutional encoder-decoder network. *IEEE Access*, 2020, 8: 134602–134618.

[20] Zou Q, Zhang Z, Li Q, *et al.* Deepcrack: Learning hierarchical convolutional features for crack detection. *IEEE Transactions on Image Processing*, 2018, 28(3): 1498–1512.

[21] O'Byrne M, Pakrashi V, Schoefs F, *et al.* Semantic segmentation of underwater imagery using deep networks trained on synthetic imagery. *Journal of Marine Science and Engineering*, 2018, 6(3): 93.

[22] Fan X, Wu J, Shi P, *et al.* A novel automatic dam crack detection algorithm based on local-global clustering. *Multimedia Tools and Applications*, 2018, 77(20): 26581–26599.

[23] Ma J, Fan X, Wu Z, Zhang X, Shi P, Wang G. Underwater crack image enhancement algorithm based on dark channel prior. *Journal of Image and Graphics*, 2016, 21(12): 1574–1584.

[24] Chen W. *Research on Image Detection Method of Underwater Dam Crack*. North China University of Water Resources and Electric Power, 2019.

[25] Chen C, Wang J, Zou L, *et al.* A novel crack detection algorithm of underwater dam image. *2012 International Conference on Systems and Informatics (ICSAI2012)*. IEEE, New York, 2012: 1825–1828.

[26] Van Engelen JE, Hoos HH. A survey on semi-supervised learning. *Machine Learning*, 2020, 109(2): 373–440.

[27] Sung F, Yang Y, Zhang L, *et al.* Learning to compare: Relation network for few-shot learning. *Proceedings of the IEEE Conference on Computer Vision and Pattern Recognition*. 2018: 1199–1208.

[28] Tan C, Sun F, Kong T, *et al.* A survey on deep transfer learning. *International Conference on Artificial Neural Networks*. Springer, Cham, 2018: 270–279.

[29] Pires de Lima R, Marfurt K. Convolutional neural network for remote-sensing scene classification: Transfer learning analysis. *Remote Sensing*, 2020, 12(1): 86.

[30] Wurm M, Stark T, Zhu XX, *et al.* Semantic segmentation of slums in satellite images using transfer learning on fully convolutional neural networks. *ISPRS Journal of Photogrammetry and Remote Sensing*, 2019, 150: 59–69.

[31] Wang M, Deng W. Deep visual domain adaptation: A survey. *Neurocomputing*, 2018, 312: 135–153.

[32] Motiian S, Piccirilli M, Adjeroh DA, *et al.* Unified deep supervised domain adaptation and generalization. *Proceedings of the IEEE International Conference on Computer Vision*, 2017: 5715–5725.

[33] Tzeng E, Hoffman J, Darrell T, *et al.* Simultaneous deep transfer across domains and tasks. *Proceedings of the IEEE International Conference on Computer Vision*, 2015: 4068–4076.

[34] Tsai Y H, Hung W C, Schulter S, *et al.* Learning to adapt structured output space for semantic segmentation. *Proceedings of the IEEE Conference on Computer Vision and Pattern Recognition*, 2018: 7472–7481.

[35] Cui L, Qi Z, Chen Z, *et al.* Pavement distress detection using random decision forests. *International Conference on Data Science*. Springer-Verlag New York, Inc. 2015.

[36] Yang F, Zhang L, Yu S, *et al.* Feature pyramid and hierarchical boosting network for pavement crack detection. *IEEE Transactions on Intelligent Transportation Systems*, 2019, 21(4): 1525–1535.

[37] Liu Y, Yao J, Lu X, *et al.* DeepCrack: A deep hierarchical feature learning architecture for crack segmentation. *Neurocomputing*, 2019, 338: 139–153.

[38] Benz C, Debus P, Ha HK, *et al.* Crack segmentation on UAS-based imagery using transfer learning. *2019 International Conference on Image and Vision Computing New Zealand (IVCNZ).* IEEE, New York, 2019: 1–6.

Chapter 6

Marine Organism Detection Algorithm Based on an Improved Faster-RCNN

6.1 Introduction

Marine organisms are an important part of the marine ecosystem and have always garnered significant attention. Marine ecological protection organizations conduct studies on the distribution and living habits of marine organisms through methods such as manual diving and underwater robot photography. However, low-quality underwater imaging makes it difficult for researchers to accurately detect marine organisms. Therefore, there is an urgent need for an effective object detection algorithm to replace human vision in detecting marine organisms.

Object detection is one of the key tasks in computer vision, and it is a computer technology related to computer vision and image processing. It involves detecting specific semantic objects (such as people, cars, or animals) in digital images or videos. Research fields in object detection include edge detection [1], multi-object detection [2–4], salient object detection [5, 6], and more.

Traditional object detection methods suffer from poor recognition performance, low accuracy, and slow detection speeds, making them ineffective for detecting marine organisms. In recent years, the rapid development of deep learning has led to significant breakthroughs in the field of object detection. Deep learning-based object detection algorithms, with their high detection accuracy and strong robustness, have been widely applied in real-world scenarios such as security monitoring [7], autonomous driving [8], and unmanned airport scene analysis [9].

However, due to low-quality underwater imaging, the complexity of underwater environments, the varying sizes and shapes of marine organisms, and issues such as overlapping occlusions, conventional deep learning-based object detection algorithms do not perform well in detecting marine organisms. Therefore, this paper aims to improve deep learning-based object detection models to achieve effective marine organism detection.

6.2 Related Work

Currently, deep learning-based object detection is divided into two categories: two-stage object detection algorithms and one-stage object detection algorithms.

One-stage object detection algorithms can simultaneously complete both object localization and classification tasks in a single stage. YOLOv1 [10] integrates the prediction of the object region and the prediction of the object class into one step using prior anchor boxes, significantly enhancing detection speed. However, each grid cell can only predict one object, leading to lower detection accuracy. YOLOv2 [11] improved upon YOLOv1 by adding batch normalization to the convolutional layers to reduce model overfitting and effectively enhance model convergence capability. YOLO9000, based on YOLOv2, employs a hierarchical view approach for object classification, allowing it to detect over 9,000 categories simultaneously. YOLOv3 [12] further developed YOLOv2 by removing all pooling layers and using enhanced convolution kernel strides to achieve the effect of pooling layers, significantly increasing detection speed and enabling multi-scale feature map outputs, which improved the detection capability for small objects. YOLOv4 [13], building on YOLOv3, filtered several techniques that have been used in various detectors since YOLOv3's release that can improve detection accuracy. It also replaced the backbone network Darknet-53 with CSPDarkNet53, further enhancing both detection speed and accuracy.

Two-stage object detection algorithms generate some candidate regions in some way and then classify and refine the content of these candidate regions. In 2014, Ross B. Girshick proposed R-CNN [14], which first generates candidate regions through selective search and then uses CNN to extract features from these candidate regions, replacing the traditional sliding window method and improving object detection accuracy. However, R-CNN involves a lot of redundant computation, severely affecting detection performance. Fast R-CNN [15] addressed the computation redundancy issue in R-CNN by first extracting features from the input image using the CNN and then extracting candidate regions through selective search. This approach reduces redundant computations by passing the CNN only once to obtain all candidate regions, but detection speed remains unsatisfactory. Faster R-CNN [16] further improved upon Fast R-CNN by replacing the selective search algorithm with a Region Proposal Network (RPN) to filter candidate regions, leading to a further increase in detection speed. The core process of Faster R-CNN detection involves using a backbone feature extraction network to extract object features, generating candidate regions through the Region Proposal Network, determining whether the candidate regions contain objects, refining the dimensions of the candidate regions, and finally classifying the candidate regions using ROI Pooling. The overall structure of Faster R-CNN is shown in Fig. 6.1.

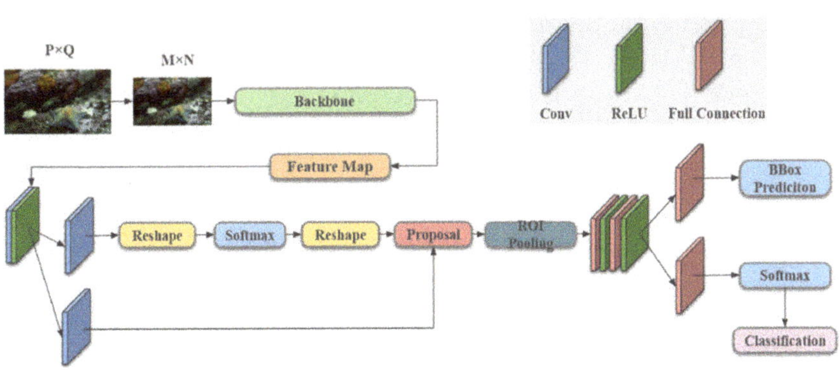

Figure 6.1. Faster-RCNN overall structure.

In this paper, the following three improvements are made to the traditional Faster-RCNN for the marine organism detection scenario:

1. To address the issue of low detection accuracy caused by low-quality underwater imaging and the varying sizes and shapes of marine organisms, ResNet is used to replace the VGG backbone feature extraction network in Faster-RCNN, and BiFPN is added after ResNet to form a ResNet-BiFPN structure. This enhances the feature extraction capability of the network model and improves multi-scale feature fusion.
2. EIoU is used to replace the IoU in Faster-RCNN, reducing the proportion of redundant bounding boxes in the training data by adding a centrality weight, thereby improving the quality of the bounding boxes.
3. The K-means++ clustering algorithm is used to generate more suitable anchor boxes for the marine organism dataset, improving detection accuracy.

6.3 Marine Organism Detection Algorithm Based on an Improved Faster-RCNN

6.3.1 *ResNet-BiFPN*

Optical scattering causes low-quality underwater imaging, and underwater scenes are often highly complex. Features such as rocks and aquatic plants on the seabed interfere with target feature extraction. The varying sizes and shapes of marine organisms also challenge the network model's multi-scale feature fusion capability. Therefore, this paper selects ResNet [17], known for its strong feature extraction ability, as the backbone feature extraction network for Faster-RCNN. Additionally, BiFPN [18] is added after ResNet to enhance the network model's multi-scale feature fusion capability.

ResNet introduces a residual structure with identity mapping, allowing gradients to pass smoothly from shallow layers to deep layers, thus enabling the training of very deep neural networks and improving feature extraction capabilities. Compared to the VGG network model, ResNet, with its residual mechanism, better retains shallow features and transfers them to deeper layers for training.

For any given input, ResNet processes it through five stages (Stage0 to Stage5) to obtain the processed features. Stage0 can be regarded as the preprocessing stage for the input, while the subsequent four stages are composed of bottleneck layers (BTNKs), with similar structures. Stage1 contains two bottleneck layers, while the remaining three stages contain 4, 6, and 3 bottleneck layers, respectively. The input dimension (3, 224, 224) refers to the number of channels, height, and width. In Stage0, the input of shape (3, 224, 224) passes through a convolutional layer, a batch normalization (BN) layer, a ReLU activation function, and a MaxPooling layer, resulting in an output of shape (64, 56, 56). There are two types of bottleneck layers corresponding to different situations: BTNK2 applies when the number of input and output channels is the same, and BTNK1 applies when the input and output channel numbers differ. For BTNK2, let the input be x with dimensions (C, W, W), and let the three convolutional blocks on the left side of BTNK2 be the function $F(x)$. The sum of $F(x)$) and x, followed by the ReLU activation function, gives the output of BTNK2. For BTNK1, which adds an extra convolutional layer on the right side, let this layer be represented by the function ggg. BTNK1 corresponds to cases where the input and output channel numbers differ. The added convolutional layer transforms x into $G(x)$ matching the dimensional differences between the input and output. The specific network structure of ResNet is shown in Fig. 6.2.

In 2020, the Google Brain team proposed the BiFPN structure in EfficientDet. Figure 6.3 illustrates the formation process of BiFPN:

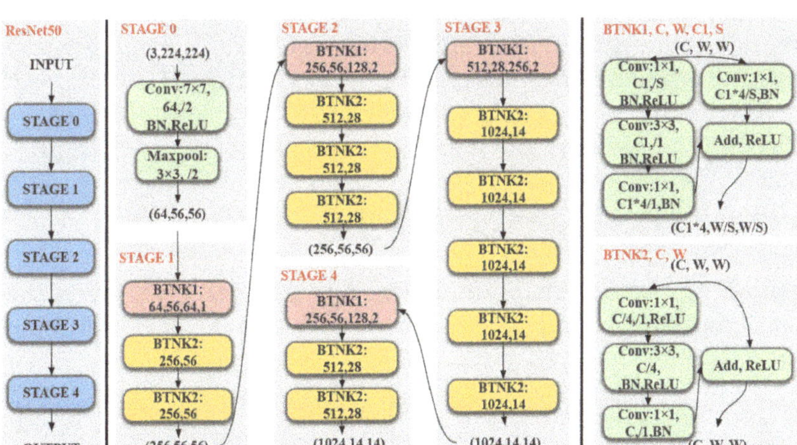

Figure 6.2. ResNet overall structure.

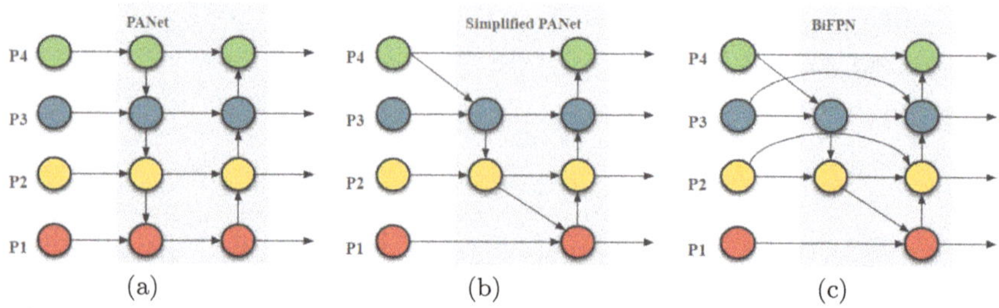

Figure 6.3. The formation process of BiFPN. (a) PANet: bidirectional top-down and bottom-up feature aggregation for multi-scale fusion. (b) Simplified PANet: redundant cross-layer connections removed to reduce computation. (c) BiFPN: adds cross-layer connections and learnable weighted fusion for more efficient and accurate feature integration.

inspired by the PANet structure (Fig. 6.3(a)), the authors simplified the PANet structure by removing redundant nodes (Fig. 6.3(b)), and then added shortcut connections to the Simplified PANet, resulting in BiFPN (Fig. 6.3(c)). BiFPN introduces learnable weights to determine the importance of different input features and repeatedly applies top-down and bottom-up multi-scale feature fusion.

To introduce learnable weights to determine the importance of different input features, you simply need to multiply the features by a learnable weight:

$$O = \sum_i w_i \cdot I_i \tag{6.1}$$

Here, w_i can be a scalar (for each feature), a vector (for each channel), or a multi-dimensional tensor (for each pixel). I_i represents the input features, and O represents the output features. However, without restrictions, the weights can easily lead to unstable training, so Softmax is applied to each weight:

$$O = \sum_j \frac{e^{w_i}}{e^{wj}} \tag{6.2}$$

However, the actual computation speed of Softmax is relatively slow, so it is replaced with:

$$O = \sum_j \frac{w_i}{\varepsilon + \sum_j w_j} \tag{6.3}$$

where $\varepsilon = 0.0001$ is used to avoid numerical instability, a ReLU activation function is applied to ensure that the weights are greater than zero. This paper uses Eq. (6.3) to implement the weighting mechanism in BiFPN. The specific implementation of ResNet-BiFPN is shown in Fig. 6.4. Four groups of features with different scales, P1–P4, are obtained from the STAGE1–STAGE4 of the ResNet50 backbone feature extraction network. A 1×1 convolution is used to adjust the number of channels, and P4 is reshaped through upsampling to match the scale of P3P3P3. The features ① from P4 and the convolved features ② from P3 are then stacked and convolved.

In the Weight Module, all stacking and convolution operations learn the importance of different input features using the mechanism described in Eq. (2.7). Taking the features from P4 and P3 as an example, the stacking and convolution operation in the upper left corner will determine whether to focus more on feature ① or feature ② through the weighting mechanism. After filtering through the weighting mechanism, the remaining features will continue to undergo the same stacking, convolution, and weight filtering operations with the convolved features of P2 and the convolved and skip-connected features of P3, thus forming the BiFPN network.

To achieve better detection results, EfficientDet stacks the BiFPN structure multiple times. Experiments have shown that, to a certain extent, stacking BiFPN can lead to improved accuracy, but it also increases the number of parameters, thereby affecting the model's operational performance. This paper tests the number of BiFPN stacks to select the optimal stacking number for the Faster-RCNN model.

6.3.2 *Effective intersection over union (EIoU)*

In the Faster R-CNN object detection algorithm, we generate a large number of candidate bounding boxes in one pass. These boxes are then sorted based on their confidence scores, and the Intersection over Union (IoU) is calculated between each pair of boxes. Non-Maximum Suppression (NMS) is used to determine which boxes should be kept and which should be discarded.

However, the IoU metric is not perfect. In reality, because the shapes of detection targets vary, the anchor boxes often contain not only the features of the target but also some background information. This non-target information can interfere with the model's performance. For example, in Fig. 6.4, the white box represents the ground truth (GT) box, while the red box (Box A) and the blue box

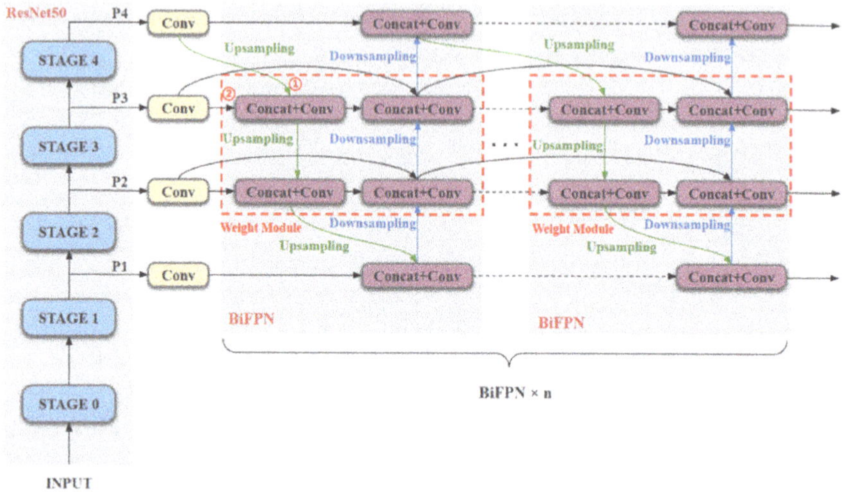

Figure 6.4. Specific implementation of ResNet-BiFPN.

(Box B) are two predicted boxes. According to the IoU calculation, Box A has an IoU of 0.71 with the GT, and Box B has an IoU of 0.65 with the GT. If we rely solely on IoU for selection, Box A would be chosen. However, Box A includes a significant amount of irrelevant background information, whereas Box B captures more of the actual target. Therefore, Box B is a more effective sample.

Therefore, this paper uses EIoU (Effective Intersection over Union) [19] instead of IoU (Intersection over Union) in the Region Proposal Network (RPN) of Faster R-CNN as the criterion for distinguishing positive and negative samples. EIoU incorporates a "centerness" measure to evaluate the degree to which a predicted bounding box is centered within the target. Centerness is defined as the normalized distance from the center of the predicted box to the center of the ground truth box. EIoU posits that predicted boxes that are closer to the center of the ground truth box are more likely to contain more relevant information about the detection target and should be considered more important.

In Fig. 6.5, assume a bounding box $A = (\hat{x}_1, \hat{y}_1, \hat{x}_2, \hat{y}_2)$, where $\hat{x}_1, \hat{y}_1, \hat{x}_2, \hat{y}_2$ represent the coordinates of the top-left and bottom-right corners, respectively. The center coordinates of the predicted bounding box A are $C_A = (\hat{x}_c, \hat{y}_c) = (\frac{\hat{x}_1+\hat{x}_2}{2}, \frac{\hat{y}_1+\hat{y}_2}{2})$. The corresponding ground truth bounding box for A is $GT = (x_1, y_1, x_2, y_2)$, where

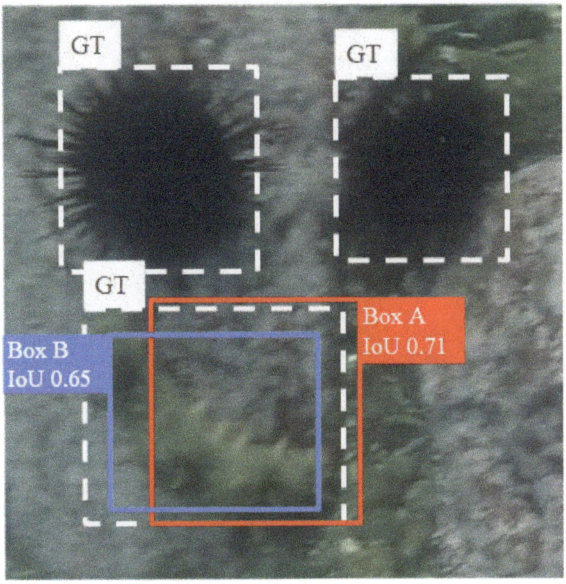

Figure 6.5. IoU example.

x_1, y_1, x_2, y_2 represent the coordinates of the top-left and bottom-right corners of the ground truth box. Next, we calculate the distance C_A from the center of the predicted bounding box to the boundaries of the ground truth box. We define d_l, d_r, d_t, d_b as the distances from the center point C_A of the predicted bounding box A to the four sides of the ground truth box:

$$\begin{aligned} d^l &= |\hat{x}_c - x_l| \\ d^r &= |x_2 - \hat{x}_c| \\ d^t &= |\hat{y}_c - y_1| \\ d^b &= |y_2 - \hat{y}_c| \end{aligned} \tag{6.4}$$

Define the Centerness Weight W_A for a Bounding Box as:

$$W_A = \sqrt{\frac{min(d^l, d^r) \cdot min(d^t, d^b)}{max(d^l, d^r) \cdot max(d^t, d^b)}} \tag{6.5}$$

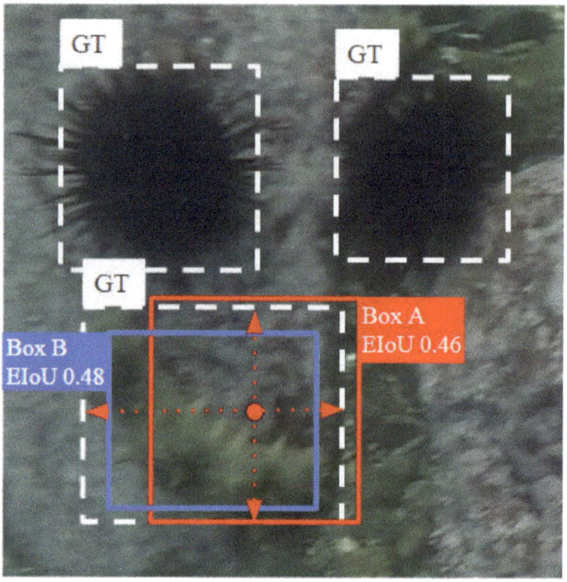

Figure 6.6. EIoU example.

Final Definition of $EIoU$:

$$EIoU = W_A \cdot IoU \tag{6.6}$$

where IoU is the Intersection over Union (IoU) between the predicted bounding box A and the ground truth bounding box.

In Fig. 6.6, we can see that after adding the centerness weight to the IoU, the predicted bounding boxes that are closer to the center of the ground truth bounding box receive higher scores, which better aligns with our detection objectives.

6.3.3 *K-means++ clustering algorithm*

K-means [20] is a commonly used clustering method. Its core idea is that "things of the same kind cluster together." The algorithm starts by randomly selecting several center points, then classifies the remaining points into clusters based on their distance to these center points, thereby completing the clustering of all the data. The clustering process of the K-means algorithm is as follows:

(1) **Initialization:** Randomly select K points from the dataset to serve as the initial cluster centers.
(2) **Assignment:** For each of the remaining points, calculate the distance to each of the K cluster centers and assign the point to the cluster whose center is the closest.
(3) **Update:** Recalculate the cluster centers by moving them to the centroid (geometric center) of the current points in each cluster.
(4) **Iteration:** Repeat steps 2 and 3 until all points are assigned to a cluster and the cluster centers no longer change significantly, or a predefined number of iterations is reached.

The anchor box sizes in Faster R-CNN are manually set. A total of three anchors are defined, each with three areas: $[128^2, 256^2, 512^2]$ and three aspect ratios: [1:1, 1:2, 2:1]. The combination of these three areas and three aspect ratios results in nine anchor boxes. While these manually set anchor boxes have a certain level of generality on common datasets, they do not achieve the best detection performance on the URPC2018 marine life dataset used in this paper. Additionally, in clustering algorithms, the selection of initial cluster centers is crucial and often determines the quality of the clustering results. The K-means algorithm selects cluster centers randomly, making it difficult to determine how to choose the cluster centers to achieve better results.

Therefore, this paper will use the optimized version of the K-means clustering algorithm, K-means++ [21], to perform clustering analysis on the URPC2018 dataset, generating a set of anchor boxes that are more suitable for marine life, thereby improving detection accuracy. The K-means++ clustering algorithm is described as follows:

(1) **Initialization:** Randomly select K points from all the points that need to be clustered to serve as the initial cluster centers.
(2) **Distance calculation:** For the remaining points, calculate their distances to the nearest cluster center and sum these distances.
(3) **Selection of next center:** Choose a random point that falls within the sum of the distances calculated in step (2). Then, sequentially subtract this random value from the distances in step (2) until the random value is no longer greater than 0. The point at which this occurs is selected as the next cluster center.

(4) **Repeat:** Repeat steps (2) and (3) until all K cluster centers are selected.
(5) **K-means Clustering:** Perform the K-means clustering algorithm.

K-means++ improves the clustering results by selecting initial cluster centers that are as far apart as possible during the initialization phase (steps 1 to 3), leading to better generalization. In the actual marine life dataset, appropriate anchor box sizes can enhance the model's detection accuracy.

Figure 6.7 shows the distribution of ground truth bounding box sizes in the marine life dataset used in this paper. From the figure, it can be observed that the majority of the points are concentrated in the lower left corner. Since the K-means++ clustering algorithm selects cluster centers that are as far apart as possible, to avoid the influence of some special points on the clustering results, approximately 5% of the data was discarded. Only bounding boxes with lengths not exceeding 225 and widths not exceeding 125 were used for clustering with the K-means++ algorithm.

The clustering results are shown in Fig. 6.8. This paper will use the coordinates of these nine cluster centers as the dimensions (width and height) of the anchor boxes for training the Faster R-CNN network model.

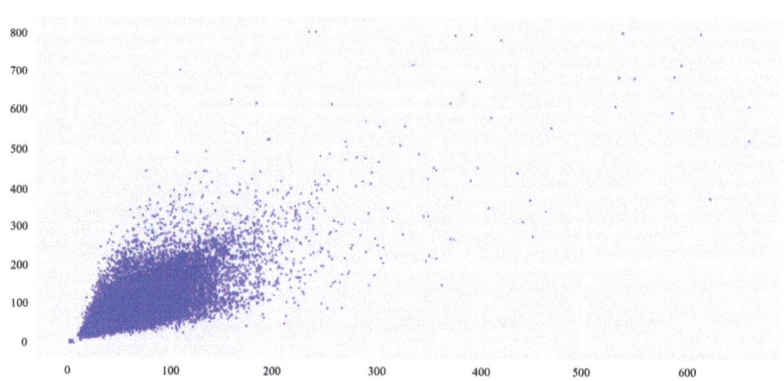

Figure 6.7. Distribution of bounding box sizes in the URPC2018 dataset.

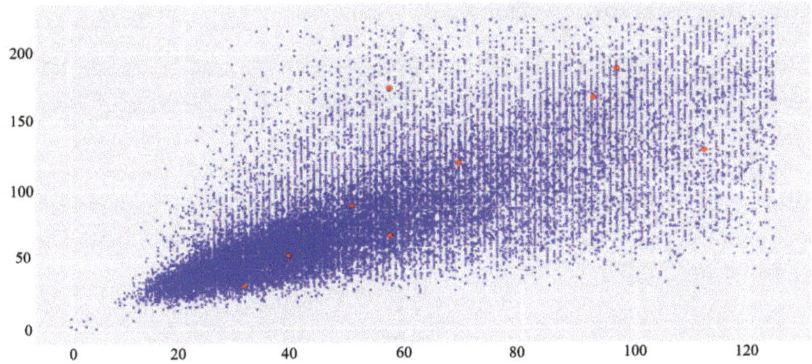

Figure 6.8. Anchor boxes generated using the K-means++ clustering algorithm.

6.4 Experiment

6.4.1 *Experiment configuration and dataset*

The network training was conducted on a workstation equipped with an Intel Xeon(R) CPU E5-2620 v4 @ 2.10GHz processor, 32GB of RAM, and an NVIDIA GeForce RTX2080 GPU. The deep learning platform used was PyTorch.

The dataset used in this paper is the official dataset provided by the URPC2018 Underwater Object Detection Competition. The URPC2018 dataset consists of 5543 images, including four categories: sea cucumbers, sea urchins, scallops, and starfish. The dataset is divided into training, validation, and test sets in an 8:1:1 ratio.

For the pre-trained weights, we chose the weights file of Faster R-CNN pre-trained on the VOC dataset. The input image size was set to 800×800. The learning rate was adjusted using a cosine annealing decay strategy, with an initial learning rate of 1×10^4 and a minimum learning rate of 1×10^5. The number of iterations per learning rate cycle was set to 5.

The entire model training process was divided into two steps:

Step 1: Freeze the ResNet parameters and train for 100 epochs to avoid destroying the initial weights. The batch size was set to 16.

Step 2: Unfreeze the ResNet parameters and train for another 100 epochs. The batch size was set to 4. All the experiments with the network models reached convergence within 200 epochs.

6.4.2 *Evaluation metrics*

To quantitatively analyze the object detection performance of the proposed algorithm, this paper adopts the Mean Average Precision (mAP) as the evaluation metric.

mAP is based on Precision and Recall. Precision P for a class C in an image is defined as the ratio of the number of true positive detections (TP) to the total number of detections of class C (including true positives TP and false positives FP):

$$p = \frac{TP}{TP + FP} \tag{6.7}$$

Recall r for a class C in an image is defined as the ratio of the number of true positive detections (TP) to the total number of actual instances of class C (including true positives TP and false negatives FN):

$$r = \frac{TP}{TP + FN} \tag{6.8}$$

The Average Precision *(AP)* for a single class C is calculated by plotting the Precision-Recall (P-R) curve, with recall rr on the x-axis and precision p on the y-axis, and computing the area under the curve (AUC):

$$AP = \int_0^1 p(r)dr \tag{6.9}$$

For a test set with NN classes, the mAP is calculated as follows:

$$\text{mAP} = \frac{\sum_{k=1}^{N} AP}{N} \tag{6.10}$$

6.4.3 *Experimental results*

In the experiments, we conducted a detailed comparison of three improvements with the Faster R-CNN network while keeping the training parameters consistent. Under the default settings of IoU 0.5 and confidence threshold 0.5, the mAP of the Faster R-CNN model was 80.68%. After using the ResNet-BiFPN feature extraction network, the mAP improved by 4.61%, with detection performance for all four categories showing some improvement. The largest AP improvement was for scallops, at 7.66%, and the smallest improvement was for starfish, at 1.96%.

Using EIoU improved the mAP by 0.36% and also enhanced the detection performance for three of the four categories, with the largest AP improvement for sea cucumbers, at 0.92%. However, the detection performance for starfish slightly decreased, with an AP reduction of 0.27. We believe this decrease in precision is because EIoU primarily improves the "quality" of the predicted bounding boxes, making them more aligned with our "subjective intention," i.e., closer to the ground truth bounding boxes, rather than focusing on improving the objective detection accuracy. This is why the improvement in detection accuracy for the other three categories was not as significant.

Using PredMix for data augmentation improved the mAP by 1.11%, with the largest AP improvement for sea cucumbers, at 1.44%.

This experiment also fully verified that combining any two improvements can further enhance the detection performance beyond the single improvement. The combination of ResNet-BiFPN and EIoU improved the mAP by 5.66%, with the largest AP improvement for scallops, at 8.30%. The combination of EIoU and PredMix improved the mAP by 1.19%, with the largest AP improvement for sea cucumbers, at 2.15%. The combination of ResNet-BiFPN and PredMix provided the highest mAP improvement, at 6.24%, with the largest AP improvement for scallops, at 8.74%.

Ultimately, the improved Faster R-CNN algorithm proposed in this paper achieved an 8.26% improvement in mAP compared to the traditional Faster R-CNN algorithm. The AP improvement for the four categories ranged from 4.97% to 10.49%, and the experimental results fully demonstrate the effectiveness of the proposed improvements.

Table 6.1 provides a detailed comparison of the experimental results. Here, ① represents the use of the ResNet-BiFPN improved feature extraction network alone on Faster R-CNN, ② represents the use of EIoU alone on Faster R-CNN, ③ represents the use of the K-means++ clustering algorithm alone on Faster R-CNN, and ①+②, ②+③, ①+③ represent the combinations of the corresponding two improvements. "Proposed" refers to the improved Faster R-CNN marine life detection algorithm proposed in this paper.

Table 6.1. Test results on the URPC2018 dataset.

Algorithm	mAP (%)	Sea Urchin (%)	Starfish (%)	Scallop (%)	Sea Cucumber (%)
Baseline	80.68	87.39	86.62	75.55	73.17
①	85.29	90.03	88.58	83.21	79.36
②	81.04	87.48	86.35	76.23	74.09
③	81.79	88.80	87.39	76.34	74.61
①+②	86.34	91.36	89.02	83.85	81.14
②+③	81.87	88.14	87.20	76.81	75.32
①+③	86.92	91.93	90.25	84.29	81.24
Proposed	88.94	92.36	90.78	86.04	82.93

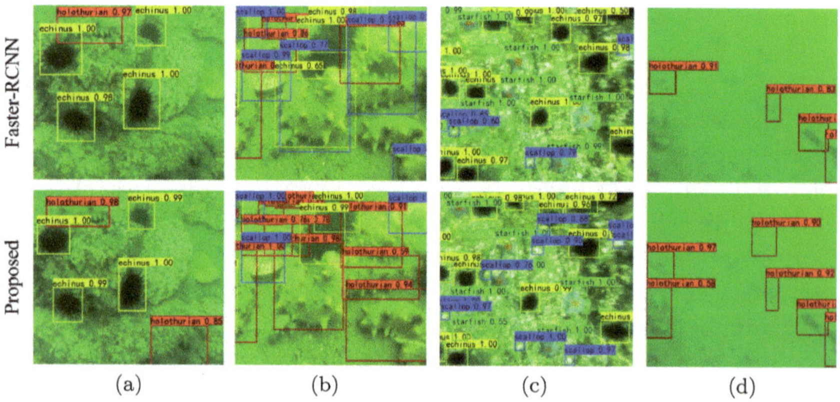

Figure 6.9. Comparison of detection results. (a)–(d) illustrate the detection results of each image using Faster R-CNN, before and after the improvements.

Figure 6.9 shows some of the detection results of Faster R-CNN before and after the improvements. It can be observed that the improved Faster R-CNN demonstrates excellent detection performance for blurry objects, dense objects, multi-scale objects, and occluded objects.

The improved Faster R-CNN-based marine life detection method shows better performance in detecting partially visible marine organisms. For example, in column (a), the improved Faster R-CNN can detect the partially visible sea cucumber in the lower right corner with high confidence. The proposed algorithm also performs better in detecting dense clusters of organisms. As shown in column (b), the original Faster R-CNN had numerous false positives and missed detections: the sea cucumber in the lower left corner was not detected, and multiple sea cucumbers were misidentified as scallops and sea urchins. The bounding boxes were also not very precise. In contrast, the improved Faster R-CNN can accurately "distinguish" between overlapping and occluded organisms, providing precise localization and identification for each organism in the image, with high confidence for most detected objects.

The improved Faster R-CNN also demonstrates strong capability in detecting multi-scale targets. As shown in column (c), the addition of the BiFPN bidirectional feature pyramid structure enhances the detection of small-scale targets like scallops. Compared to the original model, the improved Faster R-CNN not only detects more scallops but also assigns them high confidence scores. The detection of blurry targets has also been significantly enhanced. As shown in column (d), due to severe image distortion and low clarity, the original Faster R-CNN missed two sea cucumbers. However, the improved Faster R-CNN with ResNet-BiFPN has stronger feature extraction capabilities, allowing it to achieve higher detection accuracy even under such blurry conditions.

EIoU helps the predicted bounding boxes to better "fit" the target organisms. For example, in column (a), the predicted bounding box for the sea urchin by the improved Faster R-CNN is more closely aligned with the actual sea urchin.

In summary, the improved Faster R-CNN, which enhances feature extraction and multi-scale feature fusion through ResNet-BiFPN, improves the quality of predicted bounding boxes with EIoU, and generates more suitable anchor boxes using the K-means++ clustering algorithm, achieves higher detection accuracy in marine life detection.

Additionally, this paper conducted experiments to determine the optimal number of BiFPN stacks in the ResNet-BiFPN. Considering both detection accuracy and detection speed, the number of BiFPN stacks was chosen to be 3. The specific data are shown in Table 6.2.

This paper conducted experimental tests on the performance of the Faster R-CNN network with various improvements. Since the size of the anchor boxes does not affect the network's runtime performance, no additional performance tests were conducted for the model with the K-means++ improvement. The ResNet-BiFPN backbone feature extraction network has significantly more parameters

Table 6.2. Test results with different numbers of BiFPN stacks.

	0 (stack)	1 (stack)	2 (stacks)	3 (stacks)	4 (stacks)	5 (stacks)
mAP(%)	83.47	84.95	85.18	85.29	85.32	85.30
FPS	5.31	4.63	4.50	4.39	4.22	4.10

Table 6.3. Impact of various improvements on network runtime performance.

Algorithm	FPS
Baseline	5.31
ResNet-BiFPN	4.39
EIoU	5.18
K-means++	/
ResNet-BiFPN + EIoU	4.30
EIoU + K-means++	/
ResNet-BiFPN + K-means++	/
Proposed	4.30

than the VGG backbone, thus having the greatest impact on the overall network performance. EIoU, which adds a centerness weight to IoU, only introduces a small amount of additional computation, so it has a minimal impact on the network's runtime performance. The specific test results are shown in Table 6.3.

6.5 Conclusion

This paper proposes a marine life detection algorithm based on an improved Faster R-CNN. The algorithm replaces the original VGG backbone feature extraction network with ResNet and incorporates BiFPN to enhance the network's feature extraction and multi-scale feature fusion capabilities. It also uses the Effective Intersection over Union (EIoU) to replace IoU, reducing bounding box redundancy. Additionally, the K-means++ clustering algorithm is used to generate more suitable anchor boxes. Experimental data show that the marine life detection algorithm based on the improved Faster R-CNN effectively improves the detection accuracy of marine life and can achieve effective detection of marine organisms.

References

[1] Wang T, Chen Y, Qiao M, *et al.* A fast and robust convolutional neural network-based defect detection model in product quality control. *International Journal of Advanced Manufacturing Technology*, 2018, 94(9): 3465–3471.

[2] Wang R, Zhang Y, Tian W, *et al.* Fast implementation of insect multi-target detection based on multimodal optimization. *Remote Sensing*, 2021, 13(4): 594.

[3] Xu X, Li X, Zhao H, *et al.* A real-time, continuous pedestrian tracking and positioning method with multiple coordinated overhead-view cameras. *Measurement*, 2021, 178: 109386.

[4] Brys T, Harutyunyan A, Vrancx P, *et al.* Multi-objectiveization and ensembles of shapings in reinforcement learning. *Neurocomputing*, 2017, 263: 48–59.

[5] Gao SH, Tan YQ, Cheng MM, *et al.* Highly efficient salient object detection with 100k parameters. *European Conference on Computer Vision*. Springer, Cham, 2020: 702–721.

[6] Fan DP, Zhai Y, Borji A, *et al.* BBS-Net: RGB-D salient object detection with a bifurcated backbone strategy network. *European Conference on Computer Vision*. Springer, Cham, 2020: 275–292.

[7] Yu WD, Liao HC, Hsiao WT, *et al.* Automatic safety monitoring of construction hazard working zone: A semantic segmentation based deep learning approach. *Proceedings of the 2020 the 7th International Conference on Automation and Logistics (ICAL)*. 2020: 54–59.

[8] Huval B, Wang T, Tandon S, *et al.* An empirical evaluation of deep learning on highway driving. arXiv preprint arXiv:1504.01716, 2015.

[9] Zhao Y, Ma J, Li X, *et al.* Saliency detection and deep learning-based wildfire identification in UAV imagery. *Sensors*, 2018, 18(3): 712.

[10] Redmon J, Divvala S, Girshick R, *et al.* You only look once: Unified, real-time object detection. *Proceedings of the IEEE Conference on Computer Vision and Pattern Recognition*. 2016: 779–788.

[11] Redmon J, Farhadi A. YOLO9000: Better, faster, stronger. *Proceedings of the IEEE Conference on Computer Vision and Pattern Recognition*. 2017: 7263–7271.

[12] Redmon J, Farhadi A. Yolov3: An incremental improvement. arXiv preprint arXiv:1804.02767, 2018.

[13] Bochkovskiy A, Wang CY, Liao HYM. Yolov4: Optimal speed and accuracy of object detection. arXiv preprint arXiv:2004.10934, 2020.

[14] Girshick R, Donahue J, Darrell T, *et al.* Rich feature hierarchies for accurate object detection and semantic segmentation. *Proceedings of the IEEE Conference on Computer Vision and Pattern Recognition.* 2014: 580–587.

[15] Girshick R. Fast r-cnn. *Proceedings of the IEEE International Conference on Computer Vision.* 2015: 1440–1448.

[16] Ren S, He K, Girshick R, *et al.* Faster r-cnn: Towards real-time object detection with region proposal networks. arXiv preprint arXiv:1506.01497, 2015.

[17] He K, Zhang X, Ren S, *et al.* Deep residual learning for image recognition. *Proceedings of the IEEE Conference on Computer Vision and Pattern Recognition.* 2016: 770–778.

[18] Tan M, Pang R, Le QV. Efficientdet: Scalable and efficient object detection. *Proceedings of the IEEE/CVF Conference on Computer Vision and Pattern Recognition.* 2020: 10781–10790.

[19] Ma J, Chen B, Sun X. General object detection framework based on improved Faster R-CNN. *Journal of Computer Applications*, 2021, 41 (09): 2712–2719.

[20] Estlick M, Leeser M, Szymanskii JJ, *et al.* Algorithmic transforms in the implementation of k-means clustering on reconfigurable hardware. Los Alamos National Lab., NM (US), 2000.

[21] Vassilvitskii S, Arthur D. k-means++: The advantages of careful seeding. *Proceedings of the Eighteenth Annual ACM-SIAM Symposium on Discrete Algorithms.* 2006: 1027–1035.

Chapter 7

Real-Time Object Localization and Recognition Algorithm for Video Images Based on YOLOv4

7.1 Introduction

7.1.1 *Basic concept of overlay analysis*

Marine organisms are an important component of the marine ecological environment and have always been a focus of attention. Marine ecological conservation organizations conduct research on the distribution and living habits of marine organisms through methods such as manual diving and underwater robot photography. However, low-quality underwater imaging significantly hinders researchers' studies of marine organisms. Therefore, there is an urgent need for a method to detect marine organisms instead of relying solely on the human eye.

Traditional object detection methods suffer from poor recognition accuracy and slow detection speeds, making them ineffective for underwater object detection. In recent years, the rapid development of deep learning has brought significant breakthroughs to the field of object detection. Object detection is a computer technology related to computer vision and image processing, dealing with semantic objects of specific categories in digital images or videos. Due to recent technological breakthroughs, object detection has received sufficient attention in academia and has been widely applied in reality, such as in security surveillance [1], autonomous driving [2], and unmanned aerial vehicle (UAV) scene analysis [3]. Most object detection methods rely on deep learning networks as the backbone to extract features, classify, and locate objects from input images. Research areas in object detection include edge detection [4, 5], multi-object detection [6], and salient object detection [7].

In many scenarios, object detection algorithms based on deep learning have achieved promising results. However, as pointed out in references [8, 9], factors such as poor underwater imaging quality, complex underwater environments, and the varying sizes and shapes of marine organisms can interfere with the effectiveness of object detection in underwater scenes. Additionally, overlapping and occlusion among marine organisms (in this paper, "overlapping" refers to coverage between objects of the same category, while "occlusion" refers to the same situation between objects of different categories) can also interfere with detection effectiveness.

Existing data augmentation methods [10] lack a thorough study on the overlapping and occlusion of underwater objects. Figure 7.1 demonstrates the phenomenon of overlapping and occlusion among underwater objects, which can cause certain interference to object detection. If the model is only trained on the original dataset, it is prone to issues such as missed detections and false positives in scenes where target objects are relatively dense, and the detection accuracy may also decrease to some extent. The data augmentation method proposed in this paper will focus on addressing such issues.

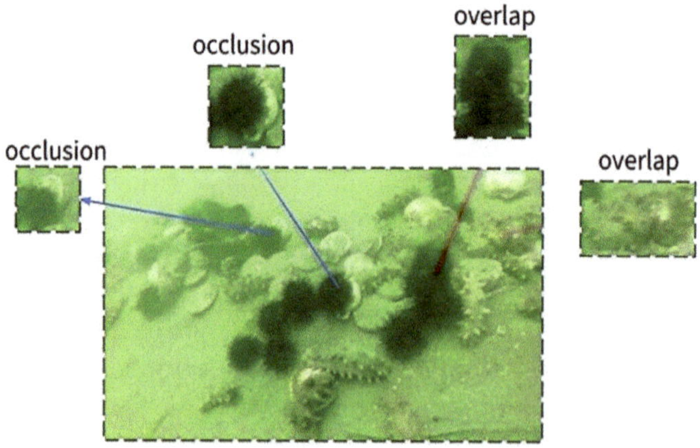

Figure 7.1. Obstruction and coverage of underwater objects.

Currently, the main object detection frameworks based on deep learning are two-stage and one-stage. The most typical two-stage object detection framework is the R-CNN series: In 2014, Ross B. Girshick proposed R-CNN [11], which first generates candidate regions through selective search and then uses CNN to extract features from these regions, thereby replacing the traditional sliding window method and improving the accuracy of object detection. However, R-CNN has a large amount of repeated calculations, which seriously affects detection performance. Fast R-CNN [12]. Addressing the computational redundancy of R-CNN, an approach was selected where the input image first undergoes feature extraction through a CNN, and then candidate regions are extracted using selective search. This method allows for obtaining all candidate regions after just one pass through the CNN, reducing repeated calculations, but the detection speed was still not ideal. Faster R-CNN [13], building upon Fast R-CNN, uses a Region Proposal Network (RPN) to replace the selective search algorithm for screening candidate regions, further improving detection speed. The most typical single-stage object detection framework is the YOLO series: YOLOv1 [14] abandons the candidate region generation step of two-stage object detection algorithms, using pre-defined anchor boxes to directly integrate object region prediction and object category prediction into a single step, significantly boosting detection speed. However, each grid cell can only predict one object, leading to lower detection accuracy. YOLOv2 [15] improves upon YOLOv1 by adding batch normalization to the convolutional layers to reduce model overfitting and effectively enhance model convergence. YOLO9000, based on YOLOv2, utilizes a method of hierarchical views for object classification, enabling the simultaneous detection of over 9,000 categories. YOLOv3 [16], building upon YOLOv2, eliminates all pooling layers and uses increased convolutional kernel strides to achieve the effect of pooling layers, thereby significantly improving detection speed. It can also simultaneously output multi-scale feature maps, enhancing the detection capability for small objects. YOLOv4 [17], based on YOLOv3, selects a number of techniques (tricks) that have been used on various detectors since the release of YOLOv3 to improve detection accuracy, and replaces the backbone network Darknet-53 of YOLOv3 with CSPDarkNet53, further enhancing detection speed and accuracy. The specific structure of YOLOv4 is shown in Fig. 7.2.

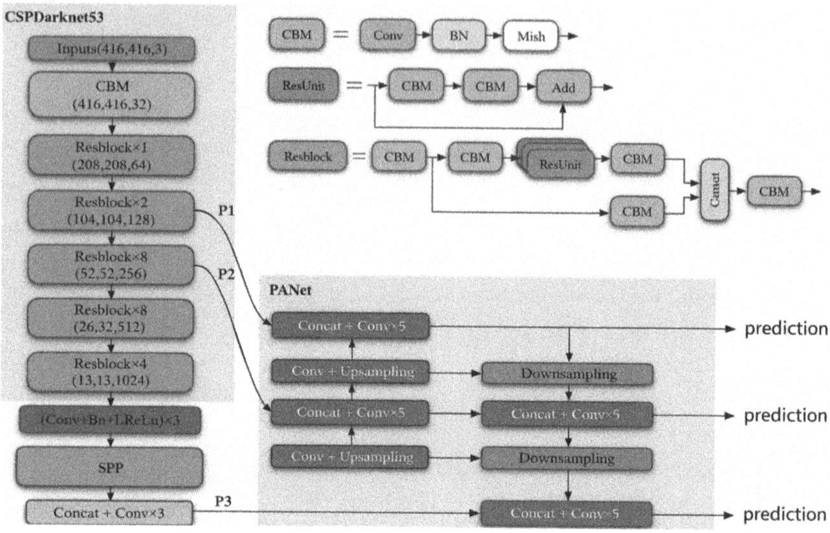

Figure 7.2. Overall Structure of YOLOv4.

Data augmentation is a method to expand the size of the data sample set and can enhance the generalization ability of the model. Common data augmentation techniques include spatial geometric transformations, pixel color transformations, Gaussian blurring, random erasing, and more. AutoAugment [18] uses a search algorithm to find image augmentation schemes suitable for specific datasets. RandAugment [19] directly searches for the optimal strategy for a given dataset on that dataset. CutOut [20] occludes parts of the input image to simulate scenarios where detection objects are partially occluded. HideAndSeek [21] divides the input image into several regions and generates masks for each region with a certain probability. MixUp [22], based on the principle of neighborhood risk minimization, uses linear interpolation to blend two input images to obtain new sample data. RoIMix [23], specifically addressing issues such as low contrast and occlusion among underwater images, applies linear interpolation to the candidate regions generated by the RPN.

The contributions of this paper mainly lie in the following three improvements made on the basis of YOLOv4, making it more suitable for underwater target detection:

1. Addressing the issue of low detection accuracy caused by low-quality underwater imaging and complex underwater environments, a CBAM feature attention module is added to the CSPDarknet53 backbone feature extraction network of YOLOv4. This allows the network model to learn to focus on content in the channel dimension and location in the spatial dimension, enhancing the feature extraction capability of the network model.
2. Addressing the issue of low detection accuracy due to the varying sizes and shapes of underwater targets, a same-layer skip connection and cross-layer skip connection structure are added to the PANet module in YOLOv4. This allows for a more thorough combination of deep features rich in semantic information with shallow features rich in location and detailed information, thereby enhancing the multi-scale feature fusion capability.
3. Addressing the issue of low detection accuracy caused by overlapping and occlusion among marine organisms, a novel data augmentation method called PredMix is proposed for YOLOv4. This method simulates the overlapping and occlusion of underwater targets by linearly blending target images.

7.2 The Underwater Target Detection Algorithm That Combines Data Augmentation with Improved YOLOv4

7.2.1 *CBAM-CSPDarknet53*

Optical scattering leads to poor underwater imaging quality, and underwater scenes are often extremely complex, with underwater rocks, seaweed, and other elements interfering with the extraction of target features. Therefore, it is highly meaningful to make the model more targeted in feature extraction. In this paper, we choose to add the CBAM attention mechanism to the CSPDarknet53 backbone feature extraction network of YOLOv4.

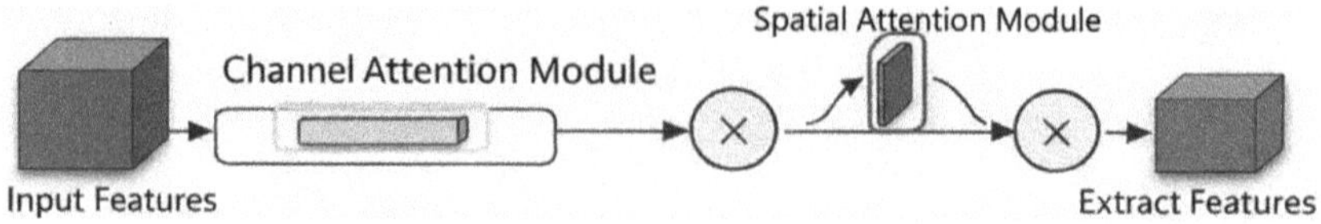

Figure 7.3. Overall structure of CBAM.

CBAM [24], proposed by Sanghyun Woo *et al.* in 2018, is a simple yet effective attention mechanism structure for feedforward convolutional neural networks. For this attention mechanism, given a feature map, CBAM sequentially infers attention maps along two separate dimensions: channel and spatial. These attention maps are then multiplied with the input feature map to perform adaptive feature refinement. The CBAM attention mechanism not only "tells" the model where to focus but also enhances the feature representation of key regions, paying attention only to important features while suppressing or ignoring irrelevant ones. CBAM is mainly composed of channel attention and spatial attention modules, with its structure illustrated in Fig. 7.3.

The channel attention module primarily generates a channel attention map by utilizing the relationships among the feature channels. In the network model, for any input feature map with C dimensions, average pooling and max pooling layers are applied to aggregate spatial information, resulting in two C-dimensional pooled feature maps. These two pooled feature maps are then fed into a multi-layer perceptron (MLP) with a hidden layer to obtain two $1 \times 1 \times C$ channel attention maps. Finally, the two channel attention maps obtained from the MLP are element-wise added to produce the final channel attention map. The structure of the channel attention module is illustrated in Fig. 7.4.

The spatial attention module primarily generates a spatial attention map by utilizing the spatial relationships among features. In the network model, for the feature map refined by the channel attention map, it first undergoes max pooling and average pooling along the channel dimension to obtain two two-dimensional feature maps. These two $1 \times H \times W$ feature maps are then concatenated along the dimension. For the concatenated feature map, a convolution layer with a kernel size of 7×7 is used to generate the spatial attention

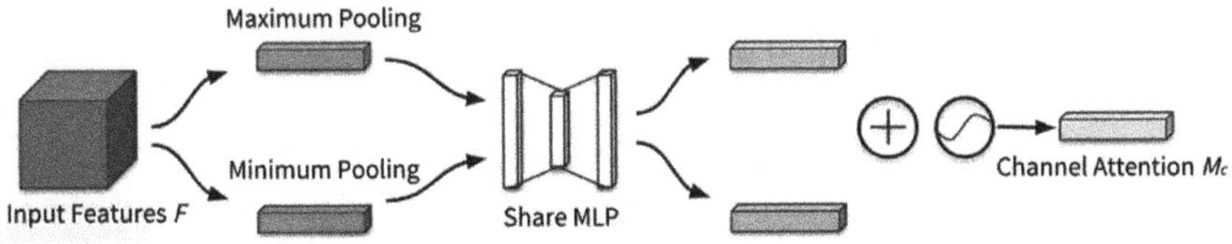

Figure 7.4. Structure of the channel attention module.

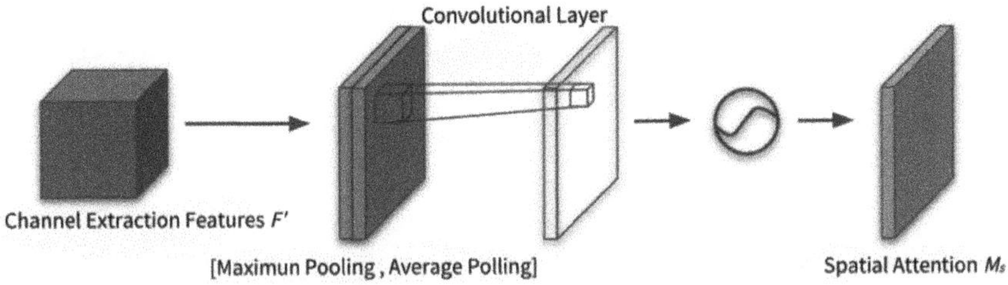

Figure 7.5. Structure of the spatial attention module.

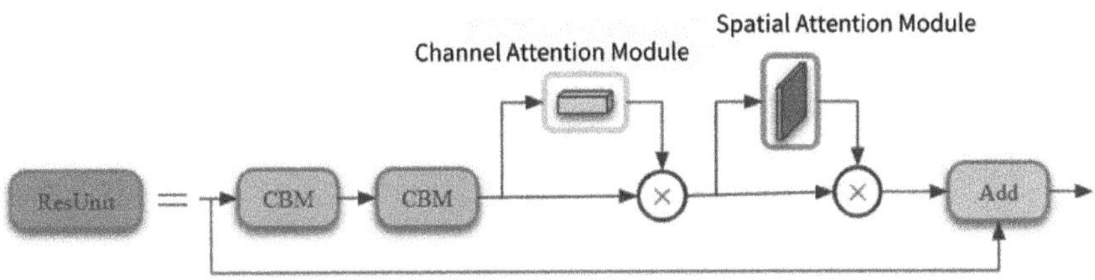

Figure 7.6. Structure of ResUnit with CBAM added.

map$M_s \in R^{\mathrm{H}\times\mathrm{W}\times 1}$. The structure of the spatial attention module is illustrated in Fig. 7.5.

CSPDarknet53 consists of five consecutive residual blocks (Resblocks), with the number of ResUnits stacked in each of the five residual blocks being [1,2,8,8,4], respectively. In this paper, we choose to insert CBAM into the first ResUnit of each residual block. After passing through two CBMs (assuming CBM refers to some preceding layers or operations, though typically it's not a standard abbreviation; here we interpret it contextually), a channel attention module is added first, followed by a spatial attention module to form a serial structure. The specific implementation structure is illustrated in Fig. 7.6.

7.2.2 *DetPANet*

Due to factors such as varying growth conditions of marine organisms and different shooting angles, the size and shape of marine organisms presented vary greatly. The original Path Aggregation Network (PANet) in YOLOv4 struggles to cope with the complexity and diversity of marine organisms. Therefore, this paper introduces intra-layer skip connections and cross-layer skip connections into the original PANet module, fully integrating deep features rich in semantic information with shallow features abundant in positional and detailed information. The deep features rich in semantic information are conducive to object classification, while the shallow features rich in positional and detailed information are beneficial for object localization and the detection of small objects. The specific structural comparison is shown in Fig. 7.7. In this paper, the modified PANet is named DetPANet (Detailed-PANet).

In the CSPDarknet53 feature extraction network of YOLOv4, a large number of convolutional layers are already used to extract image features, which significantly reduces the resolution. This leads to the loss of image details, which is not conducive to accurate object localization and correct classification in the future. Therefore, to avoid significant loss of details, this paper introduces skip connections at the same level, allowing the features from shallower convolutional layers to be referenced in deeper layers. The abundant shallow information can contribute to more precise object localization and correct classification. During the training process, skip connections facilitate the flow of gradients to deeper networks.

Furthermore, in order to combine low-resolution, semantically strong features with high-resolution, semantically strong features,

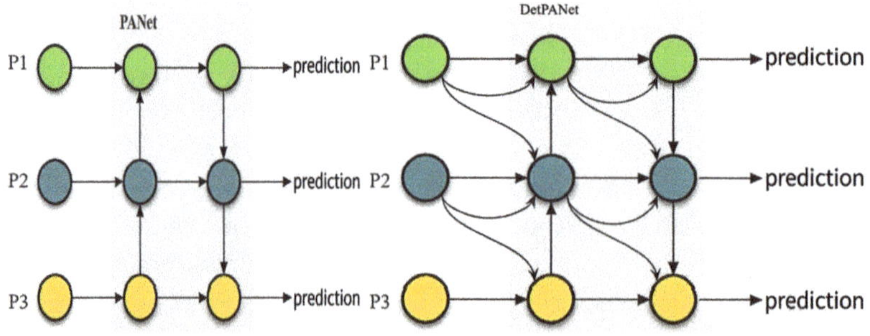

Figure 7.7. Structural comparison between PANet and DetPANet.

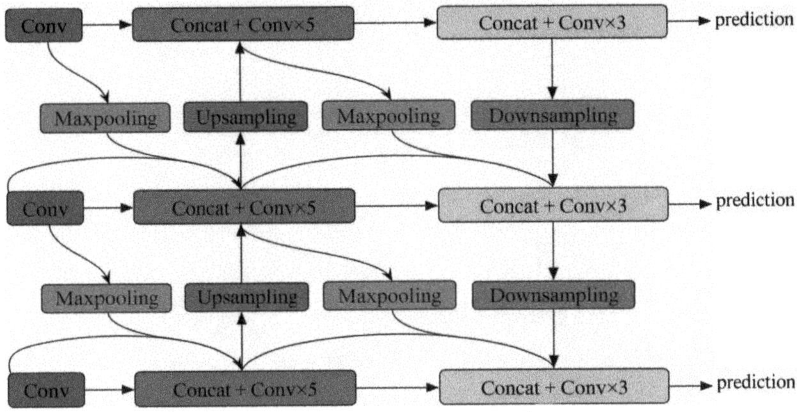

Figure 7.8. Detailed structure of DetPANet.

this paper introduces four max pooling layers between prediction layers of different sizes, thereby achieving feature fusion between shallow and deep layers and enabling accurate prediction of multi-scale objects. By integrating low-level features with high-level features, the network is able to retain more high-resolution detail information contained in the high-level feature maps, thus improving the accuracy of image localization. The specific implementation of the network structure is shown in Fig. 7.8.

7.2.3 *PredMix*

The data augmentation method proposed in this paper, PredMix, is applied to the input stage of YOLOv4. The entire data augmentation process is divided into two steps.

The first step is to generate prediction data for the training set.

The first step involves generating prediction data for the training set. The entire dataset is divided into four parts: training set A, training set B, validation set, and test set. The YOLOv4 network with the improved PANet is trained separately on training sets A and B. Then, the two trained models, A and B, are used to perform cross-predictions on the other part of the training set. The detection results (specific coordinate positions) of each training image are saved for subsequent data augmentation operations. The specific operation method is shown in Fig. 7.9.

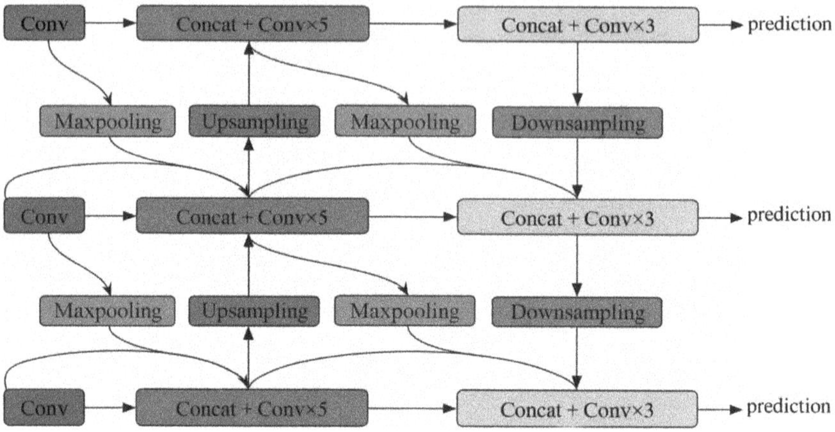

Figure 7.9. Pre-processing workflow of the dataset.

The second step involves generating new training samples by mixing the labeled images with the predicted images using a randomly selected weight ratio, and then using these new samples for training.

Let $\mathrm{x}^{\mathrm{truth}} \in \mathrm{R}^{\mathrm{H}\times\mathrm{W}\times\mathrm{C}}$ represent a labeled portion of a certain image during training, y^{truth} represents the label; $x^{\mathrm{pred}} \in \mathrm{R}^{\mathrm{H}\times\mathrm{W}\times\mathrm{C}}$ represents a predicted bounding box portion of a certain image from the prediction results in the first step, y^{pred} represents the predicted classification. PredMix aims to generate new training samples by combining a randomly selected labeled portion of an image $(x_i^{\mathrm{truth}}, y_i^{\mathrm{truth}})$ from one dataset with a randomly selected predicted bounding box portion of an image $(x_j^{\mathrm{pred}}, y_j^{\mathrm{pred}})$ from another dataset. The sizes of the predicted bounding box and the labeled bounding box are usually inconsistent, so first, the size of x_j^{pred} is adjusted to match the size of x_i^{truth}. The generated training sample $(\tilde{x}\tilde{y})$ is then used for model training.

The specific operation is defined as follows:

$$\tilde{x} = \lambda' x_i^{\mathrm{truth}} + (1 - \lambda')\, x_j^{\mathrm{pred}}, \tilde{y} = y_i^{\mathrm{truth}} \tag{7.1}$$

Since we consider y_i^{pred} to be an occlusion of y_i^{truth}, y_i^{truth} is assigned the label of $\tilde{y}$. Here, λ' represents the mixing ratio between the labeled bounding box portion image and the predicted bounding box portion image. The formula for generating λ' is as follows:

$$\lambda' = \max(\lambda, 1 - \lambda) \tag{7.2}$$

where max() is a function that selects the larger value between the two. Using PredMix to augment data can simulate the overlapping and occlusion of underwater targets. In this paper, these newly mixed regions are used to replace the original region x_i^{truth}, and new training samples are generated.

The definition of λ is as follows:

$$\lambda = \beta(\alpha, \alpha) \tag{7.3}$$

The reason for choosing to mix the prediction results with the true labels, rather than directly mixing two true labels, is to simulate the diverse underwater scenarios of overlapping, covering, occlusion, and blurring, as shown in Fig. 7.10. The predicted bounding boxes may sometimes have certain deviations, and sometimes they may mistakenly predict other objects (such as rocks, aquatic plants, etc.) as the labeled objects. Mixing different prediction results with label images can simulate various incomplete displays of underwater objects.

By simulating the overlapping and occlusion of objects through PredMix, the detection capability of the model for dense and partially displayed targets can be improved. From a statistical perspective, PredMix can be viewed as a linear interpolation between the predicted bounding box area and the labeled bounding box area, which

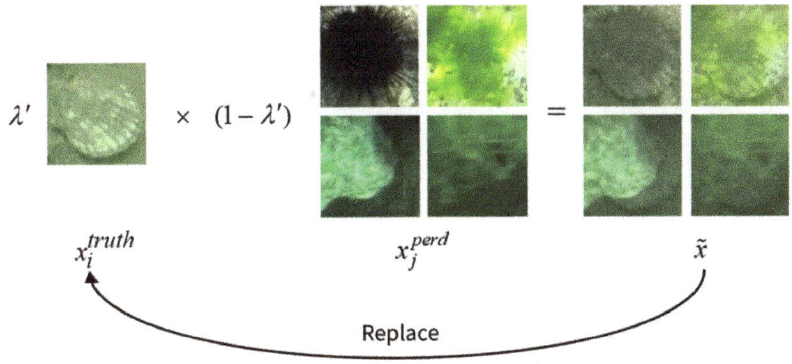

Figure 7.10. Example of PredMix operation.

can make the decision boundary smoother without sudden transitions. PredMix follows the principle of VRM (Vicinal Risk Minimization) rather than ERM (Empirical Risk Minimization). This allows the model to have better robustness and generalization ability. A model trained according to the ERM principle minimizes empirical risk, which helps the model fit the training data better. We define empirical risk as:

$$R_\delta(f) = \frac{1}{n}\sum_{i=1}^{n} l(f(x_i), y_i) x_j^{\text{pred}} f \tag{7.4}$$

where represents a nonlinear expression between x and y, n is the number of samples, and l is a loss function that measures the distance between $f(x_i)$ and y_i. However, this training strategy may cause the decision boundary to overfit the training data, leading to overfitting. PredMix follows the VRM principle to generate a vicinal distribution of the training data. Then, we can use the vicinal data $(\tilde{x}, \tilde{y})$ to replace the training data $(x_i^{\text{truth}}, y_i^{\text{truth}})$. The approximate expected risk e is defined as follows:

$$R_v(f) = \frac{1}{n}\sum_{i=1}^{n} l(f(\tilde{x}), \tilde{y})(\tilde{x}, \tilde{y}) \tag{7.5}$$

Therefore, the training process is transformed into minimizing the expected risk. Using vicinal data for training with PredMix can effectively enhance the robustness of the model.

7.3 Experiment

7.3.1 *Experimental configuration and dataset*

The network training was conducted on a workstation equipped with an Intel Xeon(R) CPU E5-2620 v4 @ 2.10GHz processor, 32GB of RAM, and an NVIDIA GeForce RTX2080 graphics card. The deep learning platform used was Pytorch.

The dataset used in this paper is the one officially provided by the URPC2018 Underwater Object Detection Competition. The URPC2018 dataset contains a total of 5543 images, including four categories: sea cucumbers, sea urchins, scallops, and starfish. In the first step of the PredMix operation, the dataset was divided into a training set A, a training set B, a validation set, and a test set in the ratio of 4:4:1:1. Subsequently, the training sets A and B were merged, resulting in a division of the dataset into training set, validation set, and test set in the ratio of 8:1:1. The PredMix data augmentation operation was only performed on the training set and not on the validation set or test set.

In this paper, the pre-trained weight file of YOLOv4 on the VOC dataset is selected as the pre-trained weight. The hyperparameter α in PredMix is set to 0.2, and the input image size is set to 416×416. The learning rate is adjusted using a cosine annealing decay strategy, with one cycle of learning rate iteration set to 5, an initial learning rate of 1×10^{-5}. The entire model training process is divided into two steps:

Step 1: Freeze the CSPDarknet53 parameters and train for 80 epochs to avoid weight destruction in the early stages of training, with a batch size set to 16;

Step 2: Unfreeze the CSPDarknet53 parameters and train for an additional 80 epochs, with a batch size set to 4. All experimental network models converge before reaching 160 epochs.

7.3.2 *Experimental results*

During the experiment, this paper conducted detailed comparisons between three improvements and the YOLOv4 algorithm while controlling the training parameters consistently. Additionally, the detection performance of the SSD model and Faster-RCNN model on the URPC2018 dataset was also tested. With the default IoU set to 0.5 and confidence threshold set to 0.5, the mAP of the SSD model was 63.43%, the mAP of Faster R-CNN was 75.25%, and the mAP of the YOLOv4 model was 71.36%. It can be observed that, as single-stage object detection algorithms, the detection performance of the SSD model is far inferior to that of the YOLOv4 model. Meanwhile, the detection performance of the two-stage object detection algorithm Faster R-CNN is slightly better than YOLOv4, except for in the category of scallops, where YOLOv4 outperforms Faster R-CNN. This is because scallops are relatively small, and Faster R-CNN has weaker detection capabilities for small objects.

After applying PredMix data augmentation, the detection mAP of YOLOv4 improved by 2.06% compared to the previous result, with improvements observed in all four categories. Among them, the largest improvement in *AP* was seen in sea urchins, with an increase of 3.30%. This is because sea urchins are pure black and can easily be confused with shadows in the background during actual detection. PredMix effectively simulates situations where sea urchins are obscured by other objects, allowing the network model to fully learn and improve its detection capabilities for such cases. After adding the CBAM feature attention module, the detection mAP of YOLOv4 improved by 2.43%, with the largest improvement in *AP* observed in sea cucumbers. This is due to the fact that sea cucumbers can resemble rocks in some scenarios, leading to confusion during detection. By adding the CBAM attention mechanism, the network model pays more attention to the features of sea cucumbers. DetPANet showed the largest improvement in mAP among the three improvements, with an increase of 3.26%. Among the four categories, the detection performance for scallops improved by 4.10%. This is because scallops are mostly small-scale targets and can be easily overlooked during detection. DetPANet effectively combines shallow and deep features, fully integrating semantic information, location information, and detailed information, thereby significantly improving the detection performance for small targets.

This experiment also fully verifies that the combination of any two improvements can further enhance detection performance on top of the original single improvement. The combination of CBAM and PredMix results in an improvement of 5.06% in mAP, with the largest increase observed in the detection of sea cucumbers among the four categories. The combination of DetPANet and CBAM leads to an improvement of 3.66% in mAP, with the largest increase in the detection of scallops, which is 4.06%. The combination of DetPANet and PredMix results in the largest overall improvement in mAP, which is 5.31%.

Compared to the original YOLOv4 network, the improved YOLOv4 network proposed in this paper achieves a 7.03% increase in mAP. It also outperforms the SSD network by 14.29% in mAP and the Faster R-CNN network by 3.14% in mAP. For the four categories of objects detected, the improvement in *AP* ranges from 4.71% to 9.58%. The experimental results demonstrate that the underwater object detection algorithm combining data augmentation and improved YOLOv4 proposed in this paper can achieve higher accuracy in underwater object detection.

Table 7.1. Test results on the URPC2018 dataset.

Algorithm	mAP/%	Sea urchin	Sea star	Scallop	Sea cucumber
baseline	71.36	83.40	79.66	61.46	60.93
SSD	63.43	76.68	69.44	49.15	58.47
Faster R-CNN	75.25	85.39	**86.62**	55.81	**73.17**
①	73.38	86.70	80.71	63.99	62.12
②	73.79	85.31	82.27	63.36	64.23
③	74.62	86.09	81.79	65.56	65.07
①+②	76.42	87.18	83.61	65.99	68.91
②+③	75.02	86.94	83.27	65.52	64.35
①+③	76.67	86.37	83.39	67.37	69.05
①+②+③	**78.39**	**88.11**	85.97	**68.95**	70.51

Note: The bold font indicates the optimal values in each column.

Table 7.1 presents the detailed experimental results. SSD and Faster R-CNN represent the test results of the SSD model and the Faster R-CNN model, respectively. ① indicates the use of PredMix data augmentation method alone on YOLOv4, ② indicates the use of CBAM feature attention mechanism alone on YOLOv4, and ③ indicates the use of DetPANet network alone on YOLOv4. ①+②, ②+③, and ①+③ represent the combinations of the two corresponding improvements indicated by the numbers. ①+②+③ represents the underwater object detection algorithm proposed in this paper, which combines data augmentation and improved YOLOv4.

The comparison of detection results before and after the improvement of YOLOv4 is shown in Fig. 7.11. It can be observed that in various scenarios, such as the detection of dense objects and the detection of multi-scale objects, the underwater object detection algorithm combining data augmentation and improved YOLOv4 exhibits better detection accuracy.

The CBAM feature attention mechanism enhances the network model's ability to extract target features, leading to better detection performance in cases where the image is blurred or the target features are similar to the background. In the comparison shown in group (c), due to the similarity between the features of the two sea cucumbers and the rocks, YOLOv4 failed to detect their presence. However, the proposed algorithm is able to detect these two sea cucumbers with high confidence. In group (g), the improved YOLOv4 successfully detects a sea cucumber that is extremely similar to the background, while the pre-improvement YOLOv4 fails to detect it.

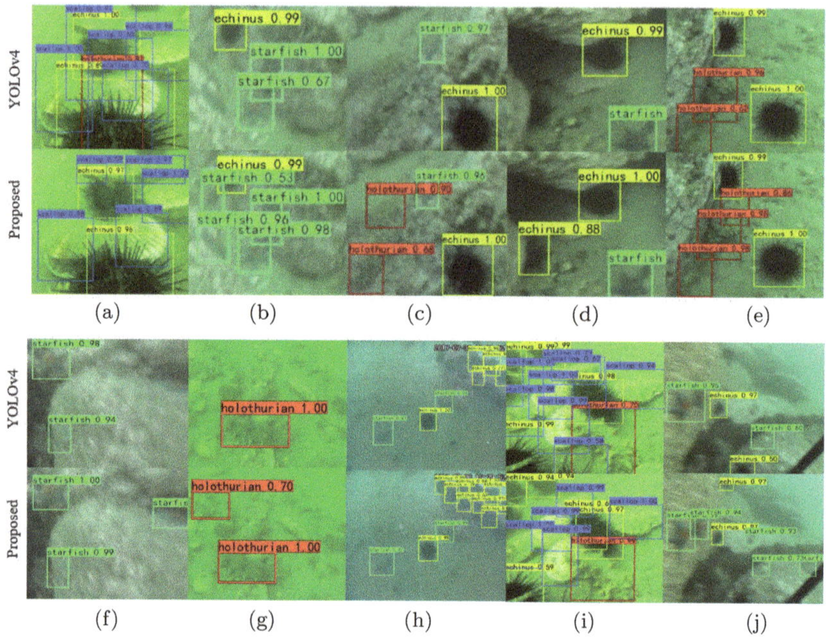

Figure 7.11. Comparison of detection results. (a)–(j) Comparison of target recognition results between YOLOv4 and the improved YOLOv4.

This demonstrates the significant improvement in feature extraction capability of the network model brought about by CBAM.

DetPANet enhances the multi-scale feature fusion capability of the network model through cross-layer and intra-layer skip connections. Due to the thorough fusion of shallow and deep features, the YOLOv4 network model equipped with DetPANet achieves better detection performance for targets of varying sizes and shapes. In the comparison shown in group (b), one sea star is only displayed from the side and is easily overlooked by YOLOv4, while another small-sized sea star is also ignored. However, the proposed algorithm is able to detect the side-facing sea star with high confidence and also detects the small-sized sea star. In group (h), a large number of sea urchins attached to the rocks in the distance are missed by YOLOv4 due to their small size and high density. In contrast, the improved YOLOv4 can accurately distinguish between them. This effective detection capability for targets of different sizes and shapes is also demonstrated in groups (f) and (j).

PredMix can effectively simulate the incomplete display phenomena of underwater organisms, such as overlapping and occlusion, thereby enhancing the robustness of the model and making it more capable of detecting partially displayed objects. In the comparison shown in group (a), YOLOv4 fails to detect the two scallops at the top and also exhibits classification errors and inaccurate localization in the central part of the image. However, the proposed algorithm is able to detect the two scallops at the top and can also accurately distinguish between the dense biological objects in the central part of the image. In group (d), the improved YOLOv4 is able to detect the sea urchin that is partially occluded by rocks with high confidence. This effective detection capability for partially displayed objects is also evident in the comparisons shown in groups (e), (g), and (i).

The above detection results fully demonstrate that the underwater object detection proposed algorithm, which combines data augmentation and improved YOLOv4, can achieve higher detection accuracy in underwater object detection.

This paper also conducted comparative experiments on PredMix data augmentation to demonstrate the necessity of mixing predicted bounding boxes with labeled bounding boxes. The specific experimental results are shown in Table 7.2, where GTMix (GroundTruth Mix) represents the mixing of two labeled bounding boxes from different training images, and RandMix (Random Mix) represents the mixing of random regions and labeled bounding boxes from different training images.

Table 7.3 presents the impact of various improvements on the network's operational performance. Since PredMix is applied to the dataset before the network model, it does not affect the network's operational performance. The improvements with CBAM and DetPANet reduce the detection speed of the network model.

Table 7.2. PredMix comparative experiment.

Algorithm	mAP/%	Sea urchin/%	Sea star/%	Scallop/%	Sea cucumber/%
baseline	71.36	83.40	79.66	61.46	60.93
GTMix	72.30	84.05	79.72	64.02	61.42
RandMix	72.22	84.93	79.71	63.29	60.98
PredMix	**73.38**	**86.70**	**80.71**	**63.99**	**62.12**

Note: The bold font indicates the optimal values in each column.

Table 7.3. Impact of various improvements on network operational performance.

Algorithm	FPS
Baseline	**15.62**
SSD	9.72
Faster R-CNN	3.19
①	/
②	11.60
③	13.37
①+②	/
②+③	10.84
①+③	/
①+②+③	10.84

Note: The bold font indicates the optimal values in each column. "/" indicates FPS less than 1.

Ultimately, the detection speed of the proposed algorithm is 10.42 frames per second (fps). Additionally, this paper also tested the detection speed of the SSD and Faster R-CNN models, both of which are slower than the original YOLOv4 model and the improved YOLOv4 model proposed in this paper.

7.4 Conclusion

This paper proposes an underwater object detection algorithm that combines data augmentation with an improved YOLOv4. The algorithm incorporates the CBAM feature attention mechanism into the CSPDarknet53 backbone feature extraction network of YOLOv4 to enhance the network's feature extraction capabilities. Additionally, intra-layer and cross-layer skip connections are added to the Path Aggregation Network (PANet) to improve the network's multi-scale feature fusion ability. A novel data augmentation method is also proposed to bolster the robustness of the model. Experimental results demonstrate that the underwater object detection algorithm, which combines data augmentation with the improved YOLOv4, effectively improves the detection accuracy for underwater objects.

References

[1] Yu WD, Liao HC, Hsiao WT, *et al.* Automatic Safety Monitoring of Construction Hazard Working Zone: A Semantic Segmentation based Deep Learning Approach. *Proceedings of the 2020 the 7th International Conference on Automation and Logistics (ICAL)*. 2020: 54–59.

[2] Huval B, Wang T, Tandon S, *et al.* An empirical evaluation of deep learning on highway driving. arXiv preprint arXiv:1504.01716, 2015.

[3] Zhao Y, Ma J, Li X, *et al.* Saliency detection and deep learning-based wildfire identification in UAV imagery. *Sensors*, 2018, 18(3): 712.

[4] Wang T, Chen Y, Qiao M, *et al.* A fast and robust convolutional neural network-based defect detection model in product quality control. *International Journal of Advanced Manufacturing Technology*, 2017, 94(9–12), 3465–3471.

[5] Yin XT, Dan YF. Photovoltaic cell internal defect detection based on improved Faster R-CNN. *Journal of Electronic Measurement and Instrumentation*, 2021, 35(01): 40–47.

[6] Li X, Liu Y, Zhao Z, *et al.* A deep learning approach of vehicle multi-target detection from traffic video. *Journal of Advanced Transportation*, 2018, 7075814.

[7] Gao SH, Tan YQ, Cheng MM, *et al.* Highly efficient salient object detection with 100k parameters. *European Conference on Computer Vision*. Springer, Cham, 2020: 702–721.

[8] Lin S, Zhao Y. Review on key technologies of target exploration in underwater optical images. *Laser & Optoelectronics Progress*, 2020, 57(6): 060002.

[9] Wang SH, Zhao JW, Chen YQ. Robust tracking of fish schools using CNN for head identification. *Multimedia Tools and Applications*, 2017, 76(22): 23679–23697.

[10] Shorten C, Khoshgoftaar TM. A survey on image data augmentation for deep learning. *Journal of Big Data*, 2019, 6(1): 1–48.

[11] Girshick R, Donahue J, Darrell T, *et al.* Rich feature hierarchies for accurate object detection and semantic segmentation. *Proceedings of the IEEE Conference on Computer Vision and Pattern Recognition*. 2014: 580–587.

[12] Girshick R. Fast r-cnn. *Proceedings of the IEEE International Conference on Computer Vision*. 2015: 1440–1448.

[13] Ren S, He K, Girshick R, *et al.* Faster r-cnn: Towards real-time object detection with region proposal networks. arXiv preprint arXiv:1506.01497, 2015.

[14] Redmon J, Divvala S, Girshick R, *et al.* You only look once: Unified, real-time object detection. *Proceedings of the IEEE Conference on Computer Vision and Pattern Recognition.* 2016: 779–788.

[15] Redmon J, Farhadi A. YOLO9000: Better, faster, stronger. *Proceedings of the IEEE Conference on Computer Vision and Pattern Recognition.* 2017: 7263–7271.

[16] Redmon J, Farhadi A. Yolov3: An incremental improvement. arXiv preprint arXiv:1804.02767, 2018.

[17] Bochkovskiy A, Wang CY, Liao HYM. Yolov4: Optimal speed and accuracy of object detection. arXiv preprint arXiv:2004.10934, 2020.

[18] Cubuk ED, Zoph B, Mane D, *et al.* Autoaugment: Learning augmentation strategies from data. *Proceedings of the IEEE/CVF Conference on Computer Vision and Pattern Recognition.* 2019: 113–123.

[19] Cubuk ED, Zoph B, Shlens J, *et al.* Randaugment: Practical automated data augmentation with a reduced search space. *Proceedings of the IEEE/CVF Conference on Computer Vision and Pattern Recognition Workshops.* 2020: 702–703.

[20] DeVries T, Taylor GW. Improved regularization of convolutional neural networks with cutout. arXiv preprint arXiv:1708.04552, 2017.

[21] Singh KK, Lee YJ. Hide-and-seek: Forcing a network to be meticulous for weakly-supervised object and action localization. *2017 IEEE International Conference on Computer Vision (ICCV).* IEEE, New York, 2017: 3544–3553.

[22] Zhang H, Cisse M, Dauphin YN, *et al.* mixup: Beyond empirical risk minimization. arXiv preprint arXiv:1710.09412, 2017.

[23] Lin WH, Zhong JX, Liu S, *et al.* RoIMix: proposal-fusion among multiple images for underwater object detection. *ICASSP 2020-2020 IEEE International Conference on Acoustics, Speech and Signal Processing (ICASSP).* IEEE, New York, 2020: 2588–2592.

[24] Woo S, Park J, Lee JY, *et al.* Cbam: Convolutional block attention module. *Proceedings of the European Conference on Computer Vision (ECCV).* 2018: 3–19.

Chapter 8

RetinaNet-Based Algorithm for Image Dense Target Detection

8.1 Introduction

Remote sensing imagery frequently captures densely distributed critical objects such as aircraft and maritime vessels, whose precise identification holds significant military and civilian applications. As illustrated in Fig. 8.1, the characteristic tight spatial arrangement of these targets often results in ambiguous inter-object boundaries. Such boundary uncertainty may lead to detection errors including false positives and target omissions, ultimately compromising detection accuracy. To address this challenge, this chapter specifically investigates detection methodologies for various categories of densely packed targets in remote sensing images, aiming to enhance recognition precision for such clustered objects.

As evidenced by the preceding chapter's analysis, three principal components critically influence target detection performance: detector architecture, feature extraction backbone networks, and feature fusion mechanisms. Currently, the field maintains two dominant detector paradigms: the two-stage architecture exemplified by Faster R-CNN and the single-stage approach represented by YOLO variants and RetinaNet. Subsequent innovations predominantly adhere to these established frameworks. Regarding feature extraction, networks such as ResNet and DenseNet continue to prevail as industry standards. The advent of Feature Pyramid Networks

Figure 8.1. Target dense arrangement scenario.

(FPN) has solidified feature pyramid-based fusion as a cornerstone technique in contemporary detection systems, with numerous studies demonstrating its efficacy in enhancing algorithmic performance. While these structural elements have become relatively standardized, extant methodologies still inadequately address boundary ambiguity induced by target-dense configurations—a persistent issue that notably compromises detection accuracy in cluttered environments.

To address these challenges while balancing detection accuracy with computational efficiency, this study selects RetinaNet—a representative single-stage detector—as the foundational framework, introducing structural modifications specifically optimized for dense target recognition in remote sensing imagery. The proposed enhancements comprise two strategic components: First, a Multidimensional Attention (MDA) module integrating coordinated spatial and channel attention submodules is incorporated into the feature extraction pipeline to mitigate interference from inter-target noise in clustered configurations. Subsequently, the conventional Non-Maximum Suppression (NMS) algorithm [1] is replaced with its softened counterpart (Soft-NMS) [2], effectively preserving overlapping detection boxes characteristic of densely packed targets. The subsequent sections provide comprehensive technical specifications of both the baseline RetinaNet architecture and the proposed improvement modules.

8.2 Remote Sensing Image Target Detection Algorithm Based on Multidimensional Attention Module

8.2.1 *Algorithm body framework*

The overall network block diagram of the remote sensing image target detection algorithm based on multidimensional attention module proposed in this chapter is shown in Fig. 8.2.

As illustrated in the schematic diagram, the proposed framework adopts the RetinaNet architecture as its computational backbone. The hierarchical feature maps (denoted C2, C3, C4) generated by the deep convolutional backbone network undergo multiscale fusion through a FPN, producing enhanced pyramidal features (P2, P3, P4). The algorithmic workflow comprises four sequential phases: (1) Multiscale feature extraction via the backbone network; (2) Cross-scale feature integration using FPN; (3) Boundary noise suppression through a MDA module to amplify discriminative target signatures; (4) Final target classification and coordinate regression. A technical overview of the baseline RetinaNet architecture precedes the detailed exposition of the proposed enhancements.

Introduced by Lin *et al.* (2018), RetinaNet represents a seminal advancement in single-stage detection methodology. Prior to its development, two-stage detectors dominated the field due to their inherent mitigation of class imbalance through hierarchical

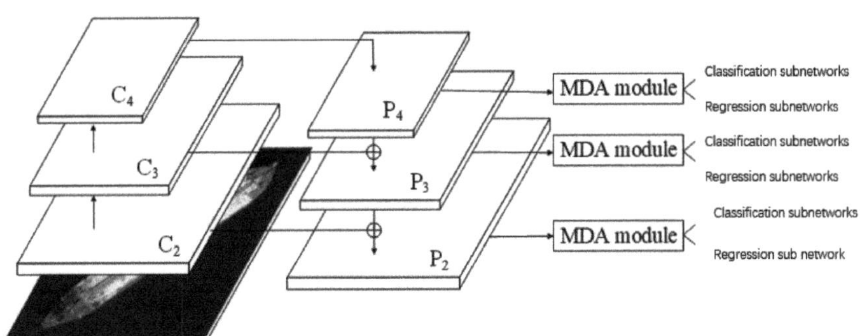

Figure 8.2. Block diagram of the overall network of algorithms in this chapter.

sample selection: Region Proposal Networks (RPN) initially filter background regions, followed by Online Hard Example Mining (OHEM) [3] for foreground-background equilibrium in the second stage. In contrast, single-stage detectors suffered severe performance degradation from extreme foreground-background ratio disparities (often exceeding 1:1000). RetinaNet's principal innovation lies in its focal loss function, which dynamically adjusts cross-entropy weights to counteract this imbalance, ultimately achieving superior accuracy over contemporary two-stage counterparts.

Figure 8.3 schematizes the detector's streamlined architecture comprising three core components: (1) A backbone network (typically ResNet-50/101) for hierarchical feature extraction (C3-C5 layers); (2) A Feature Pyramid Network (FPN) constructing multi-scale representations (P3-P7) through top-down and lateral connections; (3) Twin task-specific fully convolutional networks (FCNs) [4] for parallel classification and bounding box regression.

The FPN generates pyramidal features with progressive downsampling (P3: 1/8 to P7: 1/128 of input resolution), each level optimized for specific target scales. Anchor generation employs a combinatorial strategy: three base areas $\{32^2, 64^2, 128^2\}$ multiplied by aspect ratios $\{1{:}2, 1{:}1, 2{:}1\}$ yield nine anchors per spatial position. This configuration achieves dense spatial coverage with 36–81 anchors per pixel across pyramid levels.

The classification subnet architecture features four sequential 3×3 convolutional blocks (each with 256 channels, ReLU activation), culminating in $K \cdot A$ filters for class predictions (K: classes, A: anchors). Notably, the focal loss operates on these outputs to penalize easily classified negatives. Parallel to this, the regression subnet employs

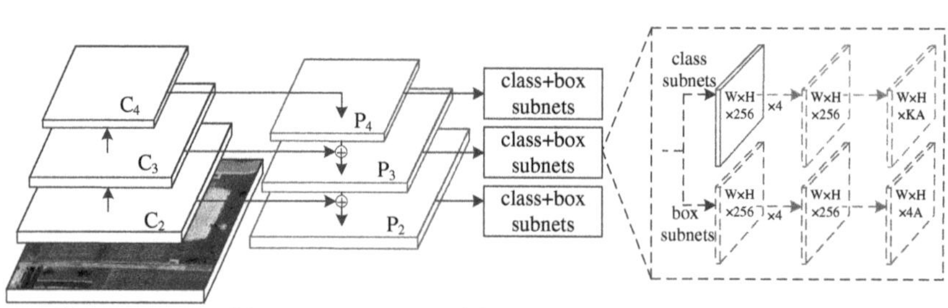

(a) ResNet (b) Feature pyramid net (c) Class subnet (top) (d) Box subnet (bottom)

Figure 8.3. Schematic diagram of RetinaNet detector structure.

identical topology (four 3 × 3 conv layers) but with 4 · A output filters for coordinate offsets (center_x, center_y, width, height). Crucially, parameter sharing occurs only within pyramid levels, preserving scale-specific discriminability.

To evaluate the performance of the RetinaNet detector, Lin *et al.* conducted experiments on the COCO dataset [5], a widely used benchmark for generic object detection. The results demonstrated that RetinaNet achieved higher detection accuracy compared to methods such as Faster R-CNN. Generally, two-stage detectors are more commonly employed in scenarios with sparse target alignment. In contrast, single-stage detectors are preferable in scenarios with dense target alignment due to their faster detection speed and more streamlined structure. Therefore, this chapter adopts the single-stage RetinaNet detector as the foundation and proposes improvements to address the challenging issue of dense target arrangement in remote sensing imagery.

8.2.2 *Multidimensional attention module*

So far, target detection, as a crucial component of computer vision, has achieved significant progress. However, some existing target detection algorithms still struggle with densely arranged scenes, a problem that is particularly pronounced in remote sensing images with dense target arrangements. This is because densely arranged target images are often more complex, and the extracted candidate frames tend to contain more noise information. As noise accumulates, it can overwhelm the target information, blurring the boundaries between targets. This, in turn, leads to incorrect target detection and omission, ultimately reducing detection accuracy.

To address this issue, many algorithms have incorporated attention mechanisms [6, 7] to highlight target information and reduce noise interference. For instance, Hu *et al.* [8] employed an attention module to model the relationships between targets, proposing a target relationship model. In another example, Hu *et al.* [9] learned feature weights based on network losses, specifically by increasing the weights of feature maps with significant effects and decreasing those with less noticeable effects. This approach is essentially an attention mechanism. However, these attention mechanisms are unsupervised and cannot be tailored to specific targets.

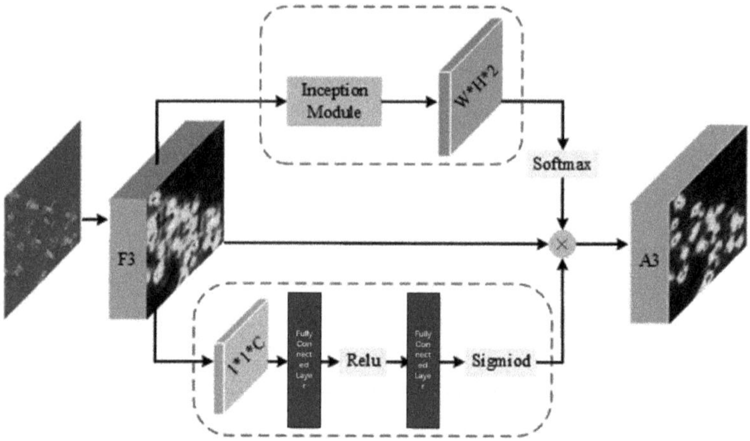

Figure 8.4. Diagram of the structure of the multidimensional attention module.

To overcome this limitation, this chapter introduces a supervised multidimensional attention module into the network. This module is designed to suppress noise and emphasize target features. It consists of two sub-modules: a spatial attention sub-module and a channel attention sub-module. The goal is to address the issue of dense target arrangements in certain remote sensing scenes and thereby improve detection accuracy. The structure of this multidimensional attention module is schematically illustrated in Fig. 8.4.

In the spatial attention sub-module, the feature map **F3** (obtained from the original image after three down-sampling operations with a sampling factor of 8) first passes through the Inception module to perform feature extraction at different scales, as shown in Fig. 8.5. After feature extraction, a convolution operation with 2 channels is applied to produce a two-channel saliency map, representing the confidence levels of the foreground and background, respectively. This two-channel saliency map is then binarized to obtain a binary image containing the target region. The binary image is subsequently normalized using the Softmax function. It is worth noting that after normalization by the Softmax function, the values of the saliency map are constrained to the range $[0, 1]$, with regions of high saliency assigned a value of 1 and regions of low saliency assigned a value of 0. This process effectively reduces noise information while enhancing target information.

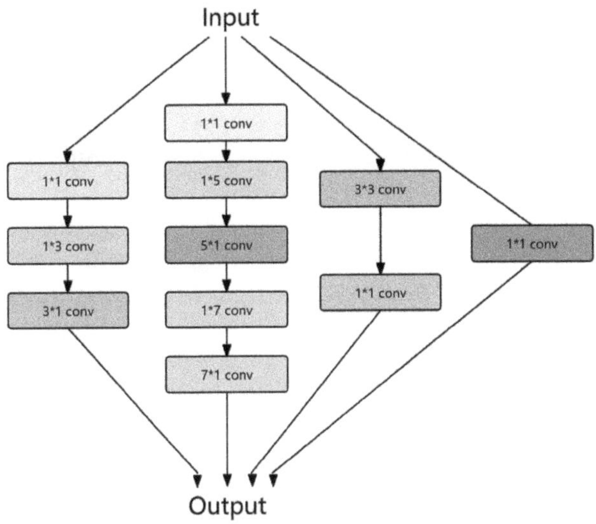

Figure 8.5. Schematic diagram of inception module structure.

In the channel attention sub-module, global average pooling is first applied to obtain the numerical distribution of the **C** feature channels. A fully convolutional neural network (FCN) is then used to reduce the feature dimensionality to $1/r$ of the input. Another FCN, following the ReLU activation function, restores the feature dimensionality to its original size. Finally, the values are normalized using the sigmoid function.

The outputs of the spatial attention sub-module, the channel attention sub-module, and the feature map **F3** are multiplied together to obtain the feature map **A3** via the multidimensional attention module. Comparing **F3** and **A3**, it is evident that the multidimensional attention module significantly reduces the noise information between targets and clarifies the boundaries between them. This enhancement is beneficial for subsequent classification and regression tasks.

8.2.3 *Weak non-maximal value suppression algorithm*

The non-maximal suppression (NMS) algorithm is commonly used to identify the maximum value within a local neighborhood. In target detection algorithms, candidate regions are first generated in the image. Then, a classification network determines the category and confidence level (i.e., the probability that the target category is correctly predicted) of the targets within these regions, while a regression network refines the detection regions for greater accuracy. As the image passes through the classification network, multiple detection frames and their corresponding confidence levels are produced. However, each target should be represented by only one detection frame. Therefore, the non-maximal suppression algorithm is employed to eliminate redundant or low-confidence detection frames. The detection frame rejection strategy in the non-maximal suppression algorithm is shown in Eq. (8.1):

$$S_i' = \begin{cases} S_i, & IoU(B, b_i) < N_t \\ 0, & IoU(B, b_i) \geq N_t \end{cases} \tag{8.1}$$

where i is the serial number of each detection frame, S_i is the initial confidence of the output of the classification network, N_t is the set threshold, S_i' is the confidence after NMS processing, and the intersection and concatenation ratio, $IoU(B, b_i)$, between the detection frame with the largest confidence, B, and the individual detection frames, b, is shown in Eq. (8.2):

$$IoU(B, b_i) = \frac{B \cap b_i}{B \cup b_i} \tag{8.2}$$

The following is an example to explain the flow of the non-maximal value suppression algorithm in detail, as shown in Fig. 8.6:

(1) Assume that six vehicle detection frames have been obtained in the figure, namely, A, B, C, D, E, and F, with increasing confidence in order.
(2) Take the detection frame F with the highest confidence level as the reference frame, and judge whether the overlap between the five detection frames A, B, C, D and E and the detection frame F is greater than the set threshold value, respectively. If it is greater than the threshold, it is rejected; conversely, it is retained.
(3) Assuming that the overlap portion of the two detection frames B and D with the F detection frame is greater than the threshold, they are rejected. And the overlapping part of the three detection frames A, C, and E with the F detection frame is smaller than the threshold value, then it is retained. Meanwhile, the F detection

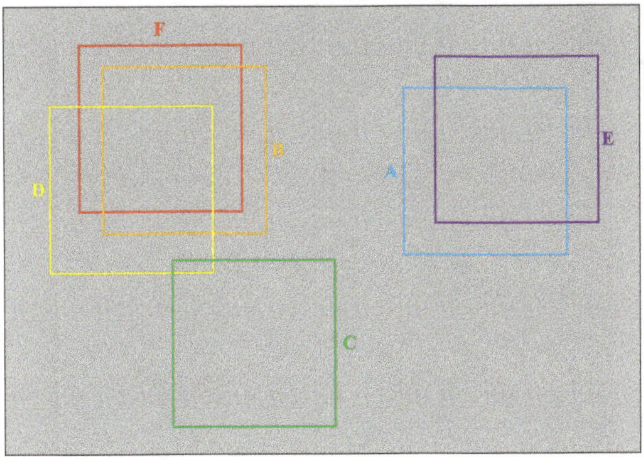

Figure 8.6. Schematic diagram of the non-maximal value suppression algorithm.

frame is marked and recognized as one of the final detection frames.

(4) The E detection frame with the highest confidence level is selected from the remaining three detection frames A, C, and E. Then the overlap portion between the two detection frames A and C and the E detection frame is judged separately, and the A detection frame is finally rejected, and the E detection frame is marked, and the detection frame is recognized as one of the final detection frames.
(5) In this way, the three detection frames C, E and F are retained as the final vehicle detection frames.

The standard NMS algorithm performs well in many generalized target detection tasks. However, some remote sensing images contain a large number of densely arranged targets, such as airplanes and ships. The spacing between these targets is often small, and in some cases, there is even mutual occlusion between them. In such scenarios, the standard NMS algorithm may reject closely spaced correct detection frames, leading to target misses, as illustrated in Fig. 8.7.

In Fig. 8.7, the two ships are classified into two detection frames by the classification network, with confidence levels of 0.94 and 0.81, respectively. According to the principle of the NMS algorithm, if

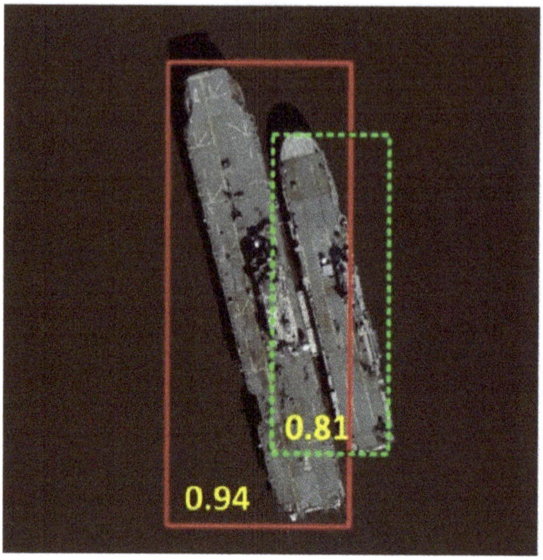

Figure 8.7. Schematic diagram of the problems with the non-great value suppression algorithm.

the overlap between the two detection frames reaches the predefined threshold, only the frame with the higher confidence level (the red detection frame) is retained, while the frame with the lower confidence level (the green detection frame) is discarded. As a result, larger ships are correctly detected, while smaller ships are missed.

In summary, the primary drawback of the NMS algorithm is that it indiscriminately rejects all detection frames with IoU values exceeding the threshold. To address this issue, this chapter proposes the use of the Soft-NMS algorithm, which employs a more nuanced detection frame rejection strategy, as shown in Eq. (8.3):

$$S_i' = \begin{cases} S_i, & IoU(B, b_i) < N_t \\ S_i(1 - IoU(B, b_i)), & IoU(B, b_i) \geq N_t \end{cases} \tag{8.3}$$

where i is the individual detection frame serial number, S_i is the initial confidence of the output of the classification network, N_t is the set threshold, S_i' is the confidence after being processed by the weakened non-maximal value suppression algorithm, and the intersection and concatenation ratio, $IoU(B, b_i)$, between the detection frame with the largest confidence, B, and the individual detection frames, b_i,

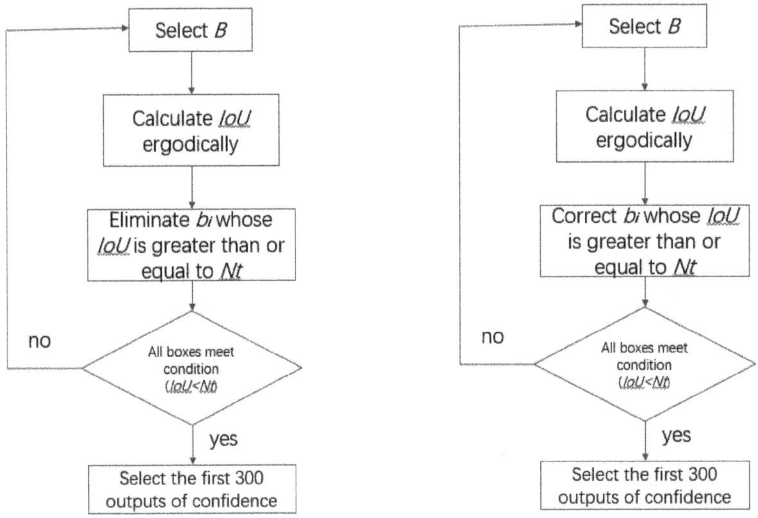

(a) Flowchart of NMS algorithm (b) Flowchart of Soft-NMS algorithm

Figure 8.8. Flow comparison of NMS and Soft-NMS.

is shown in Eq. (8.2). From Eq. (8.3), it can be seen that in the weakened non-maximal value suppression algorithm, when encountering an IoU value greater than the threshold, instead of rejecting the detection frames directly, the confidence of such detection frames is weakened and they continue to be involved in the ranking of the confidence in the subsequent process. The flow comparison diagram between the non-maximal value suppression algorithm and the weakened non-maximal value suppression algorithm is shown in Fig. 8.8. The experimental results show that the use of the weakened non-maximal value suppression algorithm can to some extent solve the problem of leakage detection in the dense scene of target arrangement in remote sensing images, thus improving the detection accuracy of targets.

8.2.4 *Loss function*

The loss function of the proposed algorithm in this chapter consists of three components: the bounding box regression loss, the loss of the multidimensional attention module, and the categorization loss.

The loss function is formulated as shown in Eq. (8.4).

$$L = \frac{\lambda_1}{N}\sum_{n=1}^{N} t'_n \sum_{j\in\{x,y,w,h\}} L_{\text{reg}}(v'_{nj}, v_{nj}) + \frac{\lambda_2}{h\times w}\sum_{i}^{h}\sum_{j}^{w} L_{\text{att}}(u'_{ij}, u_{ij})$$
$$+ \frac{\lambda_3}{N}\sum_{n=1}^{N} L_{\text{cls}}(p_n, t_n) \qquad (8.4)$$

where the regression loss of the bounding box is $\frac{\lambda_1}{N}\sum_{n=1}^{N} t'_n \sum_{j\in\{x,y,w,h\}} L_{\text{reg}}(v'_{nj}, v_{nj})$. $\lambda 1$ represents the weight coefficient; N represents the number of candidate frames; $t'n$ is a binary number, when $t'n = 0$, it represents that the candidate frames are the background, and when $t'n = 1$, it represents that the candidate frames are the foreground; x, y, w, h represent the center coordinates of the candidate frames, respectively, width and height; L_{reg} (v' nj, v_{nj}) represents the smooth $L1$ function, while $v' * j$ represents the vector of the prediction frame and $v * j$ represents the vector of the truth frame.

The multidimensional attention module loss is $\frac{\lambda_2}{h\times w}\sum_{i}^{h}\sum_{j}^{w}$ $L_{\text{att}}(u'_{ij}, u_{ij})$. λ_2 represents the weight coefficients; h and w represent the height and width of the truth frame; L_{att} (u'_{ij}, u_{ij}) represents the Softmax function while u'_{ij} represents the predicted value at pixel point (i, j) and u_{ij} represents the true value at pixel point (i, j).

The classification loss of the category is $\frac{\lambda_3}{N}\sum_{n=1}^{N} L_{\text{cls}}(p_n, t_n)$. λ_3 represents the weight coefficient; N represents the number of candidate frames; $L_{\text{cls}}(p_n, t_n)$ represents the Softmax function, whereas p_n represents the probability distribution obtained by using the Softmax function, and t_n represents the probability distribution of the true value frames.

8.3 Experimentation and Analysis Faster-RCNN

8.3.1 *Experimental environment and data sets*

The experimental environment for this chapter is shown in Table 8.1.

The datasets used in this chapter are the DOTA dataset [10, 11] and the HRSC2016 dataset [12]. The DOTA dataset was released

Table 8.1. Experimental environment.

Sports event	Set up
Operating system	Ubuntu16.04
CPU	Intel Xeon E5-2680, 3.3 GHz
RAM	128 GB
GPU	Nvidia TITAN V, 11 GB
GPU Corresponding Driver	Nvidia Driver 435.21, CUDA10.0
Programming language	Python3.5
Deep Learning Framework	TensorFlow1.13.1

by Wuhan University Mapping and Remote Sensing Laboratory in 2017, and it contains a total of 2,806 remote sensing images, of which 1/2 of the images are used as the training set, 1/6 of the images are used as the validation set, and the remaining 1/3 is used as the test set. The DOTA dataset contains a total of ground feature 1882 target instances, covering airplane (PL), ship (SH), storage tank (ST), baseball field (BD), tennis court (TC), basketball court (BC), surface runway (GTF), harbor (HA), bridge (BR), small vehicle (SV), large vehicle (LV), roundabout intersection (RA), swimming pool (SP), helicopter (HC), soccer field (SBF), and 15 other types of feature targets. Among these 15 types of feature targets, the first 10 types of feature targets are common targets in many datasets, and the last 5 types of feature targets are very important targets in practical applications. Figure 8.9 show the comparison of the number of each type of feature target between the NWPU VHR-10 dataset and the DOTA dataset.

As can be seen in Fig. 8.9, the DOTA dataset is much more than the NWPU VHR-10 dataset in terms of the number of categories and the number of instances in each category, which also reflects the difficulty of target detection on the DOTA dataset.

In order to make the dataset more suitable for the topic studied in this chapter, five types of feature targets that are densely arranged in the DOTA dataset are selected in this chapter, including: airplane (PL), ship (SH), oil storage tank (ST), small vehicle (SV), and large vehicle (LV). The labels and images of these five types of feature targets are then extracted from the DOTA dataset in order to form the dataset used in this chapter, which is named the small-DOTA dataset for ease of representation. Table 8.2 counts the number of images, the

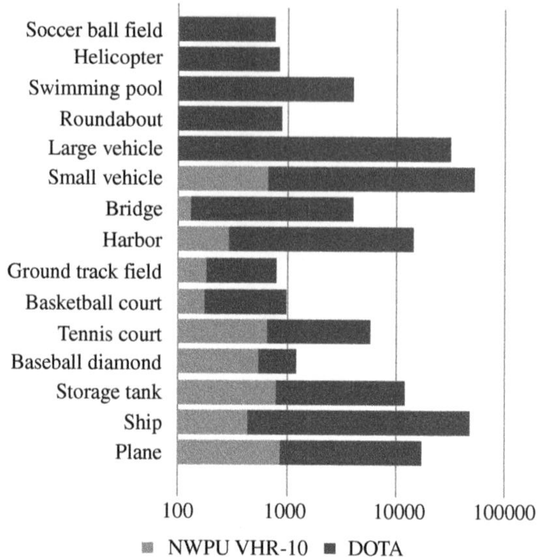

Figure 8.9. Comparison between NWPU VHR-10 dataset and DOTA dataset.

Table 8.2. Target statistics in the small-DOTA dataset.

Form	Number of images	Number of detection frames	Average number of detection frames per image	Inspection frame area as a percentage
PL	197	8055	40.89	0.0415
SH	326	28068	86.10	0.0201
ST	161	5029	31.24	0.0067
SV	486	26126	53.76	0.0128
LV	380	16969	31.24	0.0067

number of detection frames, the average number of detection frames per image and the percentage of detection frame area for each type of target in the small-DOTA dataset. As can be seen from the table, the minimum value of the average number of detection frames per image in the small-DOTA dataset is 31.24, from which the dataset is characterized by a dense arrangement of targets, which also indicates that the dataset used in this chapter is representative.

Table 8.3. HRSC2016 data set quantity information.

	Sea surface imagery	Sea-going ship	Inshore imagery	Nearshore sample	Imagery	Boats
Training set	41	55	576	1693	617	1748
Test set	29	35	415	1193	453	1228
Total	70	90	991	2886	1070	2976

The HRSC2016 dataset was released by Northwestern Polytechnical University, which has only one type of feature target, ship (SH). This dataset is the most well labeled ship detection dataset publicly available, containing 1070 remote sensing images with 2976 instances. The images in this dataset are mainly collected from Google Earth, the spatial resolution of the images ranges from 0.4 m to 2 m, the size of the images ranges from 300×300 to 1500×900, and the locations included in the images are mainly the six most famous ports in the world. The feature targets in the original HRSC2016 dataset are labeled with rotated frames, whereas they are converted to horizontal frames in this chapter. Meanwhile, the HRSC2016 dataset has been divided into training and test sets, and Table 8.3 counts the information about the number of training and test sets in the HRSC2016 dataset.

8.3.2 *Experimental parameters and evaluation indicators*

Table 8.4 lists the important experimental parameters in the algorithm of this chapter. Among them, the batch size (Batch Size) is 1, i.e., 1 image per training; the total number of training rounds (Epoch) is 20; the momentum (Momentum) is 0.9; the initial learning rate (Learning Rate) is $3e-4$; the learning rate decay rate (Learning Rate Decay Rate) is 10, i.e., the learning rate Decay rate (Learning Rate Decay Rate) is 10, i.e., the learning rate will be decayed by 10 times after every 8 rounds of training. Therefore, the learning rate becomes $3e-5$ at 8epoch and $3e-6$ at 16epoch; the three weight coefficients $\lambda 1$, $\lambda 2$, and $\lambda 3$ in the loss function are 4, 1, and 2, respectively.

Table 8.4. Experimental parameters.

Parameters	Worth
Batch Size	1
Epoch	20
Momentum	0.9
Learning Rate	3e − 4
Learning Rate Decay Rate	10
Learning Rate Decay Step	8
$\lambda 1$, $\lambda 2$, $\lambda 3$	4,1,2

The experiments in this chapter use common evaluation metrics for target detection to evaluate the performance of the algorithms in this chapter, including single-class average accuracy AP, multi-class average accuracy mAP, and the check-accuracy-check-fullness curve, i.e., P–R curve. In addition, the F1-score metrics are also used to further evaluate the performance of the algorithms in this chapter. The Precision–Recall (P–R) curve illustrates the trade-off between Precision and Recall — as Precision increases, Recall tends to decrease, and vice versa. The F1-score, defined as the harmonic mean of Precision and Recall, captures this trade-off in a single metric. Generally speaking, when the Precision, Recall and F1-score of the target detection model are all larger, it means that the model's detection performance is better. Larger Precision means that the correct rate of detected samples is higher; larger Recall means that more positive samples are detected; larger F1-score means that the model is able to find more positive samples as well as the correct rate of detected samples. The expression of F1-score is shown in Eq. (8.5).

$$\text{F1-score} = 2 * \frac{\text{Precision} * \text{Recall}}{\text{Precision} + \text{Recall}} \tag{8.5}$$

8.3.3 *Experimental procedures and analysis of results*

In order to verify the effectiveness of the proposed algorithms, this chapter first conducts an ablation experiment between each improvement module on the small-DOTA dataset as well as the HRSC2016 dataset, the main purpose of this experiment is to prove whether the proposed improvement modules based on the RetinaNet algorithm in this chapter can improve the target detection accuracy of remote sensing images. Then the algorithms in this chapter are compared with six algorithms on the small-DOTA dataset as well as the HRSC2016 dataset, and the comparison algorithms include SSD [13], YOLOv2 [14], R-FCN [15], Faster R-CNN [16], RetinaNet [17], and ICN [18], and the main purpose of this experiment is to verify whether the proposed algorithm has a higher target detection accuracy for remote sensing images compared to the comparison algorithms.

Tables 8.5 and 8.6 show the results of the ablation experiments between the multidimensional attention module (MDA module) and the improved modules such as the weakened non-maximal suppression algorithm (Soft-NMS).

As can be seen in Table 8.5, after adding the multidimensional attention module MDA module with the weakened non-maximal suppression algorithm Soft-NMS, the proposed algorithm improves the multi-class average accuracy mAP on the small-DOTA dataset by 5.01% and 0.54%, respectively, and the multi-class average accuracy mAP on the HRSC2016 dataset by 2.97% and 5.37%, respectively. This result proves that all the proposed improvement modules can help to improve the target detection accuracy of remote sensing images.

As can be seen in Table 8.6, after adding the multidimensional attention module MDA module with the weakened non-maximal suppression algorithm Soft-NMS, the proposed algorithm improves the accuracy Precision on the small-DOTA dataset by 0.99% and 3.09%, the recall Recall by 5.02% and 0.66%, and the F1-score improved by 2.56% and 2.20%, respectively, while on the HRSC2016 dataset the accuracy Precision improved by 2.14% and −1.46%, the recall Recall improved by 1.75% and 8.41%, and the F1-score improved by 1.92% and 4.57%, respectively. This result indicates that the algorithm in this chapter is able to detect feature targets more accurately and comprehensively compared to the original algorithm.

Figure 8.10 show the single-class average accuracy AP and P–R curves of the base algorithm RetinaNet and the algorithm in this chapter on the small-DOTA dataset and the HRSC2016 dataset.

Table 8.5. AP and mAP results of ablation experiments between modules.

MDA module	Soft-NMS	small-DOTA	HRSC 2016	PL	SH	ST	SV	LV	mAP
×	×	√	×	89.21	76.17	83.75	77.33	64.76	78.24
√	×	√	×	88.76	87.08	84.75	77.81	77.84	83.25
√	√	√	×	89.12	87.35	85.15	78.10	79.22	83.79
×	×	×	√	—	81.62	—	—	—	81.62
√	×	×	√	—	84.59	—	—	—	84.59
√	√	×	√	—	89.96	—	—	—	89.96

Note: Values in the table are in %.

Table 8.6. Precision, Recall, and F1-score results of inter-module ablation experiments.

MDA module	Soft-NMS	small-DOTA	HRSC2016	Precision (%)	Recall (%)	F1-score (%)
×	×	√	×	60.58	75.60	67.26
√	×	√	×	61.57	80.62	69.82
√	√	√	×	64.66	81.28	72.02
×	×	×	√	82.49	61.85	70.70
√	×	×	√	84.63	63.60	72.62
√	√	×	√	83.17	72.01	77.19

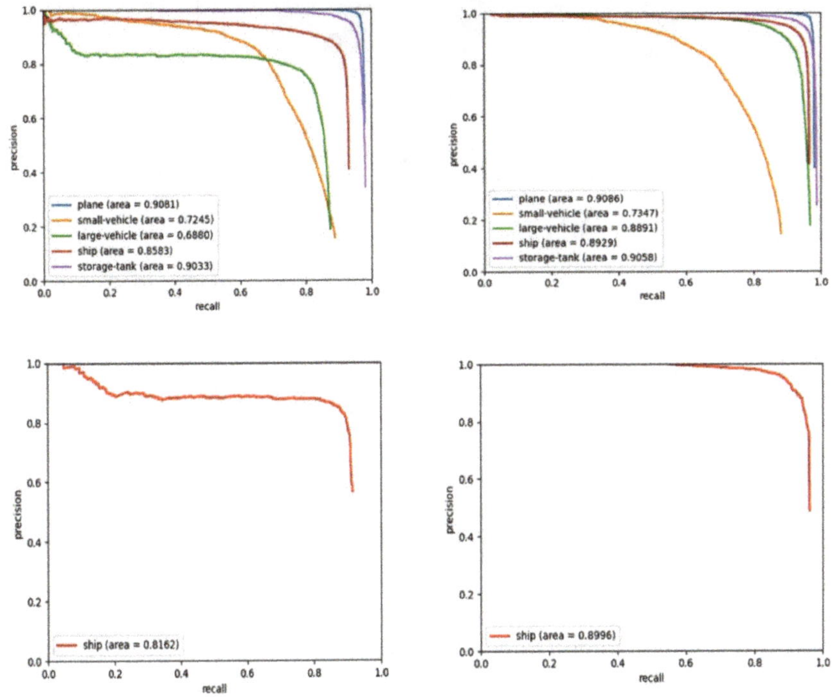

Figure 8.10. Comparison of P–R curves. (a) P–R curve of RetinaNet algorithm on small-DOTA dataset. (b) P–R curves of Proposed algorithms in this chapter on the small-DOTA dataset. (c) P–R curve of RetinaNet algorithm on HRSC2016 dataset. (d) P–R curves of Proposed algorithms in this chapter on the HRSC2016 dataset.

It can be clearly seen from the P–R curves for each category in the figure that the algorithm in this chapter has a more substantial improvement in the AP value compared to the original algorithm. At the same time, the total area of the P–R curves corresponding to the algorithm in this chapter, i.e., the multi-class average accuracy mAP, is also significantly larger than that of the original algorithm. These findings further illustrate that the algorithm in this chapter is able to solve the difficult problem of densely arranged targets in remote sensing images in order to improve the detection accuracy of densely arranged targets. Meanwhile, the improved detectability of this chapter's algorithm on both the small-DOTA dataset and the

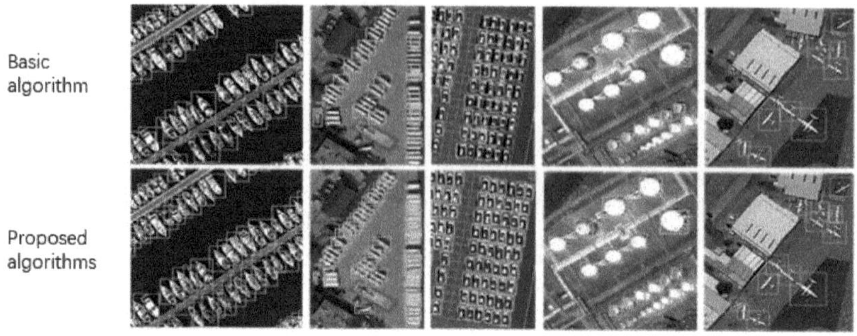

Figure 8.11. Comparison of target detection effect before and after algorithm improvement.

HRSC2016 dataset also indicates that the algorithm in this chapter has good generalization performance.

In order to visualize the improved performance of the algorithm in the effect graphs, Fig. 8.11 show the detection effect of the algorithm before and after the algorithm improvement on the five types of feature targets in the small-DOTA dataset.

As can be seen in Fig. 8.11, the base algorithm RetinaNet often misses detection when detecting densely arranged targets. For example, in the first comparison chart in Fig. 8.11, the base algorithm detects two ships as one ship, in the second comparison chart two large vehicles as one large vehicle, in the third comparison chart many small vehicles are missed, in the fourth comparison chart many oil storage tanks are missed, and in the fifth comparison chart there are airplanes that are missed. This phenomenon indicates that the base algorithm often misses detection when detecting densely arranged targets, which reduces the target detection accuracy. The main reason for this situation is that when the targets are arranged too densely, the problem of interference between neighboring targets will occur, which makes the boundary information between the targets become blurred. In addition, due to the use of the standard non-maximum suppression algorithm in the base algorithm, this will result in the elimination of targets with lower confidence in the densely arranged targets. In comparison, the detection effect of this chapter's algorithm in Fig. 8.11 is much better than that of the basic algorithm because firstly, the algorithm in this chapter uses the multidimensional attention module to make the boundary information between the targets clear, and secondly, it adopts the weakened non-extremely large value suppression algorithm to overcome the drawbacks of the standard non-extremely large value suppression algorithm, which solves the problem of the omission of the densely-arranged targets, and enhances the accuracy of the target detection.

The above ablation experiment results show that the algorithm in this chapter can solve the difficult problem of dense target arrangement in remote sensing images to a certain extent, so as to improve the detection accuracy of dense targets.

The following is a comparison experiment between the algorithms in this chapter and the remaining six classical target detection algorithms, which is mainly used to compare the detection performance of the algorithms in this chapter with many target detection algorithms. The single-class average accuracy AP as well as the multi-class average accuracy mAP of each algorithm on the small-DOTA dataset are shown in Table 8.7, and the single-class average accuracy AP as well as the multi-class average accuracy mAP on the HRSC2016 dataset are shown in Table 8.8. From the table, it can be seen that since SSD and YOLOv2 belong to the early single-stage target detection algorithms, these two algorithms are not good for remote sensing image target detection, and the mAP on the small-DOTA dataset is only 17.25% versus 46.79%, while the mAP on the HRSC2016 dataset is only 28.11% versus 54.56%. the R-FCN algorithm is an algorithm that applies R-CNN to FCN, and the target detection performance of this algorithm for remote sensing images is slightly better than the previous two algorithms. The Faster R-CNN algorithm is the classic two-stage target detection algorithm, which has better target detection performance in many applications due to the use of RPN networks. While RetinaNet, the base algorithm used in this chapter, is a single-stage target detection algorithm, the algorithm outperforms the Faster R-CNN algorithm due to the use of the feature pyramid network and the focal loss function, and the mAP on the small-DOTA dataset and the HRSC2016 dataset reaches 78.24% vs. 81.62%. The algorithm in this chapter, as an improved RetinaNet algorithm, achieves 83.79% and 89.96% mAP on the small-DOTA

Table 8.7. AP, mAP results of 7 algorithms on small-DOTA dataset.

Algorithm	SSD (%)	YOLOv2 (%)	R-FCN (%)	Faster R-CNN (%)	RetinaNet (%)	ICN (%)	Proposed algorithm (%)
PL	44.74	76.90	79.33	80.32	89.21	**90.00**	89.12
SH	11.34	52.37	47.29	50.04	76.17	78.20	**87.35**
ST	17.94	33.91	65.84	59.59	83.75	84.80	**85.15**
SV	2.00	38.73	39.38	53.66	77.33	73.50	**78.10**
LV	10.24	32.02	34.15	52.49	64.76	65.00	**79.22**
mAP	17.25	46.79	53.20	59.22	78.24	78.30	83.79

Note: Bolded text is the optimal value for the line in which it is placed.

Table 8.8. AP, mAP results of 7 algorithms on HRSC2016 dataset.

Algorithm	SSD (%)	YOLOv2 (%)	R-FCN (%)	Faster R-CNN (%)	RetinaNet (%)	ICN (%)	Proposed algorithm (%)
SH	28.11	54.56	60.58	69.25	81.62	84.30	**89.96**
mAP	28.11	54.56	60.58	69.25	81.62	84.30	**89.96**

Note: Bolded text is the optimal value for the line in which it is placed.

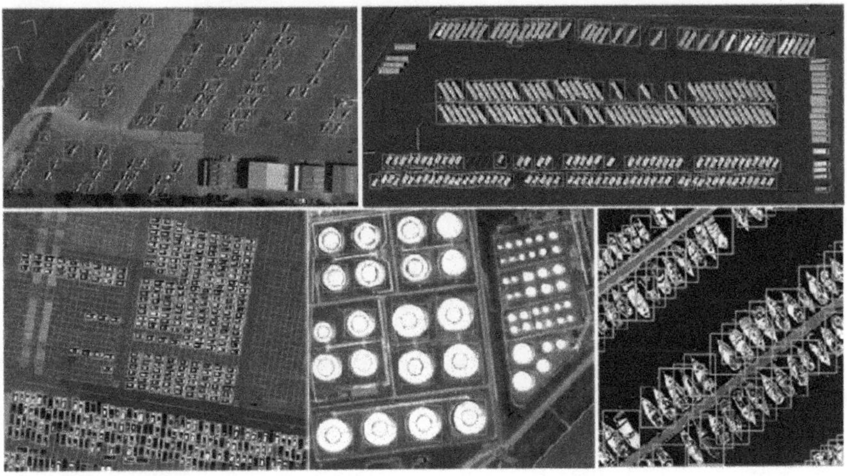

Figure 8.12. Partial image target detection effect.

dataset and the HRSC2016 dataset, which is 5.55% and 8.34% higher than the base algorithm, respectively.

Finally, Fig. 8.12 show the effect of the algorithms in this chapter on target detection in some images.

As can be seen from the figure, the targets in the detected remote sensing images are densely arranged, while the algorithm in this chapter is still able to detect most of the feature targets using the horizontal detection frame, and the position of the detection frame is more accurate, reflecting the good performance of the algorithm in this chapter in detecting the targets in the densely arranged remote sensing images.

8.4 Conclusion

This chapter proposes a remote sensing image target detection algorithm based on multidimensional attention module for the difficult problem of dense arrangement of certain feature targets in remote sensing images. The algorithm takes RetinaNet target detection algorithm as the basic algorithm and makes improvements to it. Firstly, for the interference problem of noise information between dense targets, a multidimensional attention module consisting of spatial attention submodule and channel attention submodule is added to suppress the noise information. Then a weakened non-maximum suppression algorithm is used instead of the standard non-maximum suppression algorithm to prevent certain dense target detection frames from being rejected. In this chapter, the performance of the proposed target detection algorithm is verified through ablation experiments and comparison experiments, and the datasets used are the small-DOTA dataset consisting of five types of dense targets filtered from the DOTA dataset and the HRSC2016 dataset. The results of the ablation experiments show that the improved algorithm outperforms the base algorithm in terms of detection accuracy. And the results of the comparison experiments show that the proposed algorithm outperforms the six classical target detection algorithms compared. The experiments show that the algorithm in this chapter has high detection accuracy in detecting densely arranged targets in remote sensing images, indicating that the proposed algorithm can solve the difficult problem of densely arranged targets in remote sensing images to a certain extent.

References

[1] Bodla N, Singh B, Chellappa R, *et al.* Improving object detection with one line of code. *Proceedings of the IEEE International Conference on Computer Vision.* 2017: 5561–5569.

[2] Neubeck A, Gool LV. Efficient non-maximum suppression. *Proceedings of the 18th International Conference on Pattern Recognition.* 2006: 850–855.

[3] Shrivastava A, Gupta A, Girshick R. Training region-based object detectors with online hard example mining. *Proceedings of the 2016 IEEE Conference on Computer Vision and Pattern Recognition.* 2016: 761–769.

[4] Long J, Shelhamer E, Darrell T. Fully convolutional networks for semantic segmentation. *Proceedings of the IEEE Conference on Computer Vision and Pattern Recognition.* 2015: 3431–3440.

[5] Lin TY, Maire M, Belongie S, *et al.* Microsoft COCO: common objects in context. *Proceedings of the European Conference on Computer Vision.* 2014: 740–755.

[6] Wang JF, Yuan Y, Yu G. Face attention network: an effective face detector for the occluded faces. arXiv preprint arXiv:1711.07246, 2017.

[7] Wang XL, Girshick R, Gupta A, *et al.* Non-local neural networks. *Proceedings of the IEEE Conference on Computer Vision and Pattern Recognition.* 2018: 7794–7803.
[8] Hu H, Gu JY, Zhang Z, *et al.* Relation networks for object detection. *Proceedings of the IEEE Conference on Computer Vision and Pattern Recognition.* 2018: 3588–3597.
[9] Hu J, Shen L, Sun G. Squeeze-and-excitation networks. *Proceedings of the IEEE Conference on Computer Vision and Pattern Recognition.* 2018: 7132–7141.
[10] Xia GS, Bai X, Ding J, *et al.* DOTA: A large-scale dataset for object detection in aerial images. *Proceedings of the IEEE Conference on Computer Vision and Pattern Recognition.* 2018: 3974–3983.
[11] Ding J, Xue N, Long Y, *et al.* Learning RoI transformer for detecting oriented objects in aerial images. *Proceedings of the 2019 IEEE/CVF Conference on Computer Vision and Pattern Recognition.* 2019: 2844–2853.
[12] Liu ZK, Liu Y, Weng LB, *et al.* A high resolution optical satellite image dataset for ship recognition and some new baselines. *Proceedings of the 6th International Conference on Pattern Recognition Applications and Methods.* 2017: 324–331.
[13] Redmon J, Farhadi A. YOLO9000: Better, faster, stronger. *Proceedings of the 2017 IEEE Conference on Computer Vision and Pattern Recognition.* 2017: 6517–6525.
[14] Liu W, Anguelov D, Erhan D, *et al.* SSD: Single shot multibox detector. *Proceedings of the European Conference on Computer Vision.* 2016: 21–37.
[15] Dai JF, Li Y, He KM, *et al.* R-FCN: Object detection via region-based fully convolutional network. arXiv preprint arXiv:1605.06409.
[16] Azimi SM, Vig E, Bahmanyar R, *et al.* Towards multi-class object detection in unconstrained remote sensing imagery. *Asian Conference on Computer Vision.* 2018: 150–165.
[17] Everingham M, Gool LV, Williams CK, *et al.* The pascal visual object classes (VOC) challenge. *International Journal of Computer Vision,* 2010, 88(2): 303–338.
[18] Xiao ZF, Liu Q, Tang GF, *et al.* Elliptic Fourier transformation-based histograms of oriented gradients for rotationally invariant object detection in remote sensing images. *International Journal of Remote Sensing,* 2015, 36(2): 618–644.

Chapter 9

Real-Time Detection Algorithm of Video Image Object Based on LSTM

The previous chapter mainly studied the target detection algorithm based on single frame sonar image. The advantages of this algorithm are high robustness, strong scalability, and high detection accuracy for targets with slow moving speed and no occlusion. However, in practical applications, the sonar system basically acquires continuous sonar video frames. In sonar video, dynamic targets sometimes deform and blur due to their own fast movement or reverberation noise. In such cases, the single frame image often does not provide enough feature information, resulting in low confidence in the intermediate frame, and sometimes even undetectable. Since there is no precedent for sonar video target detection, we first analyze the optical video target detection algorithm.

The existing video object detection algorithms mainly have the following research directions [1,2]: One is to compute the optical flow features between continuous frames through optical flow network to carry out feature enhancement. The other is a method based on associative feature algorithm, which correlates features at the frame level to produce high-quality detection results at the video level. Another kind of method is to use Long Short Term Memory network (LSTM) to extract the motion information between successive frames, and perform motion compensation and prediction for moving objects.

The feature aggregation algorithm based on optical flow guidance proposed by Zhu *et al.* [3] uses optical flow to align inter-frame features and aggregate the features of the front and back frames to improve the detection effect of the current frame. Although the algorithm improves the accuracy of target detection, the calculation amount of the model is too large due to the dense interframe aggregation and complex optical flow characteristics.

Considering the large number of feature redundancy between adjacent frames, Zhu *et al.* [4] also proposed a video target detection algorithm based on deep optical flow features. In order to reduce the amount of calculation, the key frames are extracted according to the pre-set interval, and only the key frames are extracted. For non-key frames, the optical flow between the current frame and the previous key frame is calculated through the optical flow network, and the feature is propagated through the optical flow. Since the computation of optical flow network is much less than that of feature extraction network, this algorithm can effectively improve the detection speed.

Feichtenhofe *et al.* [5] correlated frame-level features based on cross-frame target trajectories to produce high-quality detection results at the video level. Firstly, the feature graphs extracted from layers conv3, conv4 and conv5 in the regional full convolutional network are used to calculate the correlation features between two frames. Then, the features extracted by the two frames through the backbone network are respectively applied to the ROI-pooling layer and connection correlation features, and finally, a regression network is used to generate the RoI movement between the two frames.

Traditional video object detection algorithms will forget important timing information when applied in video detection. Liu *et al.* [6] proposed an online video object detection model for real-time operation on mobile devices and edge devices. The main idea is to combine the fast single frame target detector (such as CNN) and LSTM network to get a hybrid network structure—memory guided network. In addition, the author improves the traditional LSTM structure and proposes an efficient Bottleneck-LSTM layer, which reduces the computational load compared with the traditional LSTM. This model is implemented using Bottleneck-LSTM Motor memory perception and use this to improve and propagate features between successive frames. This method performs well and fast on the ImagenetVID dataset, achieving a real-time inference speed of 15FPS on a mobile CPU.

In summary, the method based on optical flow network can supplement the features of frames with insufficient target information through feature propagation, thus improving the accuracy of video target detection. However, optical flow network often brings more computation and is not conducive to the application of video target detection, and the noise of sonar video is more complex than that of optical image, so the effect of direct application of optical flow network in sonar video is not ideal. However, the video detection algorithm based on correlation features is mainly used in offline video target detection, but not applicable to online detection scenarios. At present, only the video target detection method based on LSTM network can better balance the accuracy and speed of video target detection. Therefore, based on LSTM and memory guided network, this chapter studies sonar video target detection.

9.1 Long Short-Term Memory Network and Memory Guide Network

9.1.1 *Long short-term memory network*

In general, CNNs are good at extracting spatial information and characteristics of images, while RNNs excel at extracting features in the time dimension and transmission of information. The research focus of this chapter is to combine the convolutional neural network detection model and recurrent neural network model to form an end-to-end video target detection framework, and fully mine the context feature information in sonar video sequences. In addition, in order to balance the accuracy and speed of video target detection, this chapter studies and proposes a cross-detection framework. For some frames, large models with deeper layers are used to extract features, and small models are used to extract features for the rest of the frames. In addition, memory-guided networks are used to aggregate the features of frames extracted from small models and the feature maps of frames extracted from large models. Improve the prediction accuracy of the model. In addition, because the detection speed of

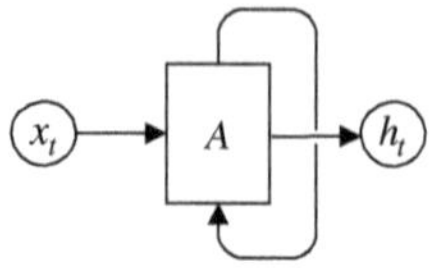

Figure 9.1. Neural network structure.

small models is faster, the detection speed of the overall framework can be improved by applying small models.

Recurrent neural network (RNN) was first proposed in the field of natural language processing, because problems such as language translation and sentiment analysis often involve the processing of temporal information, that is, considering the relevance of the input information before and after. Figure 9.1 shows the unit structure of a recurrent neural network.

As can be seen from the figure above, the recurrent neural network unit is to input the calculation result of the unit at the last moment into the current unit to calculate the output, and the cycle continues. The state output of a recurrent neural network unit at a certain time can be described by the following formula:

$$h_t = f(h_{t-1}, x_t) \tag{9.1}$$

where, h_t is the state at time t, h_{t-1} is the state at time $t-1$, and x_t is the input data at time t. The traditional recurrent neural network uses the fully connected layer to calculate h_{t-1} and x_t, then sums the results, and uses the tanh activation function to activate to get h_t. The whole process is as follows:

$$h_t = \tanh(W_{xh}h_{t-1}, W_{xh}x_t) \tag{9.2}$$

Recurrent neural networks generally connect multiple units, but RNN is prone to gradient disappearance and explosion during training, so simple RNN cannot handle the processing of long sequence data well. In order to deal with the problem of gradient disappearance and explosion during training, Hochreiter *et al.* [8] proposed a special recurrent neural network structure: Long Short-Term (LSTM) structure, which was recently improved and promoted by Alex *et al.* In speech recognition, sequence modeling, video analysis and other fields, recurrent neural network LSTM has made great progress.

Compared with RNN, LSTM has the following two main improvements: (1) Increased cell state, which can retain long-term information compared with hidden state. (2) Proposed the use of "Gate" control mechanism to control the choice of information. The gate structure is usually implemented by a fully connected layer with a sigmoid activation function that controls incoming state information through output values. The traditional LSTM structure is shown in Fig. 9.2, which contains three gated units. Input Gate determines how much of the input at the current moment is retained to the current cell state, and Forget Gate is responsible for determining how much information of the cell state at the previous moment is retained to the current state. An Output Gate is used to control how much information about the current cell state can be output to the output value at the current time. The structure of LSTM is shown as follows:

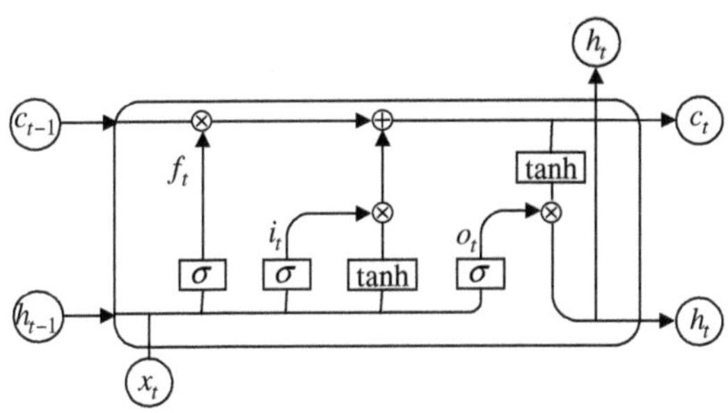

Figure 9.2. LSTM structure.

The relationship between each gate and state in the LSTM network can be described by the following formula, where i_t, f_t, o_t, c_t, h_t represent the output of the input gate, the forgotten gate, the output gate, the cell state, and the hidden state respectively.

$$\begin{cases} i_t = \sigma(W_{xi}x_t + W_{hi}h_{t-1} + W_{ci} \circ c_{t-1} + b_i) \\ f_t = \sigma(W_{xf}x_t + W_{hf}h_{t-1} + W_{cf} \circ c_{t-1} + b_f) \\ c_t = f_t \circ c_{t-1} + i_t \circ \tanh(W_{xc}x_t + W_{hc} \circ h_{t-1} + b_c) \\ o_t = \sigma(W_{xo}x_t + W_{ho}h_{t-1} + W_{co} \circ c_t + b_o) \\ h_t = o_t \circ \tanh(c_t) \end{cases} \tag{9.3}$$

In the above formula, σ is the sigmoid activation function, and the element-wise multiplication represents the multiplication of the corresponding elements of the matrix. The LSTM is depend on the connection between inside the "Gate" neural network to calculate, also known as the Fully Connected Long Short Term (FC-LSTM).

9.1.2 *Memory guide network improvement*

FC-LSTM can extract features well for timing information such as speech, but for two-dimensional or three-dimensional spatial data, these fully connected layers will bring a lot of redundant calculations. Because the data in the space has strong local features, it is difficult for FC-LSTM network to describe the local features. Therefore, Liu *et al.* proposed a combination of convolutional neural network CNN and recurrent neural network LSTM—memory guidance network, replacing the fully connected layer network in the input-to-state and state-to-state parts of FC-LSTM with convolutional layer. A BottleneckConv layer is added before the gated input to reduce bottleneckConv additional computation caused by dimensional conversion between gates. The structure of memory guide network is shown in the Fig. 9.3.

Figure 9.3 shows the connection between the input and the various "gates" is changed from the fully connected layer, and the calculation between states also becomes the convolution operation. Therefore,

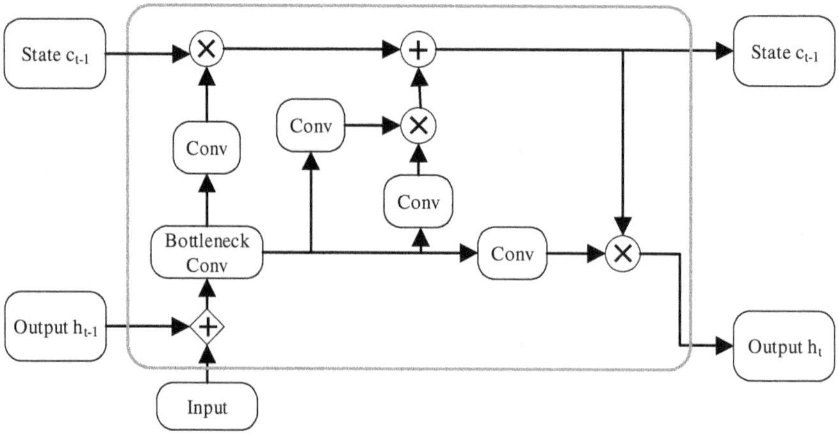

Figure 9.3. Memory guide network structure.

the working principle of a memory-guided network can be described by Eq. (9.4):

$$\begin{cases} i_t = \sigma(W_i * [x_t, h_{t-1}]) \\ f_t = \sigma(W_f * [x_t, h_{t-1}]) \\ o_t = \sigma(W_o * [x_t, h_{t-1}]) \\ c_t = f_t \circ c_{t-1} + i_t \circ \phi(W_c * [x_t, h_{t-1}]) \\ h_t = o_t \circ \phi(c_t) \end{cases} \tag{9.4}$$

In the above equation, $*$ represents the convolution operation, $\phi(\cdot)$ represents the Relu activation function. Compared with one-dimensional tensors in traditional LSTM networks, the outputs of input gate, forgetting gate, output gate, cell state and hidden state in the memory guide networks i, f, c, o, h, x are all three-dimensional tensors, which can better describe the spatial features in the image. In order to reduce the number of parameters in the memory guide network, some improvements are made to the original memory guide network.

(1) Replacement of convolutional layer in memory-guided network with Depthwise Separable Convolution [9]. Depthwise Separable Convolution integrating a standard convolution into a Depthwise Convolution and Pointwise Convolution two parts, the former is used for feature extraction of each input channel, and the latter is responsible for adjusting the output channel. The calculation process of Depthwise Separable Convolution and ordinary convolution is shown in Fig. 9.4.

Figure 9.4(a) shows the calculation process representing the ordinary convolution, assuming that the size of the input feature map is F × F × M, the size of the convolution core is K × K × M, if the number of convolution kernels is N, the size of the output feature map is F × F × N, the number of parameters for the model is K × K × M × N. Figure 9.4(b) shows the calculation process of Depthwise Convolution. Figure 9.4(c) the calculation of the Pointwise Convolution is shown, and the two together form a Depthwise Separable Convolution. First, the input feature map is deeply convoluted to extract features; then the channel is adjusted by Pointwise Convolution to make the size of the output feature map the same as that of the ordinary convolutional output feature map. At this time,

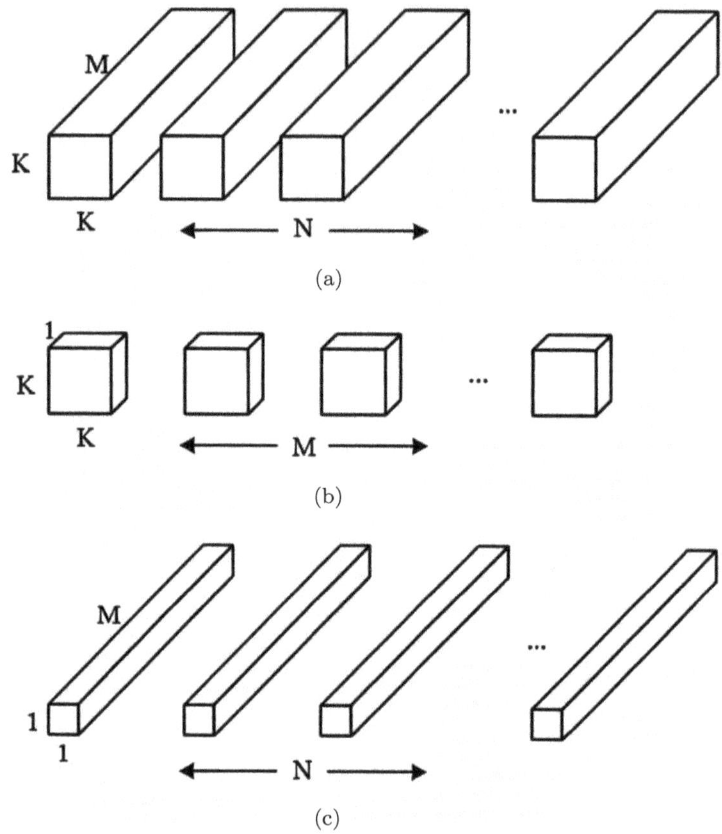

Figure 9.4. Comparison of the calculation process of depth-separable convolution and traditional convolution. (a) Standard convolution, (b) Depthwise convolution, (c) Pointwise convolution.

the total number of parameters of the Depthwise Separable Convolution is K × K × M + M × N. By splitting the convolution process, the parameters of convolution layer can be reduced effectively.

(2) The states of the original network are grouped and each state is processed separately using packet convolution. For the status h_{t-1} of the previous moment, it is divided into G group $\{{}^1h_{t-1}, {}^2h_{t-1}, \ldots, {}^Gh_{t-1}\}$, and each group of states is connected with the input feature map of the current moment after input the output data of each "Gate" in the network. The number of parameters of the model is further reduced and the inference speed of the model is improved by grouping convolution sparse layer connections.

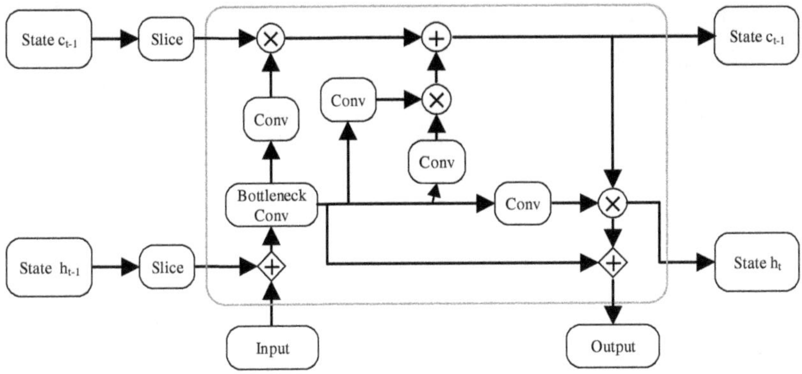

Figure 9.5. Structure of the improved memory guidance network after this chapter.

(3) Building a layer-hopping connection between the BottleneckConv layer and the output layer makes the BottleneckConv layer part of the output. The benefit of this jump connection is that it allows features of the current frame that are less time-related to be included in the output state, making the detection of the current frame more accurate. Figure 9.5 shows the final structure of the memory guide network.

9.2 Construction of Cross Detection Model

9.2.1 *Cross detection model idea*

In the past video object detection framework, in order to pursue detection speed, only the key frame is detected, and then the features of the key frame are aggregated and propagated to the non-key frame through optical flow network or other models, and the non-key frame is not detected. For objects with motion ambiguity or abnormal motion, the detection accuracy of the model will be greatly affected. However, the background similarity of adjacent frames in the video is highly changed by the position and state of the moving target. If the single-frame model is used to detect each frame, a large number of redundant calculations will be generated, which is not conducive to the application in real-time scenarios.

Therefore, based on the above problems, this paper proposes the idea of a cross-detection model. Two models, one large and one small

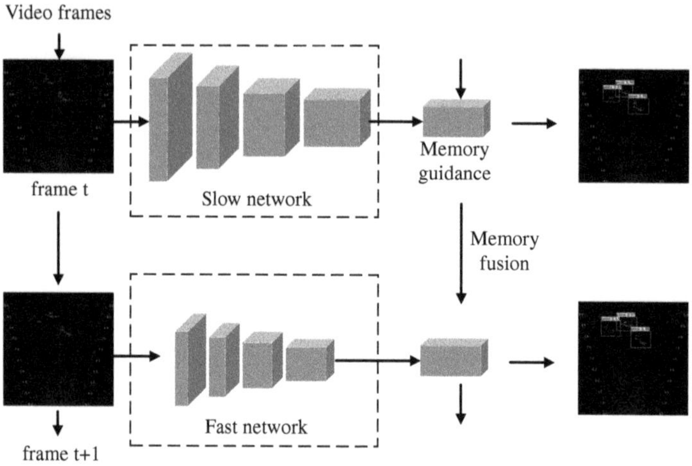

Figure 9.6. Cross-detection model.

(large model with high precision and low speed, small model with low precision and high speed), are used to extract image features on successive frames respectively. The extracted feature maps are input into the shared memory-guided network proposed in the previous section for feature fusion. The memory-guided network is then output to the detector to detect and classify the target in the sonar image. Figure 9.6 shows the overall framework of the cross-detection model.

9.2.2 *Cross detection model selection*

In terms of size model selection, this chapter takes MobileNetV3-Large [10] as the backbone network of large model f0, and MobileNetV3-Small as the backbone network of small model f1. In addition, in order to output size matching, the resolution of the image is input resize to 224×224. And the two models share YOLOv4-tiny's prediction and classification network. Figure 9.7 shows the feature extraction networks of MobileNetV3-Large and MobileNetV3-Small.

The main idea of MobileNetV1 network is to achieve lightweight network structure through deep separable convolutional stack. In the V2 network design [1], in addition to continuing to use the deep separable convolutional structure, Expansion Layer and Projection layer were used in Bottlenecklayer (the Bneck layer in Fig. 9.7). The projection layer also uses a 1×1 size network structure, its purpose

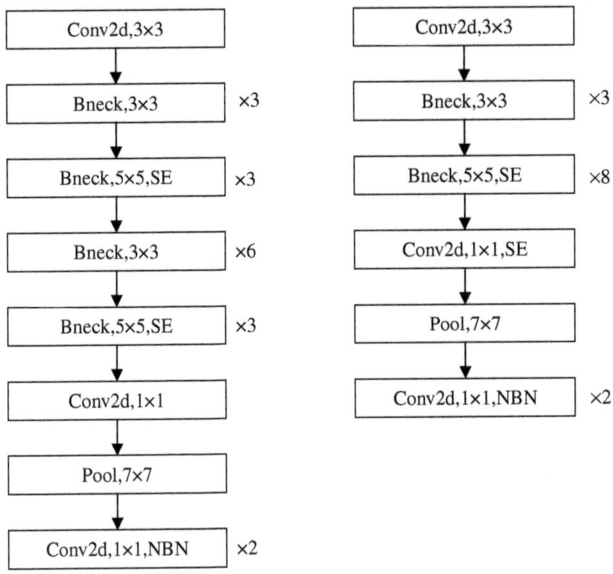

Figure 9.7. MobileNetV3-Large and MobileNetV3-Small feature extraction networks.

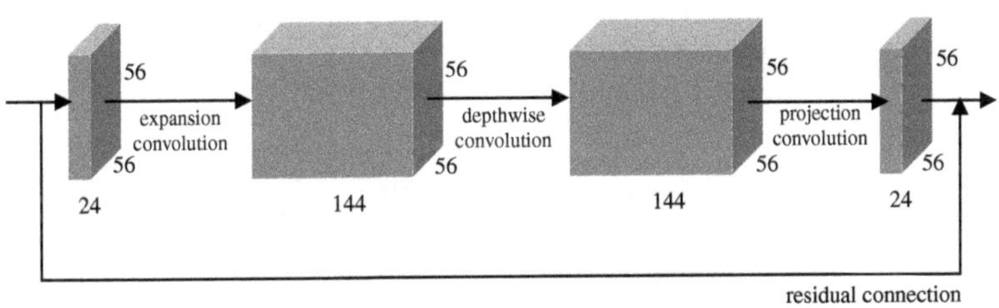

Figure 9.8. Bottleneck layer structure in MobileNetV3.

is to map the features of the high-dimensional space to the low-dimensional space. "Expansion layer" would do the opposite, using large and small network structures to map features from low to high dimensions. Here Expansion has a hyperparameter that is several times the dimension expansion. Can be adjusted according to the actual situation, the default value is 6, that is, the expansion of 6 times. Figure 9.8 shows the Bottleneck layer structure.

The above figure uses quantitative data to more intuitively demonstrate the functions of the extension layer and the mapping layer. When the input dimension and output dimension are the same,

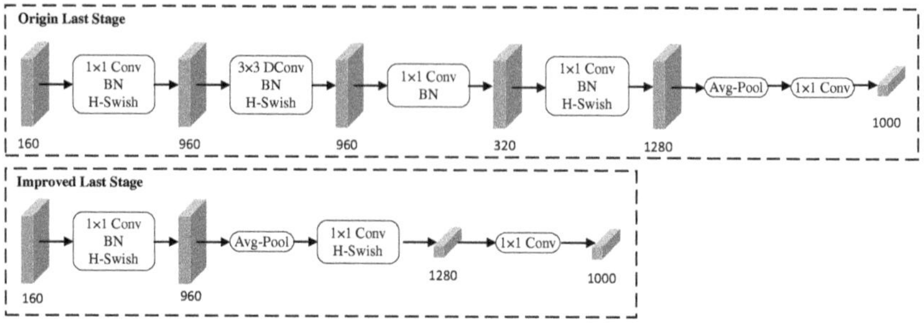

Figure 9.9. Improved tail structure in MobileNetV3.

the input channel is increased from 24 to 144 through the extension layer, and then the depth separable convolution is applied for processing, and the processed structure is compressed to the same dimension as the output through the network structure of size. The advantage of this is that more semantic information can be extracted through high-dimensional tensors. MobileNetV2 uses such a structure to balance the accuracy and speed of the model.

V3 added lightweight attention models (Squeeze and Excitation, SE) after depthwise convolution in the Bottle neck layer structure to improve precision. Due to the additional computational cost of SE module, the author reduced the number of expansion convolution channels in the SE layer structure to one-fourth of the original. Experiments show that such a structure not only reduces the inference time but also improves the model precision. In addition, V3 modifies the tail structure of V2, as shown in Fig. 9.9. In V3, the author first reduces the size of the feature map from 7×7 to 1×1 by using the average pooling layer, and then increases the dimension of the feature map by using the convolution kernel of 1×1, which reduces the computation time by 49 times compared with V2. Moreover, the 3×3 and 1×1 convolution kernels in the spindle convolution are removed directly, which further reduces the calculation amount.

9.3 Model Training and Experimental Analysis

9.3.1 *Model training strategy*

The configuration of the experimental platform in this chapter is as follows: The CPU used in the experiment is Intel Core i5-10400F with a main frequency of 2.9 GHz. The GPU is Nvidia GeForce RTX 3070, the video memory is 8 GB, and the corresponding GPU driver versions are Nvidia Driver 460.32.03 and CUDA11.2. The operating system is Ubuntu 18.04, the deep learning framework is PyTorch1.7.1 and the programming is implemented based on Python3.6. Mean average precision (mAP) and Frames Per Second (FPS) were selected for evaluation.

The test set used in this chapter includes sonar video frames of different underwater scenes, among which some of the video frames are caused by blurred target motion or strange posture caused by abnormal target motion due to noise, some are caused by interference with complex background, and some only have part of the target in the image due to the motion trajectory beyond the sonar detection range, and the feature information of the target is incomplete. These problems are difficult to solve in the single-frame target detection model. Both the model and the comparison method are tested on this test set. In this chapter, the training of the whole sonar video target detection framework is divided into two stages. Firstly, the cross model without detector is pre-trained in the sonar image data set, so that the ConvLSTM layer of the memory-guided network can obtain good initial weights. Since the detection layer was removed during training, in order to adapt the network to the classification of sonar targets, we added a mean pooling layer and a fully connected layer immediately after the ConvLSTM layer, and then a softmax classifier. When training on an image dataset, each image is copied three times and flipped randomly to simulate the movement of the target in the image. When detecting each frame, a feature extraction network (f0 or f1) is randomly selected for feature extraction. After the pre-training is completed, the prediction and classification network of YOLOv4-tiny is connected to the back of the pre-trained feature extraction network and memory guidance module, and then the overall training is carried out on the video key frame of sonar image data. In addition, the memory-guided model needs to be expanded into three steps, that is, 3 adjacent frames of pictures are selected as a set of training data, and a feature extraction network is randomly selected on each step for training. In addition, the training process is similar to the standard YOLOv4-tiny, using a batch size of 8, a learning rate of 0.002, and a cosine of the learning rate attenuation.

9.3.2 Experimental analysis

The model in this chapter concentrates several modules and is the result of the joint action of many modules. In order to verify the effectiveness of each module, we designed a module ablation experiment. The following table shows the results of the module ablation experiment. In Table 9.1, methods A and B are single-frame detection models in the cross model. Where MobilenetV3-YOLOv4-tiny (Large) is the large detection model f0 and MobilenetV3-YOLOv4-tiny (Small) is the target small detection model f1. In the above experiment, the frame interval k of the cross model is set to 2, that is, the two frames after f0 detection are detected by f1. It can be seen that the detection accuracy of model f0 is much higher than that of model f1, but f0 loses its advantage in detection speed. Method C combines single-frame models with different detection speeds and effects by combining cross-detection models. Although the detection speed is improved, the accuracy is greatly reduced compared with the large model, indicating that direct model cross-detection cannot achieve the best results. Method D is the result of combining the cross-detection model in this chapter with the original memory-guided network. Compared with method C, which only carries out a simple model crossover, the memory-guided network can effectively improve the detection accuracy. However, due to the introduction of extra computing amount, the speed of this method is significantly affected.

Method E is the detection effect of the algorithm in this chapter. Compared with method D, which uses the original memory-guided network, the algorithm in this chapter uses the improved

Table 9.1. Module ablation experiment.

Method	A	B	C	D	E
MobilenetV3-YOLOv4-tiny (Large)	√				
MobilenetV3-YOLOLv4-tiny (Small)		√			
Cross over model ($k = 2$)			√	√	√
Memory guide network (first)				√	
Memory guide network (now)					√
mAP (%)	90.5	65.1	75.5	80.2	85.8
FPS	50	190	157	105	150

memory-guided network to extract the context information in the continuous sequence, thus improving the detection accuracy of the overall model. Compared with method D, mAP improves by 5.6% without excessive loss detection speed. The experiment shows that the improved memory-guided network has better feature aggregation ability, and this chapter effectively reduces the number of parameters in the memory-guided network and improves the detection speed through state grouping and depth-separable convolution. For some problems that cannot be solved by a single frame target, such as background interference, missing part of the target, etc., the memory-guided network combines some time sequence information and feature information of the historical frame with the feature of the current frame through the gating structure of LSTM. The model effectively improves the performance of target detection in complex background and provides sufficient feature information for location and classification under the condition of target occlusion or missing.

In the crossover model, parameter k, that is, the number of frame intervals, is a hyperparameter. In order to verify the influence of parameter k on the model detection performance, we conducted tests on parameter k of different sizes, and the results are shown in Table 9.2.

As can be seen from the above table, when parameter k gradually increases from 1 to 7, the mAP obtained by the algorithm gradually decreases while the general trend of FPS gradually increases. Although the features within two frame intervals are aggregated during training, mAP is still higher than f1 model when k is 7, which indicates that the algorithm can aggregate and propagate features from a further distance during testing. However, it can be seen from the table that the capture of this long-range information also has a certain limit, when the frame interval is 7, it is basically not much worse than the single frame detection accuracy of the small model, and even the reasoning speed of the model is reduced due to the

Table 9.2. Influence of parameter k selection on the model.

Parameter k	1	2	3	4	5	6	7
mAP (%)	88.1	85.8	80.5	74.2	70.5	67.7	67.1
FPS	125	150	161	169	176	183	185

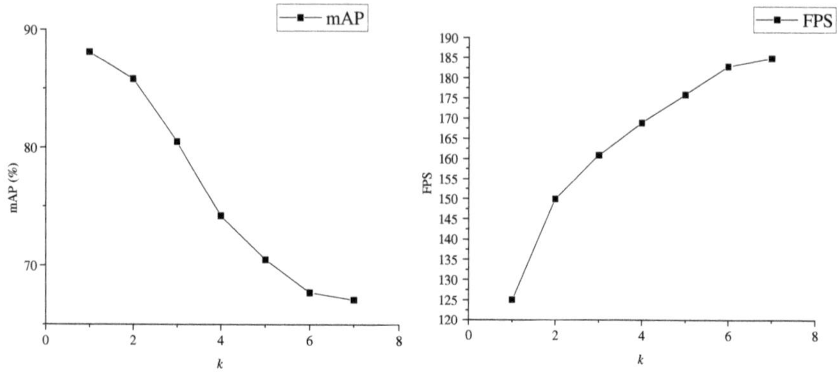

Figure 9.10. Influence of the selection of parameter k on the accuracy and speed of the model.

introduction of some additional calculations. The influence of parameter k on the accuracy and speed of the model can be intuitively seen from Fig. 9.10. As k increases, the accuracy of the model gradually decreases, and the reasoning speed of the model gradually increases. When k is equal to 2, the model speed increase is the most, and the precision loss is relatively small. Therefore, the value of k is set to 2 in the experiment to obtain better detection results.

According to the research on the current situation of video object detection in the introduction, optical flow network and LSTM-based video object detection are two mainstream research directions. The video target detection method based on optical flow network, by adding an optical flow network to the single frame target detection model, predicts the motion trajectory of the target in the video, and successfully solves the problem of target occlusion and lens out-of-focus, but the optical flow network is large, so the reasoning speed of the model cannot meet the actual application needs. In the detection method based on LSTM, by embedding LSTM structure in the network, the timing information between continuous frames in the video is fused into the current frame to improve the detection accuracy of the current frame. In order to compare the performance of the algorithm in this chapter with other models, the experiment of object detection is carried out on the same test set.

Table 9.3 shows the comparison between the algorithm in this chapter and some existing video object detection algorithms. The method of comparison is based on mobile network target detection

Table 9.3. Compares the performance of different types of mainstream detection models and the models in this chapter on sonar data sets.

Algorithm type	Model	Parameter quantity (M)	mAP (%)	FPS
Single-frame detection algorithm	MobilenetV3 (Large)-YOLOv4-tiny	5.4	90.5	50
	MobilenetV3 (Small)-YOLOv4-tiny	2.9	65.1	190
	YOLOv4-tiny	5.9	76.2	130
LSTM	MobilenetV3 (Large)-YOLOv4-tiny + LSTM	5.5	91.8	51
	MobilenetV3 (Small)-YOLOv4-tiny + LSTM	3.0	66.9	189
	LSTM-SSD	3.3	79.1	145
Optical flow network	FGFA	23.5	96.5	5
	Zhu *et al.*	9.0	91.1	20
Proposed algorithm	Cross over model + Memory guide network	7.1	85.8	150

algorithm of frame, based on LSTM algorithm, feature aggregation algorithm based on optical flow network and the algorithm in this chapter. The comparison parameters include the number of model parameters, the average precision mAP of the model and the number of frames per second detected by the model. The detection framework in this chapter is composed of two single-frame models, and the overall parameter number is 7.1 M, which is larger than that of any single detection model. However, only one model is used for detection, and the number of uses of small models accounts for the majority of cases, so it is not significant to compare the number of parameters in the framework of this chapter alone, or to combine the accuracy and speed. With the interval frame number set to 2, the model obtained 85.8% mAP and an average frame detection speed of 150FPS. Compared with the single frame detection algorithms YOLOv4-tiny and LSTM-SSD with similar detection speed, the algorithm in this chapter achieves an average accuracy improvement from 6.7% to 9.6%. This shows that the model in this chapter can effectively propagate the features and timing information of the historical frame and fuse with the feature map of the current frame, providing more feature data for the detection and classification of the current frame, and successfully improving the detection accuracy of the overall model.

In order to more intuitively compare the performance of the video target detection algorithm in this chapter with that of the single-frame target detection algorithm, the detection results of some continuous frames on the sonar video test set between the algorithm in this chapter and the single-frame target detection algorithm YOLOv4-tiny at the same detection speed are extracted and visually compared. Figure 9.11 shows the comparison results. In Fig. 9.11(a–d), the first behavior is the detection result of the single-frame model YOLOv4-tiny, and the second behavior is the detection result of the model in this paper. It can be seen from the results that the single-frame target detection algorithm has the problem of missing detection or low confidence in the detection of the above types of targets, while the algorithm in this chapter successfully detects all the targets. In these detection cases, it can be seen that most of the missed targets have complex backgrounds and a large amount of reverberation noise in the background. Without the prior conditions provided by previous frames, a single frame image cannot provide sufficient position and feature information, so it is difficult to effectively locate and classify the targets in the scene. For example, in Fig. 9.11(a), due to the diver's strange movement posture, the target in the sonar becomes very fuzzy and cannot provide enough feature information for the single-frame target detector, which brings great difficulties to the positioning and classification of the sonar target. As can be seen from the figure, with the help of prior frame target information, the framework of this chapter successfully detected the missed targets of the single-frame target detector, improving the accuracy of target detection. In Fig. 9.11(b), the imaging of some targets is not clear due to the weak sonar echo signal, which makes the single frame model unable to complete the feature extraction, thus affecting the subsequent target positioning and classification. In the detection framework of this chapter, the memory-guided network can easily spread the feature information extracted from previous frames to the affected current frame, increase the amount of information in the feature map of the current frame, and successfully complete the localization and classification of such targets. In Fig. 9.11(c), the sonar imaging of the target in the middle frame is very similar to the background features, which greatly affects the detection of the single frame model, resulting in the missing detection of the

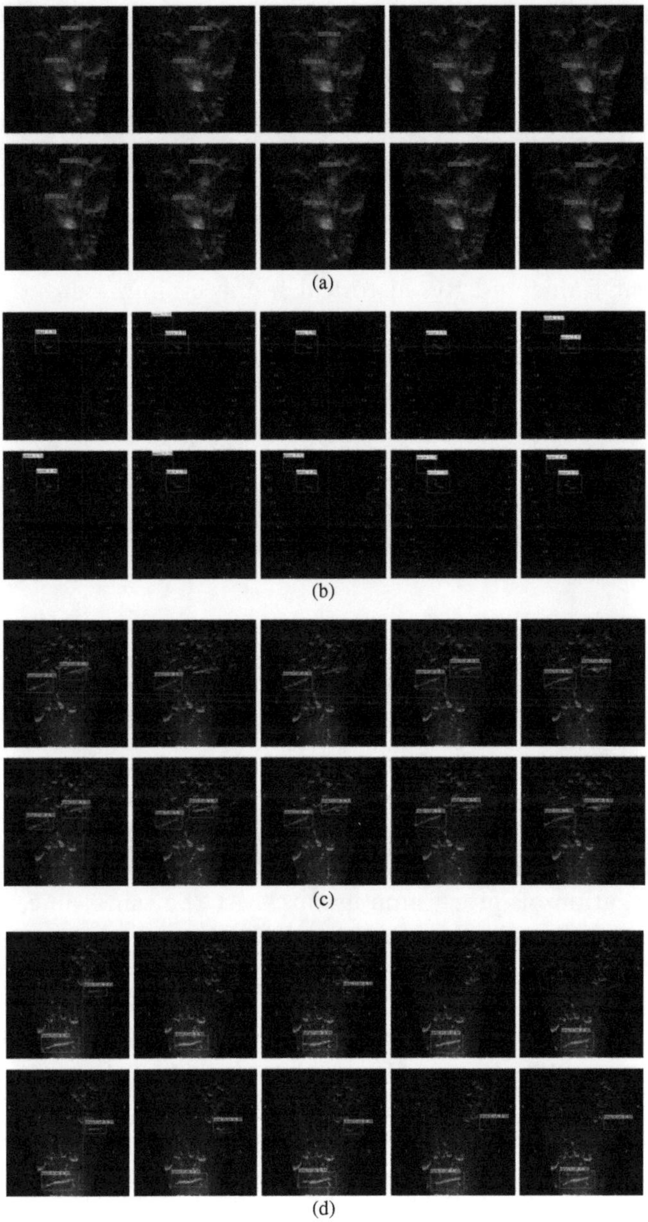

Figure 9.11. Visual comparison of detection results between the single-frame algorithm and the proposed algorithm. (a) Targets with ambiguous postures causing blurred sonar imaging. (b) Targets with weak sonar echo signals. (c) Targets with features highly similar to background reverberation. (d) Targets affected by complex background noise and low signal-to-noise ratio.

middle frame. The framework of this paper uses the timing information provided by ConvLSTM to accurately predict the location of the target and separate the target from the background. In Fig. 9.11(d), due to the fact that the motion trajectory of the target exceeds the detection range of sonar, the imaging of the target is incomplete. In this case, the problem of missing target detection will occur in the single-frame model due to the lack of feature information. The algorithm proposed in this chapter establishes the connection between the current frame and the historical frame by improving the memory guidance network, and makes full use of the timing and position information of the historical frame during detection. Therefore, the target can be successfully located even when the target is partially missing or blocked, thus effectively improving the accuracy of video target detection.

9.4 Conclusion

Aiming at the problem of missing detection in sonar video due to motion blur and noise in traditional image target detection algorithm, this chapter proposes a sonar video target detection algorithm based on memory guidance network. By improving the original memory guidance network and proposing a cross-detection model, the timing information in continuous frames of video is utilized. Improve the accuracy and speed of object detection in video. Firstly, the original memory-guided network is improved to realize the propagation and aggregation of inter-frame features. At the same time, in order to enhance the application and practice of the reasoning geographic information system model (2nd edition) two hundred and thirty. This article proposes a strategy for cross detection of video frames using models of different sizes. The larger model is responsible for improving accuracy, while the smaller model is more efficient. The model is responsible for improving speed and ultimately achieves end-to-end training on the sonar dataset. The experimental results show that compared with the single-frame object detection algorithm, the proposed algorithm solves the problem of missing single-frame model caused by the abnormal posture of the moving object, complex background interference and the missing part of the object. Compared with other video object detection algorithms, it achieves better or similar performance.

References

[1] Wei WQ, Yu J, Bai YY, *et al.* Video object detection based on SSD and Spatiotemporal feature fusion. *Chinese Journal of Image and Graphics*, 2021, 26(03): 542–555.

[2] Cui J, Hu CQ, Xu HD. Multi-beam forward-looking Sonar moving target Detection based on frame difference method. *Chinese Journal of Scientific Instrument*, 2018, 39(02): 169–176.

[3] Zhu X, Wang Y, Dai J, *et al.* Flow-guided feature aggregation for video object detection. *Proceedings of the IEEE International Conference on Computer Vision.* 2017: 408–417.

[4] Zhu X, Xiong Y, Dai J, *et al.* Deep feature flow for video recognition. *Proceedings of the IEEE Conference on Computer Vision and Pattern Recognition.* 2017: 2349–2358.

[5] Feichtenhofer C, Pinz A, Zisserman A. Detect to track and track to detect. *Proceedings of the IEEE International Conference on Computer Vision.* 2017: 3038–3046.

[6] Liu M, Zhu M. Mobile video object detection with temporally-aware feature maps. *Proceedings of the IEEE Conference on Computer Vision and Pattern Recognition.* 2018: 5686–5695.

[7] Mikolov T, Karafiát M, Burget L, *et al.* Recurrent neural network based language model. *Eleventh Annual Conference of the International Speech Communication Association.* 2010.

[8] Hochreiter S, Schmidhuber J. Long short-term memory. *Neural Computation*, 1997, 9(8): 1735–1780.

[9] Chollet F. Xception: Deep learning with depthwise separable convolutions. *Proceedings of the IEEE Conference on Computer Vision and Pattern Recognition.* 2017: 1251–1258.

[10] Howard A, Sandler M, Chu G, *et al.* Searching for mobilenetv3. *Proceedings of the IEEE/CVF International Conference on Computer Vision.* 2019: 1314–1324.

[11] Sandler M, Howard A, Zhu M, *et al.* Mobilenetv2: Inverted residuals and linear bottlenecks. *Proceedings of the IEEE Conference on Computer Vision and Pattern Recognition.* 2018: 4510–4520.

Chapter 10

Embedded Substation Instrument Detection Algorithm Based on Improved YOLOv4

10.1 Introduction

The substation is a hub for power transmission, playing a crucial role in voltage transformation and energy distribution. In a substation, the information displayed by various instruments reflects the operating conditions of the equipment, making it essential to monitor these instruments to ensure the proper functioning of the equipment. Currently, manual inspection is the primary method used in most substations, relying mainly on professional skills and subjective judgment. However, manual inspections suffer from issues such as poor reliability, low efficiency, and in some extreme weather conditions or hazardous environments, they may not be feasible, which hinders the smart management of substations. In recent years, the country has been actively promoting the use of intelligent inspection robots in substations to replace or assist in manual instrument inspections, drawing widespread attention and becoming a hot research topic [1, 2]. The instrument reading inspection scheme in substations has been progressively upgraded and optimized towards automation and unmanned solutions.

The ability of the visual system to accurately recognize instrument readings is one of the criteria for evaluating whether an intelligent inspection robot can operate stably [3]. The substation robot conducts inspections along a prearranged route, capturing images of the substation instruments, and either performs instrument recognition on the robot's front-end or sends the images back to the back-end system for recognition tasks. In the visual system, instrument detection and recognition consist of two parts: (1) instrument localization, which involves finding the position of the instrument within the substation environment image; and (2) instrument reading, which extracts information from the instrument image using computer vision techniques to obtain the reading. The accuracy of instrument localization significantly impacts the entire detection and recognition task. Localization is essentially a target detection problem in computer vision, but the special nature of the inspection robot's work makes this problem different from general target detection. The substation inspection robot has characteristics like fixed point, fixed orientation, and fixed focus for image collection. Fixed point means the robot reaches a designated image capture area according to the predefined inspection route; fixed orientation means the camera's angle is fixed when capturing the instrument; fixed focus means the camera's focal length is fixed during the shoot. Ideally, in multiple inspection tasks, the instrument's position at the same capture point remains constant. However, due to factors such as robot positioning errors and mechanical errors of the camera, the actual captured image may differ from the ideal image with unpredictable errors, mainly reflected in small position deviations and no obvious changes in the shooting angle. If a sufficient number of actual instrument images can be collected, and the features of images with varying degrees of offset are thoroughly learned, high localization accuracy can be achieved.

The instrument positioning algorithm mainly includes traditional detection algorithms based on feature detection and matching, as well as detection algorithms based on deep learning. Huan Fang *et al.* [4] used the Scale-Invariant Feature Transform (SIFT) algorithm to detect and match the features of the instrument dial area. Zhijuan Yang *et al.* [5] used the Oriented FAST and Rotated BRIEF (ORB) algorithm to locate the instrument dial area. Gao *et al.* [6] used the Speeded-Up Robust Features (SURF) method along with template image matching to detect the instrument area from images captured by inspection robots. Yan Huang *et al.* [7] used the Accelerated Robust Features (ARF) algorithm for image matching to achieve instrument dial detection. With the development of machine learning and the improvement of computer performance, machine learning applications in instrument positioning have become more widespread. Among them, Haoqiang Xing *et al.* [8] improved the SSD network to meet the task requirements of instrument dial detection. Fabing Xu *et al.* [9] adopted the improved YOLO9000 network to quickly detect the bounding box positions of instrument dials, removing redundant background information interference. Research on the application of semantic segmentation networks in instrument dial detection has also made some achievements. Yanghao Zhou *et al.* [10] used fully convolutional networks for semantic segmentation of instrument image data to accurately segment the position of the instrument dial. Liu *et al.* [11] used feature matching algorithms and the two-stage object detection algorithm Faster R-CNN to detect the location of the target instrument.

To address the issues of excessive network parameters and low detection efficiency in existing algorithms, and to achieve real-time detection tasks for substations on embedded platforms, a lightweight substation instrument detection algorithm is proposed. Common methods for generating lightweight networks include lightweight network design, model pruning, quantization, and knowledge distillation. This paper employs both the first and third methods, combining lightweight network design during the model design phase and inference phase to achieve network lightweighting, with the following improvements based on YOLOv4:

In edge computing scenarios such as mobile and embedded systems, where real-time performance is not critical and detection efficiency is low, various solutions were tested. The original YOLOv4 CSPDarknet-53 Backbone was replaced with the MobileNetV3 Backbone. After two iterations of updates, MobileNetV3 not only improved accuracy but also enhanced detection speed. Compared to CSPDarknet-53 and other lightweight networks, the number of parameters and computational complexity were significantly reduced, making real-time detection of substations on embedded devices possible.

Based on the improvement of the backbone network, the convolution operations in the Path Aggregation Network (PANet) after feature extraction were replaced with depthwise separable convolutions. By reducing the model's parameters and size, the detection speed was further improved.

To improve inference efficiency on embedded devices, the model was deployed on an embedded platform. The improved model was then quantized using TensorRT, which performed model reconfiguration and optimization to achieve network acceleration.

10.2 Methodology

10.2.1 *YOLOv4 network*

The YOLOv4 [12] network structure mainly consists of four parts: Input, Backbone, Neck, and Head. To enhance the robustness of the model, YOLOv4 employs Self-Adversarial Training (SAT) and Mosaic data augmentation. The SAT strategy allows the neural network to update images in reverse, training on images with added perturbations to achieve data expansion. Mosaic data augmentation combines four images using random scaling, random cropping, and random arrangement to expand the detection dataset.

In the backbone network, YOLOv4 utilizes the CSPDarknet-53 feature extraction network, built upon YOLOv3's Darknet-53, by incorporating the Cross Stage Partial Network (CSPNet). As shown in Fig. 10.1, CSPNet splits the residual blocks in Darknet into two parts: the right part continues to stack the original residual blocks as the backbone, while the left part undergoes minimal processing before being directly connected. This approach reduces computational load while allowing gradients to propagate through different paths, achieving a rich gradient combination and avoiding issues like gradient vanishing.

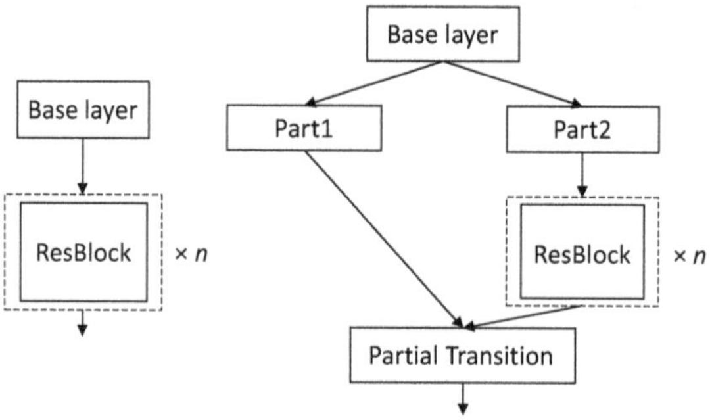

Figure 10.1. Structure of CSPNet.

Feature Fusion Network: YOLOv4 uses the SPP (Spatial Pyramid Pooling) module and the PANet (Path Aggregation Network) module. By adopting the SPP module, compared to simply using k $*$ k max pooling, it effectively increases the receptive field of the backbone features. PANet adds a bottom-up feature pyramid after the FPN layer in YOLOv3. The FPN layer conveys strong semantic features top-down, while the feature pyramid conveys strong localization features bottom-up. It aggregates parameters from different backbone layers to different detection layers, avoiding the loss of shallow information during the transmission process, thus improving the accuracy of the network's predictions.

Head (Prediction Network): YOLOv4 employs multi-scale prediction, outputting 3 feature maps of different sizes to detect small, medium, and large targets. Each grid in the feature map corresponds to 3 predicted boxes. The predicted boxes offset to predict the object's location while also outputting the probability of the object belonging to each class. The overall model architecture is shown in Fig. 10.2.

10.2.2 *Improved YOLOv4 substation instrument detection algorithm*

10.2.2.1 *Backbone network structure improvement*

Considering that most substation inspection robots in practical applications use CPU platforms, although some use GPU platforms, their performance is still limited. In practical applications, we cannot only consider the model's performance, but also need to address the deployment of large-scale network models on embedded devices. YOLOv4 experiences slow detection speeds on embedded platforms, which makes it difficult to meet real-time detection requirements for instruments. Since the backbone network is a key component of the model and plays a crucial role in extracting features from instrument images, the original backbone network is relatively complex, with a large number of parameters. Therefore, it is considered to introduce a high-performance and lightweight network into YOLOv4 to form a new network structure. Compared to other lightweight networks, MobileNetV3 achieves good results in object detection tasks while maintaining small computation and fewer parameters.

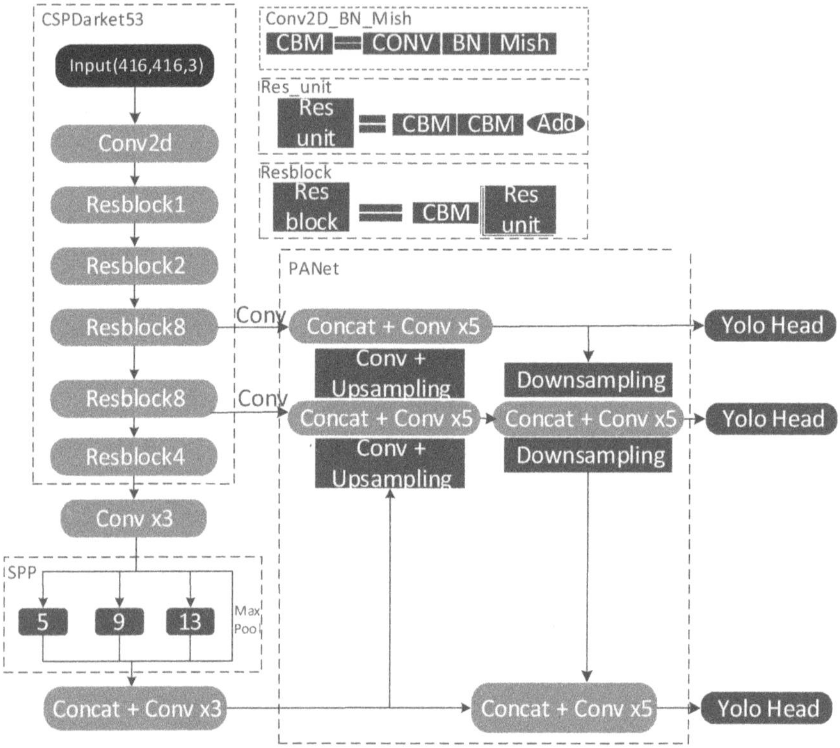

Figure 10.2. Overall structure of YOLOv4.

It is proposed to use MobileNetV3 to replace YOLOv4's backbone feature extraction network CSPDarknet-53 for instrument detection and localization, thereby accelerating the model's detection speed. MobileNet [13] has the advantages of fewer parameters, lower computation, and faster inference speed, making it suitable for applications in scenarios with limited device performance, such as mobile or embedded edge computing devices.

MobileNetV3 uses the NetAdapt algorithm to optimize the number of kernels in each layer, obtaining the optimal number of convolution kernels and channels. While inheriting the depthwise separable convolution from MobileNetV1 to reduce the model parameters, it also retains the residual structure with linear bottlenecks from MobileNetV2. The Bottleneck (linear bottleneck residual block) is an extension of the residual block, focusing on the number of layers in the residual network. After entering the block, a 1×1 convolution is used to map the low-dimensional space to a high-dimensional space, enlarging the feature dimensions, followed by lightweight depthwise convolution for filtering. Then, a Linear Bottleneck projects the features back to a low-dimensional compressed representation. MobileNetV3 also introduces a lightweight channel attention mechanism based on the squeeze and excitation structure, which performs spatial transformations to extract key information from the spatial domain of images and identify regions that need attention. The squeeze operation computes the weight of each feature channel, which is then applied to the original feature channels to learn the importance of different channels. This enhances or suppresses different channels depending on the task, resulting in a significant performance improvement with minimal additional computation. The specific implementation is as follows: the features from the previous layer are split into two paths. The first path undergoes no processing, while the second path first performs the squeeze operation, compressing each channel's feature into a one-dimensional vector to obtain a feature channel vector. Then, the excitation operation is applied, where this feature channel vector is input into two fully connected layers and a sigmoid function, modeling the correlation between feature channels and obtaining the weight for each channel. Finally, these weights are applied to the original features via scale multiplication, achieving feature channel weight distribution.

10.2.2.2 *Introduction of depthwise separable convolutions*

Deep neural networks achieve superior performance through vast network parameters. As the network structure becomes more complex and the model depth increases, the pressure on storage space and computational cost also grows. Section 10.2.1 has already introduced the overall structure of the YOLOv4 algorithm. In this paper, based on modifications to the backbone network, we plan to modify its feature fusion network to significantly reduce the complexity and parameter count of the overall network structure. While keeping the basic structures of the SPP module and PANet module in the feature fusion network unchanged to preserve their advantages, we aim to reduce their parameters. Depthwise separable convolutions will be introduced into the PANet feature fusion network to replace the original standard convolutions, further compressing the model's parameter count and making it easier to deploy on embedded devices.

A standard convolution uses a convolution kernel with the same number of channels as the input. It performs multiplication and accumulation operations across all feature channels, and the resulting data is used as the output. The computational load for a single operation is represented as $D_k \times D_k \times M$, where M is the number of input channels and D_k is the size of the filter. When a convolutional kernel filters the input data, the computational load is $D_k \times D_k \times M \times D_F \times D_F$, where D_F represents the size of the input feature map. When using N convolutional kernels, the computational load becomes $D_k \times D_k \times M \times D_F \times D_F \times N$. The computation process of standard convolution is illustrated in Fig. 10.3.

The standard convolution operation, while filtering, also involves the combination of all input channel features to generate new features. However, filtering and combination can be decomposed into two steps, significantly reducing the computational cost. Depthwise separable convolution consists of depthwise convolution and pointwise convolution. The depthwise convolution applies a single filter to each input channel, while the pointwise convolution combines the outputs of the different depthwise convolutions through a convolution operation. The process of depthwise convolution is shown in Fig. 10.4, and its computational complexity is $D_k \times D_k \times M \times D_F \times D_F$.

Depthwise convolution is much more efficient compared to standard convolution, but it only filters the input channels without

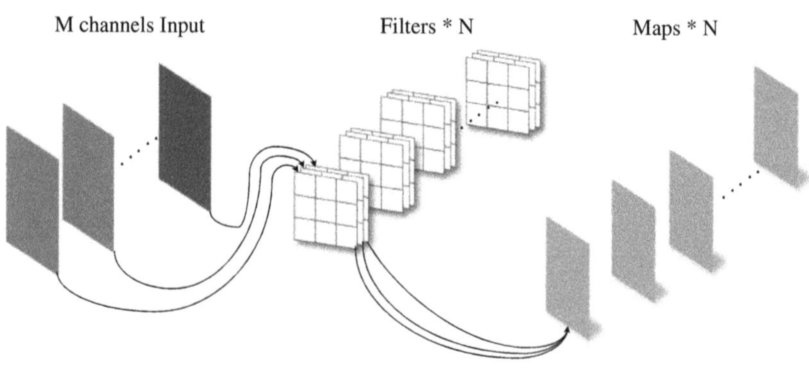

Figure 10.3. Standard convolution process.

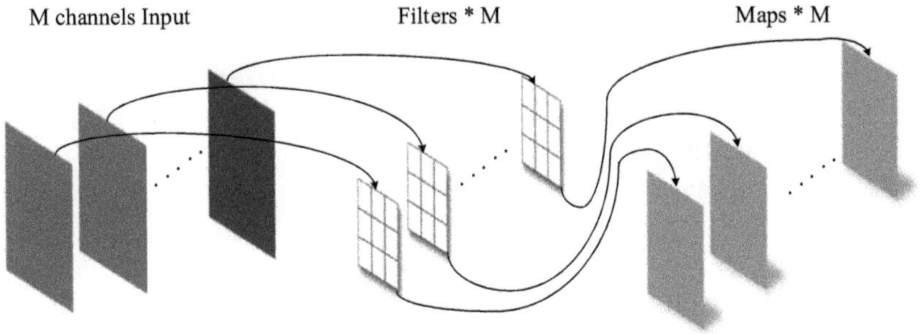

Figure 10.4. Depthwise convolution process.

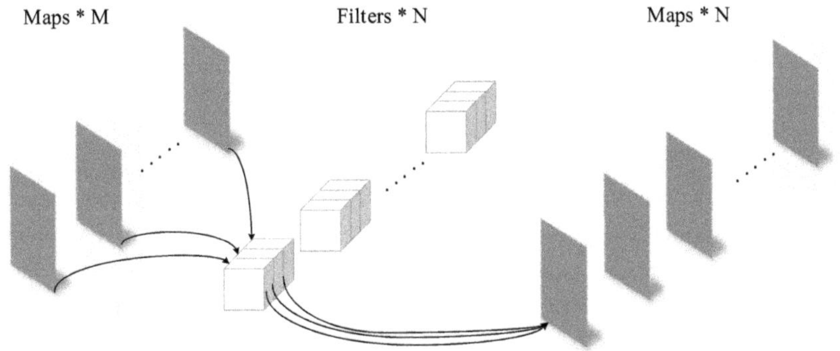

Figure 10.5. Pointwise convolution process.

combining the feature maps of different channels to generate new features. To address this issue, a 1×1 pointwise convolution is applied after the depthwise convolution. The function of pointwise convolution is to collect feature information from each point using a 1×1 convolution to combine spatial information across multiple channels. Additionally, adding a Batch Normalization BN layer and a ReLU layer after the pointwise convolution enhances the model's non-linearity, thereby improving its generalization capability. The computational complexity is $D_F \times D_F \times M \times N$, and the process of pointwise convolution is illustrated in Fig. 10.5.

In summary, the total computational complexity of a single depthwise separable convolution is $D_k \times D_k \times M \times D_F \times D_F + D_F \times D_F \times M \times N$. From the above analysis, the ratio of the total computational complexity of depthwise separable convolution to that of standard convolution is $1/(N + D_k^2)$.

10.2.2.3 *Transfer learning strategies*

Transfer learning [14] is the process of transferring the weights of each node in a trained network to a completely new network. In practical applications, it is often inefficient to train a new neural network from scratch for a new task. When the dataset is not large enough, it can be difficult to train a network model with sufficient generalization ability. Therefore, this paper adopts a transfer learning training strategy, which can accelerate the convergence speed of the network, simplify the training process, and achieve a high-precision detection model within the same training time.

10.2.2.4 *TensorRT acceleration for inference*

TensorRT is an inference framework that can run on NVIDIA GPU hardware platforms [15]. ONNX is an open format for deep learning models, allowing the design, training, and deployment of deep learning models using any framework. After improving the network and completing the training, a lightweight model is obtained. Before running inference, TensorRT quantization is applied to the model. The specific implementation involves exporting the trained PyTorch model to ONNX format. The converted ONNX model may contain many redundant operations, which can be simplified using ONNX Simplifier to obtain the optimized ONNX model. Then, the onnx2trt tool is used to generate the TensorRT engine, and finally, the TensorRT inference engine is utilized to run the model. TensorRT can decompose and then fuse our trained models, resulting in a fused model with higher efficiency. For example, fusing convolutional layers with activation layers improves computation speed. Deploying the TensorRT-accelerated model onto embedded development boards can enhance throughput and reduce inference latency, leading to higher inference efficiency.

10.3 Experimental Results and Analysis

10.3.1 *Dataset and experimental platform*

Since this paper focuses on substation instrument detection, the scenario is quite specific and there are no large publicly available specialized datasets. Therefore, in the experiments, a dataset was collected online and created manually. After screening, basic image augmentation techniques such as image cropping, adding noise, and contrast adjustment were applied, resulting in a total of 850 images. These images were manually annotated using LabelImg for model training, validation, and testing. Some images from the dataset are shown in Fig. 10.6, and the server experimental platform configuration is detailed in Table 10.1.

The experiments in this paper were conducted simultaneously on a server and the NVIDIA Jetson Nano. The Jetson Nano, as an embedded mobile platform, is a powerful small computer equipped with a 128-core GPU. It includes a rich set of API interfaces and CUDA libraries, supporting edge AI applications and enabling effective use in edge computing scenarios.

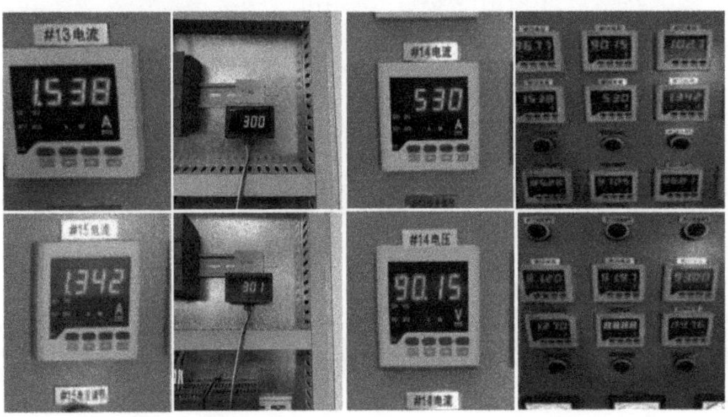

Figure 10.6. Sample images from the dataset.

Table 10.1. Specific environment configuration.

Operating System	Ubuntu 18.04
CPU	i5-10400F CPU
GPU	NVIDIA RTX 3070
Memory (RAM)	16.00GB
Programming Language	Python 3.6
Deep Learning Framework	Pytorch
Integrated Development Environment	VSCode

10.3.2 Experimental parameter settings

The training set, validation set, and test set were allocated in an 8:1:1 ratio. To improve training efficiency, a transfer learning strategy was employed using the MobileNetV3 weight file, which has already converged on the PASCAL VOC dataset. During the experiments, the images were resized to ensure uniformity of the input images. The Adam optimizer was used to calculate the adaptive learning rate for each parameter, with Mosaic data augmentation and cosine annealing decay enabled. The maximum learning rate was set to 0.001, and the learning rate cycle iteration count was 5.

The entire training process is divided into two steps: In the first step, to prevent the MobileNet weights from being damaged, the parameters of the MobileNet network are frozen. To accelerate training, the learning rate is set to 0.001, and mini-batch gradient descent is used, with 16 images inputted at a time for training. In the second step, the MobileNet parameters are unfrozen to fully learn the features of the dashboard images and achieve better convergence. The learning rate is set to 0.0001, and 8 images are trained at a time.

10.3.3 Comparison of computational complexity and model parameters

To compare the superiority of this algorithm relative to other current object detection models, this paper evaluates the computational load of different models under the same hardware platform to assess the algorithm's time complexity. The model parameter size refers to the parameters during model training, corresponding to the space complexity. Table 10.2 presents a comparison of computational complexity and model parameter size between the proposed algorithm and existing algorithms. The data indicates that by optimizing the backbone network and incorporating depthwise separable convolutions, the network has been streamlined, resulting in enhanced model efficiency. Therefore, in terms of floating-point computation, the proposed algorithm demonstrates a significant reduction in computational complexity compared to Faster R-CNN, with an 89.2% decrease relative to YOLOv3, an 88.15% reduction compared to YOLOv4, and a 46.04% decrease compared to EfficientDet-D1, while remaining considerably lower than CenterNet. Regarding model size,

Table 10.2. Comparison of computational complexity of different models.

Model	Computational quantity (FLOPs)	Weight parameter
Faster-RCNN	249.84 G	110.81 M
YOLOv3	32.76 G	235.07 M
YOLOv4	29.88 G	244.42 M
EfficientDet-D1	6.56 G	25.64 M
CenterNet	32.67 G	124.93 M
Proposed algorithm	3.54 G	53.78 M

the proposed algorithm achieves a 51.47% reduction compared to Faster R-CNN, a 71.12% decrease relative to YOLOv3, and a 78% reduction compared to YOLOv4. Although it exceeds EfficientDet-D1 in size, it is still 56.95% smaller than CenterNet. It is evident that, both in terms of computational complexity and parameter count, the proposed algorithm is considerably smaller than YOLOv4. Compared to other algorithms, it exhibits a distinct advantage, making it feasible for deployment on embedded and mobile platforms.

10.3.4 *Comparison of detection accuracy and detection speed*

In addition to analyzing computational complexity and parameter count, this paper also compares the proposed algorithm with mainstream models such as Faster R-CNN [16], YOLOv3 [17], YOLOv4, EfficientDet [18], and CenterNet [19] in terms of detection speed and accuracy. The training environment used an NVIDIA RTX 3070 GPU; however, in practical applications such as substation inspection robots, typical hardware consists of standard CPU devices or those with limited GPU computing capabilities. Therefore, to better evaluate the algorithm's performance in actual industrial applications, the model is simultaneously subjected to inference analysis under two different hardware conditions: RTX 3070 and NVIDIA Jetson Nano.

This paper conducted speed testing on the model (the time taken is the sum of the input image passing through the network model, the decoding operation of the network output, and the non-maximum

Table 10.3. Detection results on RTX 3070.

Model	Basic network	FPS	mAP
Faster-RCNN	ResNet50	15	91.23%
YOLOv3	Darknet53	31	97.75%
YOLOv4	CSPDarknet53	43	98.97%
EfficientDet-D1	EfficientNet-B1	21	97.40%
CenterNet	ResNet50	35	97.93%
Proposed	MObileNetV3	50	94.72%

suppression operation), with the input image size standardized. The test results on the RTX 3070 are shown in Table 10.3. From the table, it can be seen that Faster-RCNN only achieved 15 FPS on the RTX 3070. The algorithm proposed in this paper shows a significant improvement compared to Faster-RCNN, with an increase of 233%. It outperforms YOLOv3 by 19 FPS and achieves 50 FPS based on YOLOv4, marking improvements of 138% and 42.86% compared to EfficientDet-D1 and CenterNet, respectively. The proposed algorithm demonstrates a notable enhancement in detection efficiency compared to current mainstream detection models.

During the network training phase, 32-bit floating-point numbers are used to ensure accuracy in the training process. In the deployment phase, however, a 16-bit floating-point model is adopted to reduce computational load and improve inference speed. On the embedded platform Jetson Nano, detection is constrained by the limitations of hardware devices and performance. By leveraging TensorRT technology, the model is reconstructed and optimized using half-precision floating-point (FP16) instead of full-precision floating-point (FP32).The test results are shown in Table 10.4. Faster-RCNN has a very low frame rate, while the difference in speed between YOLOv3 and YOLOv4 on Jetson Nano is minimal. This is due to the performance limitations of the hardware during inference testing on embedded platforms. Analyzing with half-precision floating-point (FP16), the algorithm in this paper shows a significant improvement in detection efficiency compared to YOLOv3 and YOLOv4, achieving an increase of 200% over YOLOv4, with a maximum frame rate of 15 FPS. At the same time, while the speed is significantly better than other algorithms, the detection accuracy is also ensured.

Table 10.4. Detection results on Jetson Nano.

Model	FPS(FP32)	FPS(FP16)	mAP (%)
Faster-RCNN	/	/	91.23
YOLOv3	3	4	97.75
YOLOv4	4	5	98.97
EfficientDet-D1	2	3	97.40
CenterNet	4	6	97.93
Proposed	10	15	94.72

Note: "/" indicates FPS less than 1.

Table 10.5. Comparison of ablation experiment results for each module and strategy.

MobileNetV3	Depthwise separable convolution	Transfer learning strategy	mAP (%)	FPS
✗	✗	✗	98.97	43
✓	✗	✗	85.98	47
✓	✓	✗	71.71	50
✓	✓	✓	94.72	50

Compared to YOLOv3, the accuracy decreased to 94.72%, a drop of 3.03%, and compared to YOLOv4, it decreased by 4.25%. When compared to EfficientDet-D1 and CenterNet, there is a significant improvement in speed while maintaining considerable accuracy. It can be seen that in the actual detection process of substation instruments, a slight sacrifice in precision greatly enhances detection speed, enabling real-time detection tasks for substation instruments.

At the same time, to better verify the effects of various modules and strategies of this algorithm, detailed ablation experiments were conducted. These ablation experiments were performed on a server configured with an RTX 3070, and the specific results are shown in Table 10.5. From the table, it can be seen that after improving the backbone network, the feature extraction capability is weakened, making it unable to effectively extract deep features from the images, resulting in a significant decrease in accuracy, while the frame rate increased to 47 FPS. On this basis, when modifying the feature fusion network, the model's accuracy further decreased. However, when using a transfer learning training strategy, the pre-trained model retains most of the general features of the targets, significantly improving accuracy while effectively shortening the training convergence time. The accuracy of this algorithm decreased by 4.25% compared to YOLOv4, while the FPS increased by 16.28%. The results demonstrate that the modules and strategies employed can improve detection efficiency while ensuring accuracy.

To more intuitively and effectively demonstrate the detection performance of this algorithm, images from special application scenarios involving single and multiple gauges were selected for validation. Multiple images containing gauges were tested, with the gauges marked in the images using red rectangular boxes.

Due to the specific nature of substation scenes, the gauges in substations have the same model and are arranged in an orderly and regular manner, with no occlusions or overlaps. As a result, the image capture does not cause interference between the targets. Furthermore, the inspection robot in the substation has characteristics such as fixed points, orientation, and focus during photography, which minimizes significant errors during the shooting process. Figures 10.7 and 10.8 respectively selected multiple images of single gauges and multiple gauges for a comparison of detection results. From Fig. 10.7, it can be seen that the algorithm is capable of correctly detecting gauges of different models and at different positions, meeting the detection requirements. The results shown in Figure 10.8

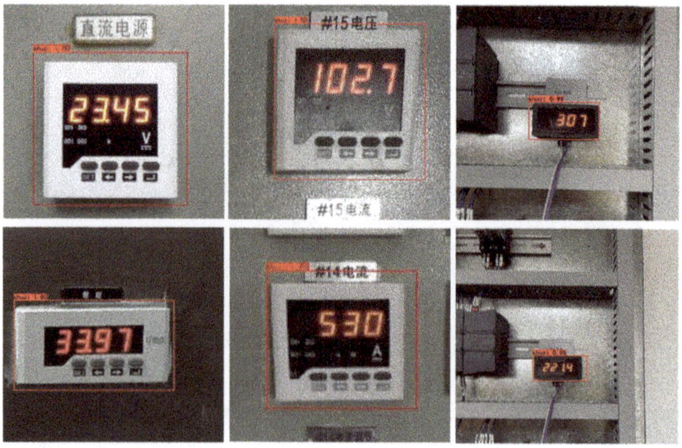

Figure 10.7. Display of single gauge detection results.

Figure 10.8. Display of multiple gauge detection results.

demonstrate that this algorithm can simultaneously detect multiple gauges located in various positions within the image, facilitating subsequent steps such as reading the gauge values. At the same time, detecting multiple gauges simultaneously takes less time than repeatedly detecting a single gauge, effectively improving detection efficiency. Based on the analysis above, the gauge detection algorithm improved from YOLOv4 can quickly and accurately detect gauges in substations, demonstrating good real-time performance and robustness, thus meeting the requirements for practical detection.

10.4 Conclusion

To address the issues of large parameter sizes, high resource consumption, and difficulty in deploying target detection models on embedded devices, a gauge detection algorithm for embedded substations based on an improved YOLOv4 has been proposed. The YOLOv4 algorithm has been lightweight modified by using MobileNet V3 as the backbone feature extraction network, incorporating depthwise separable convolutions, and employing a transfer learning strategy for network training. TensorRT is utilized to optimize the model, making it more suitable for deployment on resource-constrained embedded devices. Experimental results show that with a loss of 4.25% in accuracy, when the model data is stored in half-precision floating-point format (FP16), the detection speed (FPS) on Jetson Nano has improved by approximately 200% compared to YOLOv4. The proposed method demonstrates good robustness and real-time performance in gauge detection within substation environments, effectively meeting the requirements of substation gauge detection tasks and facilitating migration and deployment in different substations, thereby possessing significant practical application value. After detecting the gauges, the subsequent focus of research will be on reading recognition using deep learning methods based on different types of gauges.

References

[1] Gao X, Wang YL, Zeng J. Research on automatic identification of substation meters based on mobile robots. *Power Grid and Clean Energy*, 2017, 33(11): 85–90.

[2] Lu S, Zhang Y, Su J. Mobile robot for power substation inspection: A survey. *IEEE/CAA Journal of Automatica Sinica*, 2017, 4(4): 830–847.

[3] Wang H, Li J, Zhou Y. Research on the technology of indoor and outdoor integration robot inspection in substation. *2019 IEEE 3rd Information Technology, Networking, Electronic and Automation Control Conference (ITNEC)*. New York: IEEE Press, 2019: 2366–2369.

[4] Fang H, Ming ZQ, Zhou YF, *et al.* An instrument recognition algorithm suitable for substation inspection robots. *Automation and Instrumentation*, 2013, 28(05): 10–14.

[5] Yang ZJ, Yuan ZH, Qiao Y, *et al.* Research on intelligent recognition method of pointer meter based on image processing. *Computer Measurement and Control*, 2015, 23(05): 1717–1720.

[6] Gao JW, Xie HT, Zuo L, *et al.* A robust pointer meter reading recognition method for substation inspection robot. *2017 International Conference on Robotics and Automation Sciences (ICRAS)*. New York: IEEE Press, 2017: 43–47.

[7] Huang Y, Li WS, Mai XM, *et al.* Intelligent reading method of substation pointer meters based on one-dimensional measurement line mapping. *Guangdong Electric Power*, 2018, 31(12): 80–85.

[8] Xing HQ, Du ZQ, Su B. Substation pointer instrument detection and identification method. *Chinese Journal of Scientific Instrument*, 2017, 38(11): 2813–2821.

[9] Xu FB, Wu HY, Chen ZH, *et al.* Research on pointer instrument detection and recognition based on deep learning. *High-tech Communications*, 2019, 29(12): 1206–1215.

[10] Yang H, Liu YF, Li X. A method to automatically read the readings of pointer meters. *Journal of Shandong University (Engineering Science Edition)*, 2019, 49(04): 1–7.

[11] Liu Y, Liu J, Ke Y. A detection and recognition system of pointer meters in substations based on computer vision. *Measurement*, 2020, 152: 107333.

[12] Bochkovskiy A, Wang CY, Liao HYM. Yolov4: Optimal speed and accuracy of object detection. arXiv preprint arXiv:2004.10934, 2020.
[13] Howard AG, Zhu M, Chen B, *et al.* Mobilenets: Efficient convolutional neural networks for mobile vision applications. arXiv preprint arXiv:1704.04861, 2017.
[14] Zhu HL, Niu ZW, Huang KC, *et al.* Infrared image target recognition and positioning of substation equipment based on single-stage target detection algorithm. *Electric Power Automation Equipment*, 2021, 41(08): 217–224.
[15] Stepanenko S, Yakimo P. Using high-performance deep learning platform to accelerate object detection. *2019 International Conference on Information Technology and Nanotechnology*. England: IOP Press, 2019: 26–29.
[16] Ren S, He K, Girshick R, *et al.* Faster R-CNN: Towards real-time object detection with region proposal networks. *IEEE Transactions on Pattern Analysis and Machine Intelligence*, 2017, 39(6): 1137–1149.
[17] Redmon J, Farhadi A. Yolov3: An incremental improvement. arXiv preprint arXiv:1804.02767, 2018.
[18] Tan M, Pang R, Le QV. EfficientDet: Scalable and efficient object detection. *2020 IEEE/CVF Conference on Computer Vision and Pattern Recognition*. New York: IEEE Press, 2020: 10781–10790.
[19] Zhou X, Wang D, Krähenbühl P. Objects as points. arXiv preprint arXiv:1904.07850, 2019.

Index

A

ablation experiments, 63
atmospheric scattering model, 27
Att Nested U-Net, 89
attention gate, 98
attention mechanism, 27
average precision (AP), 211

B

bicubic interpolation, 81
BiFPN structure, 133
BSD100 dataset, 81

C

channel attention sub-module, 30
color correction, 47
convolutional block attention module (CBAM), 162
convolutional neural network (CNN), 26
crack image segmentation, 89
cross detection model, 203
CSPDarknet53, 230

D

dark channel prior (DCP), 25
data augmentation, 157
deep convolutional generative adversarial networks (DCGAN), 78
DehazeNet, 26
depthwise convolution, 201
depthwise separable convolution, 201
DetPANet, 165
Dice coefficient, 104
Dice loss, 103
discriminator, 119
DIV2K dataset, 81
domain adaptive method, 113
DOTA, 180

E

edge computing, 219
edge loss, 56
efficient channel attention (ECA), 76
embedded system, 219
encoder-decoder structure, 27
enhanced super-resolution generative adversarial networks (ESRGAN), 69

F

faster R-CNN, 131
feature attention module, 30
feature extraction, 197

feature fusion generative adversarial network (FFGAN), 46
feature pyramid networks (FPN), 170
focal loss, 172
frames per second (FPS), 207
FSRCNN, 81
fully convolutional network (FCN), 89

G

gated context aggregation network (GCAN), 26
gated fusion network (GFN), 26
generative adversarial networks (GANs), 43
gray edge, 47
gray world, 47

H

HRSC2016, 180

I

image dehazing, 25
image segmentation, 11

K

K-means++, 139

L

L1 loss, 79
long short-term memory (LSTM), 197

M

marine life detection, 143
Markov discriminator (PatchGAN), 53
max RGB, 47
mean average precision (mAP), 207
mean square error (MSE), 63
Middlebury Stereo dataset, 32
MobileNetV3, 204
multidimensional attention (MDA), 185
multi-level adversarial transfer learning, 123
multi-scale attention dense block (MADB), 73
multi-scale convolutional neural networks (MSCNN), 26
multi-scale dense connectivity module (MDB), 73
multi-scale feature fusion, 74
multi-stage adversarial transfer learning, 109

N

natural image quality evaluator (NIQE), 61
NYU Depth V2, 32

O

overlay analysis, 149

P

path aggregation network (PANet), 219
peak signal to noise ratio (PSNR), 33
perceptual loss, 55
pixel attention sub-module, 30
pointwise convolution, 202
PredMix, 165

R

real-time detection, 195
recurrent neural network (RNN), 197
relativistic average generative adversarial network (RaGAN), 72
remote sensing image dense target detection, 189
RESIDE, 32
residual blocks, 29
residual-in-residual dense block (RRDB), 71
RetinaNet, 191
RR-MADB, 77

S

semantic segmentation, 89
Set14 dataset, 81

Set5 dataset, 81
single-image super-resolution (SISR), 69
single-stage object detection, 10
skip connections, 27
smooth loss, 31
Soft-NMS, 178
spatial pyramid pooling (SPP), 221
SRGAN, 70
SRResNet, 70
standard convolution, 224
Structural Similarity Index (SSIM), 33
substation instrument detection, 217
surface crack image dataset, 120
synthetic objective testing set (SOTS), 33

T

transmission map, 27
two-stage object detection, 8

U

U-Net, 25
U-Net++, 89
underwater crack image dataset, 120
underwater image enhancement, 6
underwater image quality measure (UIQM), 61
underwater image restoration, 4
underwater image super-resolution, 69
underwater object detection, 150
Underwater-Imagenet, 57
unsupervised domain adaptive scheme, 124
URPC2018 dataset, 141

V

VGG19, 73

W

Wasserstein-GAN (WGAN), 55
Wasserstein-GAN with gradient penalty (WGAN-GP), 55

www.ingramcontent.com/pod-product-compliance
Lightning Source LLC
LaVergne TN
LVHW051056210926
848486LV00002B/123